The essays collected in this volume explo.
between moral philosophy and modernity. This problem consists in
defining the way distinctive forms of modern experience should orient
our moral thinking, as well as examining whether the dominant forms
of modern philosophy have not become blind to important dimensions
of the moral life.

Charles Larmore argues against recent attempts to return to the
virtue-centered perspective of ancient Greek ethics. As well as exploring the differences between ancient and modern ethics, he treats such
topics as the roles of reason and history in our moral understanding,
the inadequacy of philosophical naturalism, and the foundations of
modern liberalism. There are also extended discussions of a number
of leading contemporary philosophers: Rawls, Habermas, Williams,
and Rorty.

Written in a distinctively lucid style and covering a wide compass,
fhese essays will be of particular interest to professional philosophers
and political scientists, but they will also appeal to general readers
concerned with ethics and politics.

THE MORALS OF MODERNITY

MODERN EUROPEAN PHILOSOPHY

General Editor
Robert B. Pippin, University of Chicago

Advisory Board
Gary Gutting, University of Notre Dame
Rolf-Peter Horstmann, University of Munich
Mark Sacks, University of Essex

This series contains a range of high-quality books on philosophers, topics, and schools of thought prominent in the Kantian and post-Kantian European tradition. It is nonsectarian in approach and methodology, and includes both introductory and more specialized treatments of these thinkers and topics. Authors are encouraged to interpret the boundaries of the modern European tradition in a broad way and in primarily philosophical rather than historical terms.

Some Recent Titles
Frederick A. Olafson: *What Is a Human Being?*
Stanley Rosen: *The Mask of Enlightenment: Nietzsche's Zarathustra*
Robert C. Scharff: *Comte after Positivism*
F. T. C. Moore: *Bergson: Thinking Backwards*

THE MORALS OF MODERNITY

CHARLES LARMORE

Columbia University

Published by the Press Syndicate of the University of Cambridge
The Pitt Building, Trumpington Street, Cambridge CB2 1RP
40 West 20th Street, New York, NY 10011-4211, USA
10 Stamford Road, Oakleigh, Melbourne 3166, Australia

First published 1996

Printed in the United States of America

Library of Congress Cataloging-in-Publication Data
Larmore, Charles E.
The morals of modernity / Charles Larmore.
p.   cm. – (Modern European philosophy)
Includes bibliographical references and index.
ISBN 0-521-49717-5 – ISBN 0-521-49772-8 (pbk.)
1. Ethics, Modern – 20th century.   2. Ethics.   I. Title.
II. Series.
BJ319.L37   1996
170′.9′04 – dc20   95-37465
                                                      CIP

A catalog record for this book is available from the British Library.

ISBN 0-521-49717-5 Hardback
ISBN 0-521-49772-8 Paperback

FOR NICK

Die Vernunft als die Rose im Kreuze der Gegenwart zu erkennen und damit dieser sich zu erfreuen, diese vernünftige Einsicht ist die Versöhnung, welche die Philosophie gewährt.

Hegel, *Grundlinien der Philosophie des Rechts*

CONTENTS

ACKNOWLEDGMENTS

I would like to thank Terence Moore, my editor at Cambridge University Press, as well as Mary Racine and Cary Groner, who have all helped greatly in the preparation of this book.

I must also thank Monique Canto-Sperber, who asked me some time ago to publish in her series a collection of my essays, many of them written originally in French. That volume, *Modernité et morale* (Paris: Presses Universitaires de France, 1993), is not, despite some overlap, the same as the present book in English. But without her initiative, I would not have thought so seriously about bringing together my work of recent years.

Finally, I owe an immeasurable debt to my wife, Amey, without whose patience and careful reading I would not have been able to write this book.

The original publication of the essays, all of them substantially revised for this volume, is as follows:

Chapter 1: *Philosophia* (Israel) 20, nos. 1–2 (July 1990), pp. 15–32.
Chapter 2: Charles Larmore, *Modernité et morale,* pp. 71–92.
Chapter 3: *New Republic,* 3 July 1989, pp. 30–5.
Chapter 4: *New Republic,* 17 May 1993, pp. 50–3.
Chapter 5: Previously unpublished. The first half appeared in Larmore, *Modernité et morale,* pp. 25–44.

Chapter 6: *Political Theory* 18, no. 3 (August 1990), pp. 339–60.

Chapter 7: *Social Philosophy and Policy* 11, no. 1 (1994), pp. 61–79.

Chapter 8: Larmore, *Modernité et morale,* pp. 207–20.

Chapter 9: *Inquiry* 34 (March 1991), pp. 77–89.

Chapter 10: Originally in German in *Deutsche Zeitschrift für Philosophie* 2 (1993), pp. 321–7, and much expanded in English in *European Journal of Philosophy* 3, no. 1 (April 1995), pp. 55–68.

INTRODUCTION

Moral Philosophy and Modernity

The essays in this volume are devoted to exploring a single problem, the relation between moral philosophy and modernity. At bottom, this problem consists in defining the way distinctive forms of modern experience should orient our moral thinking. But it also gives rise to the further question of whether the dominant forms of modern philosophy have themselves been blind to important dimensions of the moral life. These are among the issues I took up in an earlier book, *Patterns of Moral Complexity* (1987), but though I have developed some of that material further, I have also had to branch out in new directions. Moreover, many of the present essays, while published before, appear here in a significantly revised and expanded form. Besides determining the claims that modern experience and philosophy should have on our moral self-understanding, this book also, I hope, gives some sense of the difficulty I have felt in finding my way through this subject to where my own convictions lie.

The meaning of the term "modernity" is far from obvious, of course. Though I trust my understanding of it emerges from the course of this book, I can help the reader by clearing away at the outset some possible misconceptions. First of all, I should emphasize that I am not principally interested here in modern culture and society as an *object* of

moral evaluation. Necessary though such evaluation be, I am concerned with what I regard as a more fundamental connection between
moral philosophy and modernity. My aim is to examine the way modern forms of experience should *constitute* or be reflected in the very
categories of our moral thinking. Clearly, modernity, so understood,
must figure as something morally positive, as an essential element in
what I believe we should value. I hope the reader will not wrongly
assume that I identify modernity in this sense with modern life as a
whole and that I celebrate everything that is distinctively modern. For
who would deny that modern times have not only known their fair
share of the usual horrors, but invented new ones all their own? It is in
the cross of the present that I, like Hegel, look for the rose.

   In addition, since my concern lies with the import of modern experience and modern philosophy for our moral thinking today, the aesthetic aspects of modernity, particularly the developments known as
"modernism," play a role (Chapter 9) only to the extent they connect
with this moral problematic. A further warning is that though I view
modernity as a phenomenon that begins to be prominent in the sixteenth century, I do not suppose there occurred at that time some
sharp and massive swerve of the *Zeitgeist,* producing hitherto unknown
forms of belief and experience that swept away all "premodern" conceptions. In this, I break with the image modern thought has often
had of itself. Early modern thinkers such as Descartes and Bacon often
saw themselves as beginning from scratch, setting aside inherited ideas
and starting out anew. The same ambition fueled the philosophies of
autonomous subjectivity in which the German Idealists announced that
modern self-consciousness can draw from itself the norms for guiding
our thought and action.[1] It is clear today how exaggerated such self-
stylizations were, and how dependent the forms of thought we might
consider distinctively modern really were on what came before. Still, an
eye for continuities should not keep us from also seeing the significant
changes modernity expresses, even if they amount more to shifts in
emphasis than to absolute breaks. In this book I try to steer a middle
way between the extremes that philosophical discussions of this subject
often take. Modernity is not a Promethean act of self-legislation, but
neither is its sense of being new a pure illusion. It represents, moreover, a condition that is still our own. I must confess little sympathy

---

1 For this understanding of the aims and difficulties of German Idealism, see the fine
   book by Robert Pippin, *Modernism as a Philosophical Problem* (Oxford: Blackwell, 1991).

with the idea of the "postmodern," which, for all its recent popularity, is very obscure. Where it does make some sense, it seems to me (as I observe in Chapter 2) still a prisoner of the very difficulties in modern thought to which it is alert.

However, probably the greatest source of misunderstanding will be the suspicion that having moral philosophy respond to something called "modernity" is a peculiarly German preoccupation, of little interest to more sober minds unimpressed by speculative philosophies of history. In reality, this project is not so parochial. The history of modern ethics since the sixteenth century, in the English-speaking world as on the Continent, cannot be understood except as the effort to devise a conception of morality appropriate to the emerging features of modern life. Nor have worries about the moral adequacy of modern ethics been confined to a German philosophical culture all too often given to antimodern rancor. After all, one of the most salient features of Anglo-American ethics today is a dissatisfaction with the dominant obligation-centered strands of modern ethics – Kantian and utilitarian – and a wish to return to ancient and medieval theories of virtue. As the essays in Part I make plain, I do not share this enthusiasm for putting notions of virtue and self-realization once again at the center of morality. And I look to ancient models, if at all, because of a different and more unusual sort of discontent with modern ethical thought, namely, with its reigning naturalism and its refusal to acknowledge the authentically normative dimension of reality. But the "neo-Aristotelian revival," as it is often called, may serve here to show that the philosophical problem of modernity is not unknown to Anglo-American ethics.

Nonetheless, the idea that moral philosophy should draw its bearings from historically specific phenomena has been rare this century in the English-speaking world. In recent years, there have been signs of a shift in this direction. (I think of such figures as Alasdair MacIntyre, John Rawls, Charles Taylor, and Bernard Williams.) But such developments stand out against the prevailing modes of thought. The dominant orthodoxy is due in no small part to the influence of "analytic philosophy." What this conception of philosophy has come to mean today is undoubtedly vague. But the specific meaning it once bore is unmistakable, and the powerful form it gave to long-standing habits of unhistorical thinking is with us still. I can best make clear the kind of project I pursue in these essays if I explain why I reject the analytic conception. Though my reasons are not unprecedented, I do not go

on to draw from them the same conclusions that many others do. The
different idea of philosophy to which I am led will show why I take so
seriously the import of modernity for moral philosophy. As will become
evident, I do not think much can be said positively about the nature of
philosophy in general. But that very fact belongs to the spirit in which
I have written this book.

The End of First Philosophy

Analytic philosophy, in the early part of this century, was guided by the
conviction that philosophy must distinguish itself, in its objects as well
as in its methods, from other forms of thought, and particularly from
the empirical sciences. Otherwise, it would have no raison d'être. (This
idea it shared, incidentally, with its Continental cousin, "phenomenology.")[2] Philosophy would focus on the "meaning" of the key concepts
of our thinking, leaving to experience or to the sciences the task of
determining the objects to which these concepts apply. To this domain
of its own it was supposed to apply a special philosophical method,
the "analysis" of concepts. Having its peculiar domain and method,
philosophy could thus determine in advance whether a given problem
was indeed "philosophical" or should be consigned to some other area
of inquiry. But most important of all, the domain of meaning seemed
to be independent of the vicissitudes of experience. That is why analytic philosophy, in investigating the meaning of our fundamental
concepts, hoped to establish the necessary features of our experience,
the structures our understanding of the world and of ourselves must
necessarily embody.

   Applied to the area of ethics, the analytic conception focused on the
analysis of key concepts such as "ought" and "good." Meta-ethics, as
this enterprise was called, aimed at determining the meaning of these
concepts without assuming the validity of any first-order claims (or at
least any disputable ones) about what one ought to do or what things
are morally good; first-order issues were to be taken up (if at all) only
on the basis of this conceptual analysis. These fundamental moral
concepts were supposed to possess an invariable meaning, untouched

---

2 Some of the material in this introduction is drawn from the essay "Convictions
  philosophiques" in my *Modernité et morale* (Paris: Presses Universitaires de France,
  1993). There I examine in detail the similarity between phenomenology and analytic
  philosophy as forms of first philosophy.

by historical changes in our ideas about the moral life. G. E. Moore's *Principia Ethica* (1903), usually considered the inaugural work of analytic ethics, fits this paradigm perfectly. Moore displayed an easy confidence in the idea that the meaning of the core ethical concepts could be settled once and for all. Nowhere did he show any inkling of the possibility that there have been in the history of ethics fundamental shifts in the content and relative centrality of these concepts. Such an awareness was not absent from the writings of his teacher at Cambridge, Henry Sidgwick (in Chapter 1 of this book I point out just how insightful Sidgwick was on this score). But not only did Moore never write, as Sidgwick did, an *Outline of the History of Ethics;* it is inconceivable he would have thought it worth his while to do so. That Moore's book did not really demonstrate any greater philosophical clarity or argumentative prowess than Sidgwick's own *Methods of Ethics* might have led one to suspect that Moore's "analytic" revolution in ethics was not all it was cracked up to be. Some indeed drew this conclusion early on. But the only decisive way to attack the rationale of analytic ethics, of course, was to show why the analytic conception in general cannot stand.

Like many others, I have always regarded W. V. O. Quine's famous essay, "Two Dogmas of Empiricism" (1951), as sounding the death knell of the analytic idea.[3] Quine revealed the failure of the best attempts to make sense of the notion of an analytic proposition – that is, a proposition that would be true or false in virtue of the meaning of its concepts and would thus be the sort of result sought by analytic philosophy. He urged that we do better to look at the supposed distinction between "truths of meaning" and experience-dependent "truths of fact" as actually forming a continuum. All are modifiable in the light of experience, though some are more directly tied to experience than others. The "meaning" of a concept is, in reality, an especially firm, if not inalterable, belief we hold about the objects to which it applies. Even our most fundamental concepts cannot be immunized against the possibility that we will find, in the light of our experience, good

---

3 W. V. O. Quine, "Two Dogmas of Empiricism," pp. 20–46 in his *From a Logical Point of View* (New York: Harper & Row, 1963). It is important to note that much the same point was made more or less simultaneously by Nelson Goodman, "On Likeness of Meaning" (1949), pp. 221–30 in his *Problems and Projects* (Indianapolis: Bobbs-Merrill, 1972), and by Morton White, "The Analytic and the Synthetic: An Untenable Dualism," pp. 316–30 in Sidney Hook (ed.), *John Dewey: Philosopher of Science and Freedom* (New York: Dial, 1950).

reason to revise them. As a result, we can no longer suppose, as Michael Dummett, for example, would like to believe, that analytic philosophy has replaced epistemology with the theory of meaning as the proper form of "first philosophy."[4] Such was indeed the goal of the analytic project. But if propositions about the meanings of concepts really express those beliefs about the world that we are least inclined to modify and that thus guide our more direct dealings with experience, epistemology has not lost at all its central role, being concerned as it is with why some beliefs should be considered more solid than others.

More important than this reshuffling, however, is that Quine's essay challenges the very idea of there being such a thing as "first philosophy." That is, we may regard his essay as demolishing the idea that philosophy should aim at knowledge of the a priori, an idea that reaches further back than the origins of analytic philosophy itself. Even before Kant, who first gave this search for the a priori something of a systematic formulation, philosophers assumed there exists some set of fundamental concepts and forms of thinking, necessary for understanding the world, that are to be determined and analyzed once and for all. "Analytic philosophy" has been but a recent and no doubt the most refined expression of this age-old ambition.

We must give up that aspiration, however, once we recognize that even our most basic ways of making sense of the world answer to the movement of experience. The point is not simply (as many would acknowledge today) that we must abandon dreams of philosophical certainty. The consequences go much deeper. The end of first philosophy means that not just the character, but also the object of philosophical reflection must be seen in the light of a new sense of contingency. Our fundamental ways of understanding the world must themselves be recognized as mutable and thus as historically contingent through and through. In reflecting upon them, philosophy can no longer sensibly aspire to stand above history. It must instead make clear the historical situation in which it proceeds. This will be as true in ethics as elsewhere.

Others before me, among them some of the most eminent moral philosophers today, such as John Rawls and Alasdair MacIntyre, have drawn encouragement from Quine's arguments for their own belief

---

4 Michael Dummett, "Can Analytical Philosophy Be Systematic, and Ought It to Be?" (1977), pp. 441, 454 in his *Truth and Other Enigmas* (Cambridge, Mass.: Harvard University Press, 1978).

that moral philosophy cannot hope for much from the timeless analysis of moral concepts.[5] Readers of this book can judge how far my way of building on this common negative result agrees with theirs. But it will be helpful if I explain why I think some of the better known "postanalytic" conceptions of philosophy in general do not point in the proper direction or offer the right sort of guidance for moral philosophy.

From the rejection of first philosophy Quine himself concluded that philosophy should assume the form of a thoroughgoing naturalism, surrendering any thought of having a subject matter distinct from that of the natural sciences. Quine's naturalism is really more a *parti pris* than a direct consequence of leaving behind the idea of first philosophy. Moreover, naturalism in general, widely espoused though it is in philosophy today, forms an ultimately untenable view of the world.[6] In Chapter 5, I explain what I find wrong in the naturalistic *Weltanschauung*. It founders for reasons that are important for moral philosophy, though not for it alone. Naturalism necessarily regards our moral judgments as expressions of preference and not as potentially a form of knowledge. But it does so on a basis that ultimately must entail denying that there are truths about how we ought not just to act, but to think as well. In this regard, it turns out to differ from the notorious irrationalism Nietzsche espoused (Chapter 4) only by being less clear about where it leads in the end. We can save the authority of reason, I argue, only if we reject modern naturalism and admit a truth the ancients more often saw – that the world must be conceived broadly enough to encompass an authentically normative dimension as well. I expect this argument will be controversial. But it should be clear, in any case, that recognizing how our ways of thinking are, even at the most basic level, subject to revision by experience says nothing by itself about the conception of reality, naturalistic or not, that we should adopt.

Another reaction to the demise of analytic philosophy as the latest avatar of first philosophy has been the "pragmatism" Richard Rorty has made so famous. My own debts to Rorty's writings are profound. I

5 See the appeals to Quine's critique of analyticity in John Rawls, *A Theory of Justice* (Cambridge, Mass.: Harvard University Press, 1971), p. 579, and Alasdair MacIntyre, *After Virtue* (Notre Dame, Ind.: University of Notre Dame Press, 1981), p. 70.

6 In my opposition to naturalism, I have been inspired by the writings of Charles Taylor, particularly his *Sources of the Self* (Cambridge, Mass.: Harvard University Press, 1989), and by parts of Thomas Nagel's *The View from Nowhere* (Oxford University Press, 1986).

.l probably not see in the breakdown of the analytic project quite
.... ignificance I do if it were not for his great book, *Philosophy and the
Mirror of Nature* (1979). But for all that, what I owe to Rorty is far more
negative than positive. His conception of what remains for philosophy,
once the charms of the a priori have been dispelled, is one in which
the very idea of there being philosophical problems seems to have
disappeared. Problems arise where our thought encounters demands
that are independent of itself. A problem we have simply invented is
no problem at all. According to Rorty's book, however, philosophy
should now view itself above all, not as the "epistemological" search for
truth, but as the "hermeneutic" quest for ever new, interesting, and
productive ways of talking.[7] In reality, this conception does not move
beyond the idea of first philosophy it disowns. It expresses instead an
inability to think of philosophy in any other way. To call for "hermeneutics" to replace epistemology supposes the only way there could be
such a thing as philosophical knowledge is that it be of the a priori.
Why must the end of first philosophy spell the end of philosophy itself?

I admit that understanding how there can be such a thing as philosophical knowledge is not an easy matter. The problem is particularly
acute once we admit that philosophy cannot hope to find a realm for
itself that is secure from the changing tides of experience. If none of
our beliefs can avoid having to answer to experience, what can philosophy tell us about the world that would not be more properly explored
by the sciences? In my view, the single greatest difficulty here is, once
again, the undue authority that naturalism exercises upon our thinking. We need to recognize how the world is not exhausted by what the
sciences can tell us of it. Reality also contains a normative dimension,
constituted by reasons for belief and action. On the basis of this
broader idea of the world, we can see how *reflection,* too – reflection
upon reasons for belief and action – can be an organ of knowledge.
Morality involves one species of such reflective knowledge, and philosophy itself typically involves another. It seeks knowledge of how we
should understand our fundamental ways of making sense of the world.

By the standards of the reigning naturalism, this conception of the

---

7 Richard Rorty, *Philosophy and the Mirror of Nature* (Princeton, N.J.: Princeton University
   Press, 1979), pp. 318–21, 359–64. Rorty also employs a very peculiar notion of
   hermeneutics. H. G. Gadamer's great book, *Wahrheit und Methode,* which Rorty frequently invokes as an authority (pp. 357–60), is devoted to the idea that hermeneutic
   thinking, though it cannot be understood in accord with the modern idea of method,
   gives us access nonetheless to truth.

world will no doubt count as "metaphysical," and I will not disown the term. But I see no reason why this metaphysics sits ill with the sense of contingency and openness to experience that the end of first philosophy demands. A "metaphysical," quasi-Platonistic view of reality can joins forces with, if you will, a "nonmetaphysical" conception of how we get in tune with the world. This eclectic outlook is perhaps unusual (it represents the extent of my defection from characteristically modern forms of thought), but it is not incoherent.

On his own image of philosophy Rorty bestows the name of "pragmatism," a term much in vogue today. (Quine has invoked it for his own philosophy, too.) I also feel an allegiance to the pragmatist tradition, but since this term has come to be so closely linked with Rorty's usage, I risk causing confusion if I make much of it. I will observe only that the classical pragmatism of C. S. Peirce, William James, and John Dewey was always keen to undo philosophical dichotomies – not just that between the empirical and the a priori, but also ones of the sort Rorty himself exploits. For example, is not a new way of talking interesting and productive precisely because of its capacity to solve problems and hook up with truth? The same goes for the dichotomy Rorty has deployed more recently between the ideal of "solidarity" he espouses, where we align our thinking with some intellectual community, and the goal of "objectivity" he rejects, where we aim to uncover the nature of things, the way things really are, and not just the way our community pictures them.[8] As I argue in Chapters 2 and 10, we do need to rethink conventional ideas about the opposition between reason and history. But Rorty's dichotomy is likely only to perpetuate these ideas. For is it not more promising to think about how solidarity can enhance objectivity, and how by relying on what we already believe, shaped by our historical situation as we are, we can make sense of the way things really are?

Philosophy and Historical Context

This last remark brings me to the very different lessons I draw from the end of first philosophy. If even our most fundamental concepts and forms of understanding follow the vicissitudes of experience, then only by attending to why we have inherited the patterns of belief and

8 Richard Rorty, "Solidarity or Objectivity?" pp. 3–19 in J. Rajchman and C. West (eds.), *Post-Analytic Philosophy* (New York: Columbia University Press, 1985).

experience we have, can we see clearly how we are to go on from there. We need, that is, a conception of philosophy that recognizes the historically conditioned character both of the problems it confronts and of the knowledge it can acquire. For other areas of inquiry, this kind of historical sensitivity may not be necessary, and a blinkered focus on isolated parts of experience may be more productive. But philosophy strives to be as reflective as possible, regarding a full awareness of any problem's complexities as not just praiseworthy, but essential to the proper investigation of it. (This, if anything, we could take as the essence of the philosophical attitude.) It cannot afford to pass by, therefore, the givens of the historical situation in which it operates.

To explain this conception of philosophy further, I should say something first about taking into account the historical circumstances that have made certain philosophical problems our own. This involves two things. It means, to begin with, that we take an undoctrinaire view of why these problems have come to count as "philosophical" ones. No doubt, philosophical problems are all, in some sense, fundamental in nature, focused on concepts and themes whose implications spread through wide stretches of experience. But that is really all that can be said about philosophy's domain by way of definition. So, too, there is little to say about philosophical method in general, except that, as I have noted, it typically aims at being maximally reflective, bringing together into consideration all the various aspects of any given problem. To give up the idea of first philosophy is to see that there is no timeless essence of philosophy, and in particular no special methods or subject matter peculiar to it. The only adequate definition of philosophy is an "extensional" one, that is, the simple enumeration of problems that for diverse, contingent reasons have come to be classified as "philosophical." Is this not, after all, what we should expect? Philosophy has a long and complex history, full of discoveries and dead ends, dynamic traditions and new beginnings. It is only reasonable to suppose that it forms a heterogeneous mixture rather than a unified discipline.

Recognizing the historical character of philosophical problems also means paying attention to the circumstances that have made certain problems truly problems – not mere curiosities, that is, but real challenges to our existing views and expectations. As our beliefs change, some problems disappear and others emerge. If even the fundamental areas of our experience that give rise to philosophical problems are not immutable, we cannot hope to understand these problems without a sense of the historical circumstances that produce them. This point is closely connected with the other part of the conception of philosophy I espouse, namely, the conviction that philosophical knowledge, like all knowledge, is historically conditioned in character.

This conviction, as I understand it, does not signal a surrender to historical relativism. On the contrary, the essential point is that we overcome the deep-seated notion that history and reason are like oil and water. The pursuit of objectivity is often assumed to require that we neutralize the effects of historical contingency on our thinking and strive to see the world from something like the standpoint of eternity. This aspiration has many sources, but one of them is not that it expresses a demand of reason itself. In Chapter 2, I present a "contextualist" theory of rational belief that dispels the supposed antagonism between objective inquiry and the recognition of historical context. It applies not just to philosophical knowledge, but to knowledge in general. Its key principle, by which I mean to break with much of traditional epistemology (and not just with so-called foundationalism, which almost everyone these days is keen to dismiss), is that no existing belief stands as such in need of justification. That need arises only when we have uncovered some positive reason, based on other things we believe, for thinking that the belief might be false. The object of justification is not belief, but rather changes in belief. And so the claims of reason govern how we go on from where we are, not whether we are entitled to be where we are at all, as that might be judged from some Archimedean standpoint transcending our historical situation.

Modern Ethics and Reasonable Disagreement

In this book I pursue these epistemological reflections not simply for their own sake, but chiefly to show how moral philosophy, on one of the pivotal issues it faces today, must come to terms with modernity. The most distinctive element of modern ethics is the idea that we all are subject to certain "categorical" moral obligations, binding on us whatever may be our various interests. Yet there has always been an undercurrent of doubt, ever more pronounced in recent years, about whether such a moral outlook can truly be authoritative for us, particularly given the waning of religious worldviews. This concern is the source of that nostalgia for "virtue-ethics," *ancien style*, mentioned earlier. As I argue in Chapters 1 and 2, insuperable difficulties stand in the way of such a return to ancient models. We can grasp the importance of these obstacles, however, only in the light of a historically sensitive conception of philosophy such as I have described, for they involve a central ingredient of our modern self-understanding.

That crucial element of modern experience is the realization that on the meaning of life reasonable people tend naturally to disagree with one another. We have come to expect that in a free and open discussion about the fulfilled life, the human good, the nature of self-realization – notions essential to the virtue-centered conceptions of ancient ethics – the more we converse, the more we disagree, even with ourselves. This outlook (see Chapter 7) is not the same as what is often called "pluralism," or the conviction that in the end the human good is not one, but many, its different forms irreducible to any single basis such as pleasure, freedom, or knowledge. Pluralism itself is one of the things about which reasonable people disagree. The expectation of reasonable disagreement is, in fact, a more unsettling view than pluralism, one that runs contrary to some of the deepest preconceptions in the Western tradition. It is the recognition that, on matters of supreme importance, reason is not likely to bring us together, but tends rather to drive us apart.

This experience was absent from ancient and medieval virtue ethics, but it loomed large in early modern thought. It was a lesson hammered home, for example, by more than a century of religious wars. In modern ethics, the expectation of disagreement has turned attention toward a core morality on which reasonable people, despite their differences about the good life, can nonetheless agree. This is the demand that the idea of categorical obligation is meant to meet. Though we associate that idea with the famous exposition Kant gave it, the "priority of the right over the good," to use his words, is by no means limited to Kantian ethics. It has also shaped the utilitarian tradition, that other great current of modern moral philosophy. We cannot, it is true, understand the whole of our moral life in terms of categorical obligations. To this extent, we may learn much from the resources of ancient ethics. But we lose touch with one of the formative experiences of modernity if we miss the importance of a core morality, binding on all whatever their views of the human good. It is an integral part of our form of life.

Clearly, this need for a core morality is particularly urgent in the political realm. The essays in Part III explore how the modern experience of reasonable disagreement has played an essential role in the liberal political tradition. The guiding liberal ideal has been that the terms of political association must be rationally transparent to those they are supposed to bind, for only so can individuals enjoy respect as persons in their own right.[9] This ideal of equal respect takes to heart the way in which political principles differ from the other moral principles we may invoke. Political principles are not just ones by which we judge people, but also ones where force may be used to ensure compliance. We therefore treat others as having the same right as ourselves to set the terms of political association – we regard them as *free and equal citizens,* only if we assume that the coercive principles we propose as binding on all would also be the object of reasonable agreement. The expectation that reasonable people tend naturally to disagree about the good life has therefore impelled the liberal tradition to seek the rules of political life within a core morality all may affirm. No doubt, that expectation has also fostered the very ideal of political transparency.

Responding to this modern experience has proven to be, however, a more complex task than liberal thinkers have often supposed. Many have cast their political principles in terms of an individualist philosophy of life, urging a critical detachment toward inherited forms of belief and cultural traditions. But such theories have themselves become the object of reasonable disagreement, particularly in the wake of the Romantic movement. As a result, this general individualism, whatever may be its truth, can no longer serve as the public philosophy of a liberal political order. Now more than ever, liberalism must take on the character of a *political* doctrine (see Chapter 6). This does not mean it ceases to be a moral conception. But the value of equal respect that is its spirit requires us to distinguish carefully between the political principles that unite us as citizens and the broader, if divergent, ideals and commitments we also affirm.

Little will be clear, therefore, about the guiding aims of modern ethics and the fundamental problems in moral philosophy we face today unless we keep in mind and understand this formative experience of modernity. The expectation of reasonable disagreement, and so the ideas of categorical obligation and political liberalism, do not,

---

9 On the liberal ideal of transparency, see Jeremy Waldron, "Theoretical Foundations of Liberalism" (1987), pp. 35–62, in his *Liberal Rights* (Cambridge University Press, 1993). I do not follow Waldron, however, in extending the liberal ideal beyond the terms of political association to social life as a whole. The "political liberalism" I espouse does not assume that a general social transparency is necessary or even desirable.

for instance, entail skepticism about other areas of the moral life. What it is reasonable to believe is not limited to what everyone will reasonably accept. The idea is, rather, as I explain in Chapter 7, that even when we have good reasons to embrace some vision of the human good, we must count on meeting with the reasoned dissent of others. Some of the controversial claims I make in this very book, such as the need to reject naturalism and adopt a quasi-Platonistic conception of reality, are no exception. This feature of modernity points, then, to the complex moral self-understanding that must be ours today. As it impresses on us the need for a core morality all must heed, it also allows that we are no less reasonable in holding to those more speculative convictions that divide us.

What Clarity Demands

I hope by now to have dispelled the suspicion that this book falls neatly into the line of historicized philosophy that springs from Hegel and is commonly associated with "Continental" thought. I acknowledge, certainly, the influence of some writers in this area, among them Hegel himself. The way I propose of bringing together reason and history, for example, owes much to his "phenomenological" method, though it also embodies a greater sense of contingency than his own trust in historical providence would admit. But not only, I repeat, is it the breakdown of the analytic project itself that points in the direction of the conception of philosophy I have advanced. I also hasten to add that the orphic style, which seems so much at home in so-called Continental thought, is not mine. Philosophy is extraordinarily difficult, I admit. But for me this means not that it is a heroic task to rise above the profound errors of common opinion, which is the sense of difficulty so many Hegel-inspired philosophers have relished, but rather that one's own philosophical vision is more likely to be wrong than right. Making mistakes is what we should expect.

The expectation of error has been, in fact, a prominent attitude throughout the course of analytic philosophy. So though I see little merit in grandiose contrasts between "Anglo-American" and "Continental" philosophy, I do feel an identification with the analytic tradition that is absent from the more exploitative, pick-and-choose relation I have to philosophy in the Hegelian mold. The sense of fallibility finds, I believe, its most enduring expression in that concern for *clarity* which has formed so much the spirit of analytic philosophy, both in the heyday of its program as first philosophy and in these latter, less self-assured times. Clarity, of course, can signify various things. Often it is only in the eyes of the beholder. In the history of philosophy, it has sometimes meant the search for intuitively perspicuous ideas or the practice of precision for its own sake. But the clarity to which I refer is something different. It is an ideal that comes from taking to heart how easy it is in philosophy to go wrong. It holds that we do not really know what we think until we have made our philosophical conceptions open to criticism. To do this, we must specify the aspects of existing opinion on which we aim to build as well as those we wish to reject, therefore exposing our views to public standards of appraisal over which others have as much control as we do. (This seems to me the element of truth in the "linguistic turn" so often associated with analytic philosophy, existing opinion generally finding expression in common forms of speech.) As a result, common opinion cannot be dismissed as but the repository of error, which a heroic philosophy must transcend. Without the bearings it provides, we lose any sense of what it is for our own thinking to go wrong. This does not mean that philosophy must be complacent and simply defer to existing views. On the contrary, only by heeding this ideal of clarity can philosophy be argumentative, for only thus do we open ourselves to criticism by others.

This ethics of thought is by no means special to analytic philosophy. It is as old as Socrates' dialectic. In hindsight we can say, indeed, that one great accomplishment of analytic philosophy has been its cultivation of the Socratic virtues in a century that has not been very hospitable to them. But its other important contribution has been, paradoxical as this may sound, the way its devotion to clarity has led to its own demise. By this I mean that it is precisely arguments such as those of Quine, working through the analytic tradition, that have so clearly brought out the failure of the analytic project and indeed the impossibility of first philosophy in general.

This same ideal of clarity now points, I believe, to a historically responsible conception of philosophy. We make ourselves clear, I have said, by holding ourselves accountable to existing opinion, even as in some regards we go beyond it. But existing opinion is historically contingent at its very core. We cannot expect to know how to go on, therefore, without understanding why we find ourselves where we do. This is the spirit in which I have written the essays in this book.

Modernity has shaped our moral thinking in fundamental ways. It has also given rise to unprecedented problems about the nature and authority of morality and the possibilities of political association. We will not see our way through these problems as clearly as we must unless we take stock of what has made us what we are.

I

MODERN ETHICS

THE RIGHT AND THE GOOD

1. Ancient and Modern Ethics

Henry Sidgwick is in many regards the greatest moral philosopher of the second half of the nineteenth century. But it was in a generally neglected chapter (I.9) of his masterpiece, *The Methods of Ethics*, that he made some of his most penetrating remarks about the foundations of ethics. The nature of moral value, he suggested, assumes two fundamentally different forms, depending on whether the notion of right or the notion of good is thought to be more basic. Furthermore, these two views of morality were in his eyes historically distinct: the priority of the good was central to Greek ethics, whereas modern ethics has embraced the priority of the right. Sidgwick's observations seem to me correct and important. In this chapter I will examine how these two views of morality differ and show why it is useful to explain the differences between ancient and modern ethics along these lines. But this discussion will also indicate how each of the two conceptions may prove unappealing to us in certain respects. In this light, we can better understand why our present moral thought seems so often disoriented, no longer fully at home in the leading currents of modern ethics, but also unable to return to the ancients. At the end, I will suggest a promising way to steer through these fundamental difficulties in the nature of morality. The exploration of this approach, however, will be the subject of the following chapter.

The place to begin is that important chapter of *The Methods of Ethics.*
To this point in his book, Sidgwick had presented the notion of "right"
as the fundamental ethical concept. The idea of right, he had claimed,
expresses the idea of an authoritative prescription, a rule or dictate to
which conduct ought to be subordinated. In this chapter, however, he
observed that alternatively the notion of good might be made basic. To
see the difference he thought this change would make, we must not
suppose that he was appealing simply to the everyday usage of these
two terms, which in fact is rather indiscriminate. The role that these
notions had played in earlier philosophical discussions, both ancient
and modern, was also in his mind. But what Sidgwick wanted most of
all was to describe two very different ways of understanding the nature
of ethics, or what he called "the moral ideal." If the notion of right is
replaced by that of good at the foundations of ethics, he wrote, then
the moral ideal will no longer be *imperative,* but rather *attractive.*[1] His
point was that ethical value may be defined either as what is binding or
obligatory upon an agent, whatever may be his wants or desires, or as
what an agent would in fact want if he were sufficiently informed about
what he desires. In the first view, the notion of right is fundamental, in
the second the notion of good. Each view makes use, of course, of the
other notion as well, but it explains it in terms of its primary notion. If
the right is fundamental, then the good is what an agent does or would
want, so long as it conforms to the demands of obligation; it is the
object of right desire. If the good is fundamental, then the right is
what one ought to do in order to attain what one would indeed want if
properly informed. So we can say that the imperative conception of
ethical value makes the right prior to the good. By contrast, the attractive conception makes the good prior to the right. I shall follow Sidgwick in using these two conceptions of ethical value to fix what is to be
meant by making the right or the good prior to the other.

Sidgwick did not present these conceptions merely as two theoretical
possibilities. In *The Methods of Ethics* and more thoroughly in his *Outlines
of the History of Ethics* he argued that they correspond to the different
perspectives of ancient and modern ethics.[2] Here, too, I believe he was
right, but I can offer only the rudiments of support for this historical
generalization. The ethical thought of both Plato and Aristotle relies

1 Henry Sidgwick, *The Methods of Ethics,* 7th ed. (London: Macmillan, 1907), p. 105.
2 Ibid., pp. 105–6; idem, *Outlines of the History of Ethics,* 5th ed. (London: Macmillan,
    1902), pp. 1–10.

upon an attractive notion of good. They both believed that the exercise of moral virtue is best conceived as forming an intrinsic part of the "happy" or fulfilled life that by nature each human being desires as his ultimate end.[3] For them, morality is fundamentally the agent's interest well-understood. This does not mean that their ethical outlook is a species of egoism, at least as that position is usually defined. For they believed that the agent's self-fulfillment *consists in* the exercise of virtue (as opposed to being a condition instrumentally advanced by it), so that one will achieve the fulfilled life one wants only by being generous, courageous, and so forth, for their own sakes. But nowhere in their writings do we find the modern idea that there are obligations unconditionally (or "categorically," as Kant would say) binding on all agents, whatever their interests or desires. In this respect, Stoic ethics was no different. All animals being predisposed to live in accord with their own nature, the value of moral virtue, for the Stoics, lies in its being the way man would live if he were to follow this predisposition (*oikeiosis*) in the light of his rational nature and so be happy as a rational being.[4] The priority of the good over the right still shaped Aquinas's ethics: the first precept of the natural law is that good is to be pursued and evil avoided, but the good itself was defined by him as that to which reason apprehends that we have a natural inclination.[5]

The priority of the right over the good is an expression that comes from Kant, when he claimed that "the concept of good and evil is not defined prior to the moral law . . . rather the concept of good and evil must be defined after and by means of the law."[6] But this conception is in reality a broad one, encompassing a great deal of modern ethics. It has its beginnings among later medieval Franciscans such as Scotus and Ockham. Rejecting the idea of a perspicuous natural order in the

---

3 Plato, *Republic*, 367c–e, 505a–e; Aristotle, *Nicomachean Ethics*, I.7.
4 See, e.g., Diogenes Laertius, H. S. Long (ed.) (Oxford University Press, 1964), VII, 85–9; and *Stoicorum veterum fragmenta,* von Arnim (ed.) (Stuttgart: Teubner, 1903), III, 16. Sidgwick included Stoicism within the ancient perspective (*Methods of Ethics,* p. 105), but he also saw it, correctly I believe, as resembling the modern outlook to the extent that it (or, most of all, its Roman forms) conceived of morality as a code of laws (*Outlines of the History of Ethics,* pp. 7, 97).
5 Thomas Aquinas, *Summa Theologica,* I–II, Q. 94, a.2. See Etienne Gilson, *Saint Thomas Moraliste* (Paris: Vrin, 1974), pp. 23, 106, 229.
6 Kant, *Kritik der praktischen Vernunft,* Akademieausgabe vol. 5 (Berlin: Preussische Akademie der Wissenschaften, 1900–42), pp. 62–3. All subsequent references to Kant's writings, both to the *Grundlegung zur Metaphysik der Sitten* and to the *Kritik der praktischen Vernunft,* will cite the Akademieausgabe and will be given in the text.

name of God's omnipotence, they shifted the source of moral principles from what men naturally desire to what God commands. Indeed, Scotus startlingly anticipated later developments we associate with Kant when he argued that the Christian rule of loving others for their own sake and thus a real sense of justice (*affectio justitiae*) cannot draw on that natural desire for self-perfection which, as he observed, underlies Aristotelian and Thomistic ethics, but only on a freedom of the will that can suspend that desire.[7] Christian theology, both in its image of God as moral legislator and in its ideal of disinterested love, played an indispensable role in the rise of an ethics of the right.

The imperative conception of morality, by no means always expressed in theological terms, has dominated much of modern moral philosophy. The utilitarian tradition, at least since the time of Sidgwick himself, is no exception. It appeals to a categorical moral "ought" as much as does Kant's moral philosophy. We go wrong if we describe, as some have done, the difference between deontological and utilitarian theories as lying in whether the right or the good is made the fundamental moral concept.[8] On the contrary, both sorts of theory turn on the priority of the right over the good. The essential principle of any "consequentialist" theory (utilitarianism being the version that conceives of the good subjectively, as felt happiness) is that right action consists in doing whatever will bring about the most good overall, for all those affected by the action, each of them "counting for one and only one." But this does not mean that the idea of right action is derived from an independent notion of the good. For the good to be

---

7 For the Franciscan emphasis on God as moral legislator and its link to the demise of a good-based ethics, see Michel Villey, *La formation de la pensée juridique moderne* (Paris: Montchrestien, 1975), pp. 182, 213, 385. For Scotus's specifically Christian rejection of the Aristotelian–Thomistic ethics of self-perfection, see Allan B. Wolter, *The Philosophical Theology of Duns Scotus* (Ithaca, N.Y.: Cornell University Press, 1990), pp. 17–19, 150–2, 188–98.

8 An influential expression of this mistake is William K. Frankena, *Ethics*, 2d ed. (Englewood Cliffs, N.J.: Prentice-Hall, 1973), pp. 14–17. In *Liberalism, Community, and Culture* (Oxford University Press, 1989), pp. 21–32, Will Kymlicka also argues that utilitarianism is best understood as a deontological theory, but his reasons for finding in it a priority of the right are not quite the same as mine. For he believes utilitarianism sometimes ceases to be deontological, namely when it makes the equal consideration of persons subordinate to maximizing the good. I, however, think it never really does this (though utilitarians may understand the idea of equal consideration differently), since it always conceives of the good impartially. And so it always views the maximization of the good as an obligation binding unconditionally on agents.

maximized is itself specified by appeal to a categorical principle of
right: the good is defined by our considering impartially, as it is
claimed we ought to do, the total good of all individuals involved,
whatever our own interests may be, and thus the duty to pursue it is
one binding upon us unconditionally. A deontological theory maintains, of course, that one is bound by certain obligations even if an
alternative course of action is known to bring about more good overall.
But it is not this principle that expresses the priority of the right
characteristic of modern ethics. It is rather the view such a theory
shares with consequentialism, the view that moral duty is independent
of the agent's own good. This common assumption explains why the
unending debate between deontological and consequentialist outlooks, which has lain at the center of modern moral philosophy, was
unknown to ancient ethics.

To glimpse the power of this way of conceiving the difference between ancient and modern ethics, recall Hegel's famous observation
that conscience has had an importance in modern thought it never
enjoyed in ancient ethics. Sidgwick himself agreed with this observation.[9] Once the right is made prior to the good, a person can expect
to find himself in situations where what he ought to do conflicts with
what he wants to do, and where this conflict will not disappear (as it
must on the ancient view) in the light of a deeper understanding of
what he wants.[10] From the moral point of view, his self-fulfillment must
then give way before the claims of morality. And to have internalized
the superiority of these claims is what it is to live under the authority
of conscience. Without this "duality" of practical reason, as Sidgwick
called it, the idea of conscience lacks a basis.[11]

However useful I find Sidgwick's contrast between the imperative
and attractive conceptions of morality, I do not think that a proper
conception of morality as a whole must take over one of these forms to
the exclusion of the other. On the contrary, I believe that our convictions are better captured by a view more complex than the outlooks

---

9 Hegel, *Vorlesungen über die Philosophie der Geschichte*, vol. 12 in *Werke* (Frankfurt:
  Suhrkamp, 1971), pp. 309, 323; Sidgwick, *Outlines of the History of Ethics*, pp. 9, 26,
  197–8.
10 A particularly clear exposition of the ancient view can be found in Cicero, *De officiis*,
  II.9–10; III.11, 34–5, 101.
11 Kant made the same point when claiming (V, 111–12) that by identifying virtue and
  happiness, the ancients had missed the complexity of the *summum bonum*, which is
  happiness in accord with virtue.

characteristic of ancient or of modern ethics: most of us recognize both a core morality unconditionally binding on all as well as a number of duties, arising from friendship or from membership in particular associations, that are ours only so long as we are interested in maintaining these social relations.[12] It would be a bizarre and hollow notion of friendship, for example, that implied that we owe our friends the special concern they deserve whatever we may feel about them. The duties of friendship differ from the duties of core morality in being contingent on a continuing pattern of affection and interest.

But despite this reservation, I remain convinced that Sidgwick's remarks express real historical insight. They will also prove helpful as we try to determine what to make of the core morality we believe binding on all – whether we ought to remain modern to the extent of viewing it (if not the whole of morality) as a system of categorical obligations, or whether we ought to return to the ancient view that the validity of our moral obligations must lie in how they foster the agent's self-fulfillment. In the rest of this essay, I shall be concerned only with the proper analysis of this core morality.

I must also note that in taking over Sidgwick's idea of the basic difference between ancient and modern ethics, I do not deny that it admits of some exceptions. Indeed, there have been several modern philosophers (including Hume, Schopenhauer, and, most influentially in our day, G. E. M. Anscombe) who have argued that "right" or "ought" should not play the fundamental role in ethical theory.[13] But the decisive point is that all of these thinkers have presented their

---

12 See my *Patterns of Moral Complexity* (Cambridge University Press, 1987), pp. 79, 131–3.

13 In *Inquiry Concerning the Principles of Morals*, appendix 4, Hume claimed that the ancient moralists were able to put the virtues (along with talents) at the center of their thought because they did not tie moral approval to voluntary action; that connection looms large in modern times, according to him, because Christian theology has treated morality like a system of civil laws. In *Über das Fundament der Moral* (§4), Schopenhauer argued that Kant's basic mistake was to assume that ethics must have a legislative, imperative form; that assumption makes sense, he claimed, only within a theological framework, so that it was not surprising that Kant was able to draw a moral theology out of his ethics: it was there from the outset. G. E. M. Anscombe's essay "Modern Moral Philosophy" (1958, reprinted in her *Collected Philosophical Papers*, vol. 3, Minneapolis: University of Minnesota Press, 1981) was therefore scarcely so novel as many have thought. In it, she announced that the modern emphatic sense of the moral "ought" makes sense only within the framework of a divine legislator and that if we lack allegiance to that framework, we must return to the ancient outlook, which makes the virtues central.

views as a protest against the dominant conception of ethics in modern times, a conception that they (like Sidgwick) believed to have been fostered by Christian theology. Hume and Anscombe (though not Schopenhauer) have seen their own thought as an effort to return to ancient models. Anscombe's essay of 1958, "Modern Moral Philosophy," in which she laid out her position, has indeed proved to be one of the charter documents of contemporary neo-Aristotelianism.

Like Hume, Anscombe has maintained that such a return to the ancient outlook would place the idea of virtue once again at the center of ethical theory. I believe that this is true. It is not that ancient ethics did not know the "ought" or had no conception of duty (as is sometimes claimed). And clearly the modern priority of the right over the good can make room for the notion of virtue, understanding it as the disposition to do what one ought to do for its own sake. The crucial issue revolves around which notion is central. In the modern outlook, the concept of virtue remains subordinate to that of duty. And what is distinctive of the ancient idea of virtue, and what present-day, often Aristotle-minded, critics of modern ethics wish to reclaim in the name of "virtue ethics," is the conception of the virtues as instead fundamentally forms of human flourishing and self-realization.[14] This understanding of the virtues is at home only in a perspective that makes the good prior to the right.

So far, I have offered only a sketch of the difference between these two moral outlooks, however. A more careful analysis is required. I believe that in Kant's moral thought we find, independent of the more specific features of his position that separate him from utilitarian thinkers, the best exposition and defense of the imperative conception of morality. Kant himself did not in fact recognize from the outset that a central feature of his moral thought had come to be a priority of the right over the good. It was a remarkable review of his *Grundlegung zur Metaphysik der Sitten*, published in 1786 by Hermann Andreas Pistorius, the pastor of Rügen, that first drew his attention to it. The focus of Pistorius's review was precisely the issue of the relative roles of the right and the good in moral theory. His insight into what is at stake in this question and his criticisms of Kant's position have indeed rarely been surpassed. The Kant–Pistorius controversy offers an excellent means to getting clearer about the difference between the imperative and attractive views of morality.

14 Cf. Anscombe, "Modern Moral Philosophy," pp. 29–31, 41.

2. Kant and the Priority of the Right

At the beginning of the *Grundlegung* Kant had claimed that the only
thing unconditionally good is a good will, the disposition to act in
accord with moral principle. This claim amounts to placing the right
above the good, although Kant did not say so at the time. It asserts that
nothing is morally good unless it accords with the principle of right,
which expresses what one ought to do. Precisely this claim is what
moved Pistorius, in his review of the *Grundlegung,* to object that Kant
had erred, that he ought instead to have begun with a definition of
good. No principle stipulating what one ought to do can be a sufficient
basis of moral action, he charged, since it must first be determined
whether that principle is good or bad.[15]

Pistorius's review makes clear what he meant by a principle of action
being good. Its goodness depends in general on its object or goal
(146). This object will be the supreme good (the *summum bonum*) only
if it is the good of all rational beings, but that is possible only if all
rational beings have a common nature that produces an interest in this
summum bonum (154). The principle of right action, he concluded,
must be to act in accord with this common nature and interest, to
pursue the good for all rational beings. The notion of good that he
placed at the foundation of ethics is plainly an attractive one: the
validity of principles of right is supposed to rest on a good in which all
have an interest who are thought to be subject to these principles.
That is why Pistorius denied explicitly that these principles can be
understood as categorical imperatives. There are only hypothetical
imperatives (153, 155, 159). He did not believe, of course, that anyone
can reasonably defect from their claims, for it was his conviction that
all rational beings have an interest in the good, which the rules of
morality serve.

I should remark that although Pistorius believed that something can
be part of the good of a rational agent only if that agent has an
interest in it, there is no evidence that he had what has been called a
"subjective" conception of the good. That is, nothing indicates that for
him, as for Hobbes, an object's being good for a person consists in its

---

15 Pistorius, "Rezension der *Grundlegung zur Metaphysik der Sitten,*" pp. 145–6, as reprinted on pp. 144–60 in Rüdiger Bittner and Konrad Cramer (eds.), *Materialien zu
Kants Kritik der praktischen Vernunft* (Frankfurt: Suhrkamp, 1975). All subsequent
references to Pistorius's essay will be given in parentheses in the text.

being desired by him, that it is nothing but the projection of his desire. A correlation between good and interest can also stem from the opposite view that the goodness of some object is what produces a person's interest in it. Either of these views can be housed within an attractive conception of morality. I believe that Pistorius (like Aristotle) was persuaded that in the end, desire must be explained by objective goodness.

In any case, he correctly perceived that Kant's conception of the rules of morality as categorical imperatives depends on not making an attractive notion of the good the foundation of ethics. And he found this idea of making the right prior to the good incoherent for the reason that a principle of right must first be shown to be good. As now must be apparent, this objection had a very specific sense. By insisting that a principle of right must be shown to be good, he meant that it had to be shown to interest the agent on whom it is supposed to be binding. The maxim of breaking a promise when this is expedient may indeed fail to be universalizable, as Kant maintained. But Pistorius observed that this fact alone would leave the will unmoved unless the agent were interested in living in accord with universalizable maxims (151). A principle purporting to be a moral law, he believed, cannot be such as to be a matter of complete indifference to the agent to whom it is thought to apply (although it may of course be overpowered by other motives). The rules of moral conduct cannot be without connection to human psychology. Having to suppose in the agent an interest in conforming with them, valid principles of right must be subordinate, he maintained, to the good that is the object of that interest (152–4).[16]

Now Pistorius realized that for Kant, too, a moral principle cannot rightly be said to be binding upon an agent who lacks any interest in conforming to it. But Kant's commitment to understanding morality as a system of categorical imperatives had forced him to accommodate this idea by means of a distinction between two sorts of interests (V, 413). Holding that our duties are ours whatever our interests may have

---

16 In his otherwise excellent book, *The Fate of Reason: German Philosophy from Kant to Fichte* (Cambridge, Mass.: Harvard University Press, 1987), Frederick Beiser seems to me to misunderstand this controversy. Contrary to what he claims (p. 191), Pistorius's point was not that reason alone cannot motivate. He agreed with Kant that all rational beings necessarily have an interest in morality. His disagreement with Kant turned on what this interest must be like – on whether it can be any other than an interest in the good.

turned out to be through experience, he had inferred that the interest
that all persons must be supposed to have in morality is an empirically
unconditioned one; it expresses our ability to act independently of the
laws of cause and effect governing the world of experience (IV, 449,
459–60). To Pistorius, however, this kind of freedom seemed only
obscure metaphysics, to which Kant need never have resorted except
for his initial mistake of making the right prior to the good (159).
There is no reason to postulate a nonempirical freedom if moral
imperatives are understood from the first as hypothetical, dependent
upon an interest in a good that experience discloses to each of us.
Besides, the distinction between empirically conditioned and unconditioned interests seems not to change the fact that, in spite of himself,
Kant had come around to tying the claims of morality to an interest
and so to an antecedent notion of the good, however perversely nonempirical.

"Truth-loving and acute and therefore worthy of respect" are the
words Kant used to describe Pistorius, in introducing his response to
these criticisms in his *Second Critique*, the *Kritik der praktischen Vernunft*
(V, 8). He recognized how forcefully Pistorius had expounded the
attractive conception of morality. Yet his conviction remained un-
shaken that it was an untenable view. One of the principal tasks of the
Second Critique was to defend, this time explicitly, the necessity of making the right prior to the good. The arguments on which Kant relied
are nowhere presented as crisply as those of Pistorius just reviewed. But
they are worth the effort of reconstruction, for in the end they yield
some of the deepest reasons for allegiance to an imperative conception
of morality. They also put us in a better position to evaluate Pistorius's
claim that, by connecting the validity of moral rules to an interest in
the agent to conform to them, Kant had contradicted his own thesis of
the priority of the right.

3. Pluralism and Reasonable Disagreement

Kant's *Second Critique* contains two separate arguments for the priority
of the right. Kant did not clearly distinguish them from one another,
and some of their elements lie scattered about the text, so I must stitch
them together from various passages. Moreover, each argument serves
a different end, though their combined import is that we must all
recognize a core morality of unconditional duties, whatever our divergent views of the human good. They combine, in other words, to give
Kant's articulation of the modern, imperative conception of morality.

The first of these arguments (V, 21, 25–6, 57–62) begins with the observation that if the good is not subordinated to a principle of right action, but instead made the ground of it, then the determining ground of the moral will must be the object of some desire. Clearly, Kant too understood the priority of the good to mean that the rules of morality have been based in what persons subject to them want or would want if properly informed. Such rules would then belong among what he called "material principles," rules of action motivated by the desire for some object. We can desire an object, Kant continued, only if we think that having it will bring us pleasure. As a result, the good will be conceived as the pleasurable, and that, he claimed, cannot be correct. Before examining why he deemed this conclusion obviously false, we should determine just what he thought it meant. Because he proceeded to add (V, 22) that all material principles belong under the general principle of self-love or our own happiness, it has seemed inescapable to many that Kant had an implausibly narrow view of the springs of human action: if our actions are not animated by supreme principles of right, they seem on his view to be given over to the egoistic pursuit of pleasure. There are many passages in the *Second Critique* that confirm this verdict (V, 28, 73). But if we lean upon other passages, a more generous interpretation is possible, and the argument for the priority of the right becomes more interesting. Sometimes Kant construed the notion of self-love very broadly to mean the agent's happiness, in the sense of the satisfaction of his desires, whether they are directed toward his own benefit or toward that of others (V, 22, 124). The point of his first argument would then be that placing the good before the right is to equate the good with the satisfaction of the agent's desires. The defect in this, according to Kant (V, 25), is that each of us has a different conception of our own happiness, shaped by our own constitution and particular experiences; even where it is an-other person whom we want to flourish, there is little likelihood that we will agree with others, or with that person himself, about just what that consists in. If conceptions of happiness vary so widely, Kant claimed, then the agent's happiness and so the agent's good cannot work as the basis for a moral law applicable to all.[17]

The dominant ancient view, articulated clearly by Aristotle and pres-

---

17 In the *Grundlegung* (IV, 395–6, 418), Kant also deployed another argument against the idea that the agent's happiness could serve as the basis of morality: every good having its drawbacks, none of us can say in unison with himself what he believes his happiness consists in.

ent still in Pistorius, was that all men share a desire for self-fulfillment that is determinate enough that, upon reflection, it will be seen to consist in the exercise of virtue. Kant was well aware that this was the outlook of ancient ethics (V, 64, 111). But he was persuaded that human nature is too variable, too malleable by circumstance and individual initiative, for this view to seem convincing. I think that we cannot help but agree. Even if the good is understood objectively as being responsible for our interest in it, the kinds of good we can pursue seem too various to serve as the basis for a common morality. Kant's first reason for rejecting the priority of the good is a characteristically modern one. It combines in fact two distinct ideas: (a) the "pluralist" insight that there are a great many valuable forms of self-realization, irreducible to any common form of good that all desire; and (b) the recognition that reasonable people tend naturally to disagree about the nature of the fulfilled life. (I explore the links and differences between these two notions in Chapter 7.) Pluralism and the expectation of reasonable disagreement about the good life are rarely found in ancient thinkers, except among the Skeptics, whose influence upon the moral thought of such modern philosophers as Montaigne, Hobbes, and Grotius was indeed pervasive, particularly in their rejection of Aristotelian and Stoic ethics. Kant stands in this modern tradition.

4. The Role of Conscience

Kant's second argument (V, 21, 26, 63) is positive rather than negative. Whereas the first aimed to explain why the good cannot be prior to the right, the second was meant to show why the right should be seen as prior to the good. (We might think of this argument as his answer to the moral skepticism he had exploited in the first argument.) If the good is made the ground of the moral law, he argued, if the desire for some object is made the determining ground of the moral will, then what this object is must be an empirical matter, since only from experience can we learn what gives us pleasure. I suggest that again we adopt the more generous interpretation of Kantian psychology so that his claim will be that only experience can teach us what satisfies our desires, whether they are directed toward ourselves or others. Now even if experience were to disclose (contrary to the first argument) some object or condition having the capacity to make all men ultimately happy, this good could still not serve as the basis of morality. Experience can inform us of what we actually want, and it can show us what we ought to do in order to attain it, but it can never instruct us in what we ought to do regardless of whatever we may want. Precisely this "necessary" or categorical form is, according to Kant, what must be recognized as characteristic of the rules of morality. Only the priority of the right over the good can make sense of this fact.

This argument may seem feeble, even circular, since Pistorius, the sort of adversary against whom the argument was directed, had explicitly denied that moral imperatives are categorical. Why was Kant so convinced that they are? In the *Grundlegung* (and earlier) he had entertained the hope that the categorical nature of morality (the Categorical Imperative, for short) could be derived from a consciousness of freedom that is empirically unconditioned, a consciousness we have in exercising our rational agency. But in the *Second Critique* he gave up this project, principally because he had realized that such a freedom, lying outside the world of experience, can never be an object of knowledge. We can only postulate that we are free, and do so precisely on the basis of the belief that we are subject to a categorical moral law. Our (nonempirical) freedom, expressed in reason's legislative activity, continued to be for Kant the *explanation* of morality. But he no longer thought this explanation could serve as a *justification* as well. The categorical or unconditional character of moral duties he now understood as a "fact of reason" (V, 31, 47, 91–2). By that he meant that we are immediately aware of it in our conscience without being able to justify it by means of anything else.

This change of mind involves a very important point for our understanding of both Kant and morality, though it is too often neglected. Thus, Bernard Williams has written that those who do not accept Kant's metaphysics of freedom, yet still believe there are categorical moral duties, must offer an alternative account to show why this is so.[18] Williams's challenge gives, first of all, the wrong impression about what Kant himself had come to expect from moral philosophy. He did not believe it could justify the view that moral duties are categorically binding. Of that we can be convinced only by the voice of conscience. The task of moral theory, he believed, can be only to explicate what we already know in our conscience. Moreover, Kant seems to me entirely right on this point. The failure of one such theory does not diminish the authority of what conscience tells us. For in general, beliefs of which we are independently certain ought not to be shaken by our

18 Bernard Williams, *Ethics and the Limits of Philosophy* (Cambridge, Mass.: Harvard University Press, 1985), p. 191.

inability to give a systematic justification of them, but only by our finding positive evidence for thinking they might be false. This epistemological thesis I shall defend in some detail in the next chapter, and with an eye to the present question about categorical obligations. I think that Kant's doctrine of the "fact of reason" expresses a glimpse of the import of this truth for the authority of conscience, though I also think (as I shall next suggest) that he wrongly saw moral conscience as a feature of human nature rather than as a social phenomenon. The authority of conscience, therefore, can be diminished only by positive grounds for doubting what it tells us. Whether such reasons exist for doubting that there are categorical moral duties is a question I take up eventually.

Kant's doctrine of the "fact of reason" must thus be added to what I have called his second argument. The gist of that argument now becomes that only the priority of the right over the good can make sense of what we know in our conscience to be the nature of moral duties. Kant rightly observed (V, 127–9), as I have done earlier, that this role of conscience, and the priority of the right it expresses, are what make modern ethics superior to ancient ethics. In the end, his reply to Pistorius must thus be that he consult his conscience once again.

There remains, however, Pistorius's objection that by conceding that valid rules of morality presuppose some interest in the agent to comply with them, Kant himself could not escape the priority of the good that he claimed to repudiate. In fact, to understand why this charge is untrue is to grasp an important feature of the imperative conception of morality. First, though, I must bring out a mistake that Kant did make at this point in his reasoning. Kant adhered (as did Pistorius as well) to a strong version of the principle that " 'ought' implies 'can' ": that no one can be said to be bound by an obligation unless his psychology is such that he can then be moved to carry it out. Otherwise, blaming someone who has failed to fulfill an obligation seemed to him to be baseless. This principle is what led him to assume that everyone must have an interest in morality, and indeed an empirically unconditioned one (the expression of a nonempirical freedom), since our moral duties are binding upon us whatever we may want in the world of experience.[19]

---

19 For evidence of Kant's commitment to the strong version of " 'ought' implies 'can,' " and for a further elaboration of this criticism, see my *Patterns of Moral Complexity*, pp. 80–90.

I think that the principle of " 'ought' implies 'can' " is far less obvious than Kant supposed. This principle does indeed suggest that our interest in a categorical morality has a source unconditioned by experience. But that is just because it can make no sense of the active role *society* plays in our developing an interest in the demands of morality. From the standpoint of society, there are things its fledging members ought to do even before they can feel moved to comply with them, since it is precisely the educative role of socialization processes to close such a gap. The coincidence of "ought" and "can" is a social achievement rather than a necessary truth. Kant failed to appreciate properly the extent to which our allegiance to morality is a social institution. In the next and following chapters, I shall have more to say about the historically and socially conditioned character of our moral knowledge. But as for the present question about obligation and motivation, we should conclude that a more reasonable view than Kant's is that no one can be said to have an obligation unless, through argument or through training, he either has or could have been brought around to have a motive to comply with it. Categorical duties need then no longer appeal to a metaphysically obscure interest in morality, one that is supposedly ours whatever our experience may have been. Instead, they presuppose only that there is an interest in categorical duties into which everyone can be socialized. Kant's exorbitant notion of freedom forms no necessary part of an imperative conception of morality.

Conceiving of this morality as thus a social institution implies that in one sense our interest in morality is empirically conditioned: we develop it only through our experience in society. But in another sense, which is the one essential to the priority of the right over the good, this interest remains empirically unconditioned. It is an *intrinsic* interest in morality – not an interest we have independently of any moral commitments and that we have learned by experience is best satisfied by acting virtuously – but instead an interest in what we ought to do, regardless of what we may want.[20] Thus, contrary to Pistorius, tying the claims of morality to an interest in the agent to comply with them, either in the strict form Kant assumed or in the looser form I have

---

20 Kant believed (V, 29), wrongly it seems to me, that if an interest does not have an object given in experience as its determining ground, the origin of this interest must be outside experience. On the contrary, we can be taught by others that we should do what is morally right, whatever may satisfy our interests.

proposed, does not reinstate the priority of the good. What we morally ought to do is not explained in terms of an interest we all have or could have, and so in terms of an attractive notion of the good, since we can describe the interest in question only as an interest in what we ought to do. The notion of right remains supreme.

I should add that by this intrinsic interest in morality I do not mean a *desire* to do one's moral duty, at least if such a desire is to be contrasted with the *belief* that one ought to do it. On the contrary, this belief is in my view precisely the form that interest takes, and it need not be supplemented by some desire to be able to move one to act. However familiar, the notion that action must proceed from desire as well as from belief is, as I argue in Chapter 5, a preconception with little warrant.[21]

5. Modern Ethics in Question

A recognition of the pluralism and controversiality of the good and an appeal to conscience are Kant's two arguments for the priority of the right. They figure prominently among the reasons many people have presented for this moral outlook. (The theological considerations we saw Scotus invoke for rejecting the priority of the good – namely, the Christian precept of loving others as one loves oneself – have also proved influential.) It is important, however, to keep in mind the difference in what the two arguments can establish. The first shows only that making the good prior to the right cannot ground a morality binding upon all; by itself it does not imply that the right must be made prior to the good, for there remains the possibility of rejecting the very idea of a universally valid morality. The second argument, which appeals to conscience, seems therefore essential to an imperative conception of morality. Taken together, Kant's two points refer to a core morality on which people of conscience can agree despite their deep differences about the nature of the good life.

But now we must look more closely at this appeal to conscience. I have insisted that conscience is a legitimate court of appeal for moral philosophy, and I doubt that anyone today would sincerely deny recognizing a basic set of duties that are ours whatever we may want to do. Nonetheless, the voice of conscience is not unimpeachable. One reason we could have for rejecting its demands is finding that they make

21 See Chapter 5, Section 3, this volume.

sense only in terms of a worldview to which we can no longer feel allegiance. And indeed an objection of precisely this form has dogged the imperative conception of morality throughout modern times.

As I observed before, Hume, Schopenhauer, and Anscombe have all argued that conceiving of morality as a set of obligations binding upon all, whatever our ideas of self-realization, cannot be coherently detached from the Christian theology that gave birth to it. There cannot be laws of conduct without a lawgiver, and only God, they have claimed, can be thought to have sufficient authority and scope to issue unconditional commands to which all human conduct is subject. Since, however, the image of the divine legislator has lost for so many its appeal (I examine the most important reasons for this in the next chapter), these thinkers have concluded that the imperative view of morality must be left behind as well. They do not deny that, without giving any thought to this theological framework, we may feel unconditionally bound by certain obligations. But for them such convictions are, as Anscombe says, mere "survivals." Having lost all intelligible meaning, they urge themselves upon us with the authority of conscience only because we have been shaped by a tradition in which we no longer truly believe. For a neo-Aristotelian such as Anscombe, the only comprehensible obligations we have must be those we can see to foster the self-fulfillment or flourishing of the agent. In other words, she, like Hume, has pleaded for restoring the ancient priority of the good.

The most common rejoinder to this argument is that the legislative source of categorical obligations can be, instead of God, practical reason itself. It has been thought that, insofar as anyone views himself as a rational agent, he must accept certain norms regulating his conduct toward other such agents, whatever other interests he may have. This approach is generally called Kantian, and with some justice, since Kant did believe that categorical obligations express the laws that rational beings impose upon themselves. But it is important to remember that (at least beginning with the *Critique of Practical Reason*) Kant did not believe that this could serve as an argument to justify that we are subject to categorical moral duties. According to him, practical reason can be legislative in this way only if it is free, only if it can transcend all empirically conditioned interests (for which, after all, it is supposedly legislating); but that means that this rational activity can never be an object of our knowledge, so it can never be used to prove anything about the nature of moral obligations. In Kant's view, we do have grounds to believe that reason is the source of morality, but only as an inference from our prior conviction (which he called the "fact of reason") that we are bound by categorical obligations.

To its contemporary adherents, however, the idea that practical reason is the source of obligations unconditionally binding upon all has seemed independent of Kant's own metaphysics of freedom. Leaving aside various differences of detail, we may understand their rationalism as resting essentially upon the following, not always fully explicit, pattern of argument:[22]

(1) To act rationally, one must act for what one believes to be good reasons.

(2) One must then also believe that all other rational agents would agree that they are good reasons. Even in the case of instrumental reasoning, where one believes a certain action is the reasonable way to satisfy some given interest, one must also believe that all rational agents would agree that it is reasonable, given that interest (which they may or may not share).

(3) If the rationality of some action must be an object of agreement among all rational agents, it seems impossible for it to depend essentially upon normative beliefs (that is, accepted norms of thought and action) that some rational agents may share, but others not.

(4) The rationality of the action must instead be ascertainable from a position of completely detached reflection, in which one stands back from all one's present norms of thought and action except the commitment to reason itself, in order to appraise the merits of the action.

(5) Thus, rational action is such that all rational agents must unconditionally acknowledge its rationality, whatever their other normative beliefs might be. Of course, they need not therefore have good reason to perform the action, since its rationality, which they must recognize, may consist in its best satisfying some interest that they may not share. But the hypothetical imperative ("Given goal

---

22 Notable examples of this "neo-Kantian" argument are Alan Gewirth, *Reason and Morality* (University of Chicago Press, 1978); Jürgen Habermas, *Diskursethik – Notizen zu einem Begründungsprogramme*, pp. 53–126 in his *Moralbewußtsein und kommunikatives Handeln* (Frankfurt: Suhrkamp, 1983); David Gauthier, *Morals by Agreement* (Oxford University Press, 1986); Thomas Nagel, *The View from Nowhere* (Oxford University Press, 1986).

G, do action *A*"), which in this case enjoins the action, implies a categorical imperative ("Either do *A,* or abandon *G*"). And the rationality of this latter unconditional demand, so it is concluded, must derive from the very nature of practical reason.

More has to be said, of course, about the nature of rationality if such unconditional claims on conduct are to become specific and begin to resemble what we ordinarily understand by moral obligations. Here differences emerge among the philosophers sharing this line of argument. In addition, it is generally supposed that practical reason can thus yield fundamental norms of moral conduct only given certain basic features of the human condition such as the relative scarcity of resources and the physical vulnerability of persons. That is another parameter of the argument that has to be spelled out.

This rationalist argument, moreover, need not be meant to show that practical reason by itself, without moral resources of some sort or other, is able to *generate* good reasons for action. The argument does presuppose, of course, that no moral obligations are already given as valid. But reason can still be said to be the source of an imperative morality, if in a posture of complete detachment it can work up an objective conception of moral value from the appearances of value contained in our less objective views – if, that is, it can *approve* or *reject* reasons for action that arise from commitments we find we have, but do not yet recognize as truly binding on us. This is the version Thomas Nagel seems to favor, for example.[23]

In any of its versions, however, and in whatever way its key terms are made specific, this argument seems to me flawed at its very heart. A commitment to rationality, however precisely understood, is simply too slender a basis for justifying the validity of any moral obligation if it may not rely upon the validity of others. The apparently more modest version, according to which practical reason by itself is able not to generate moral obligations but to evaluate the purported obligations arising from our other commitments, is in reality no more plausible. The only way to mold appearances of value into a more objective view of value is by already knowing something about what is valuable. For the evaluation of our purported obligations cannot but proceed by appealing to norms of thought and action. And if these norms do not already embody any moral obligations (as they must not on this

23 Nagel, *View from Nowhere,* pp. 141, 146–7.

argument, the aim being to show that morality has its source in practical reason), then I am convinced such an evaluation must remain mute about moral matters.

The objection I am introducing – namely, that reason is unable and indeed wrongly expected to provide by itself the basis for anything so substantial as a morality of categorical obligation – is no doubt a familiar one. In essence, it has been brought against the Kantian project since the days of F. H. Jacobi and Hegel. To prove fully convincing, my criticism needs not only more elaboration than I have given it so far, but also a diagnosis of the misconceptions about the nature of reason that make this view of morality so continually attractive. This further argument and the defense of a more "contextualist" conception of reason I shall provide in the next chapter. Here my aim is simply to map out the problematic terrain on which modern ethics finds itself today. For if there continue to be many philosophers determined to find the source of categorical obligations in the nature of practical reason, there are many, too, who suspect that the kind of objection I have sketched is on the mark. If they are right, then the priority of the right over the good cannot plausibly be defended as a requirement of practical reason itself. We may be able to show that certain categorical duties are binding on us, but only if we already believe that other such duties are ours.

Clearly, this latter sort of justification will not persuade those who truly find suspect the very notion of categorical obligation. So given the demise of its original theological framework, ought not this notion be regarded as problematic and indeed outmoded? Might not the best policy be a return to ancient models and the explanation of the rules of morality in terms of the way they promote the agent's self-fulfillment?

An insuperable obstacle blocks this line of thought as well, however. It is Kant's argument that a morality applicable to all cannot be based on the priority of the good over the right, since the forms of self-fulfillment are too various for there to be any fundamental form of good that all can be said to want, and that can prove to be of sufficient substance. And here Kant is right. Our pluralistic sensibility is indeed too developed, our expectation of reasonable disagreement about the good life too ingrained, for us honestly to share the conviction that there is a single form of life that reasonable people will agree to be the best. Neo-Aristotelians might circumvent this problem by giving up the idea that there is a core morality applicable to all. But that, too, is not a very attractive prospect, even for them. The course of Philippa Foot's thought exemplifies perfectly how the priority of the good must continually run up against our better judgment. Like Anscombe, who seems to have had a significant influence on her moral thought, Foot has recommended that in opposition to much of modern moral philosophy we replace duty by virtue as the central ethical concept. This is tantamount to reinstating the priority of the good. And indeed at one point in her thought, she claimed that the worth of the virtues lies in how they promote the agent's self-fulfillment.[24] But she also came to realize that this is unlikely to be true for everyone, especially in the case of the virtue of justice. Instead of contracting the applicability of morality to those whose self-fulfillment it would promote, however, she argued that moral judgments apply even to those who lack any motive or interest to abide by them.[25] This was a sound move, but it was also a reversion to the priority of the right over the good. Foot understood this argument as directed against Kant, and it does contradict his view that everyone subject to the claims of morality must actually have a motive to comply with them. But as I have argued earlier, this view forms no essential part of an imperative conception of morality. Foot has also insisted that in being applicable even to those who have no interest in adhering to them, the claims of morality do not differ from the claims of etiquette. This point, too, is true, but it does not really have the deflationary force she intended and is quite compatible with the moral priority of the right. As Norbert Elias has shown, the development of modern manners illustrates the same triumph of rules of conduct over the satisfaction of desire that we connect with the observance of categorical duties.[26] Modern etiquette and modern morality both issue unconditional claims. They differ (and this may be all there is to their difference) in their importance for social life.

24 See Philippa Foot, "Moral Beliefs," reprinted on pp. 110–31 in her *Virtues and Vices* (Berkeley: University of California Press, 1978), and also p. xiii of that volume.
25 Philippa Foot, "Morality as a System of Hypothetical Imperatives" and "A Reply to Professor Frankena," both reprinted on pp. 157–80 in *Virtues and Vices*.
26 Norbert Elias, *The History of Manners*, vol. 1 of *The Civilizing Process* (New York: Pantheon, 1982). Philippa Foot wrongly holds that rules of etiquette (and so those of morality, too) are but hypothetical imperatives because "they have no automatic reason-giving force independent of the agent's interests or desires" (*Virtues and Vices*, p. 176). But this claim involves an idiosyncratic notion of the distinction between hypothetical and categorical imperatives. An imperative is categorical simply if it *applies* to an agent, whatever his interests or desires; one need not assume thereby that the agent must also have a motive to *comply* with it. This was Kant's own conception of a categorical imperative, and he supposed that categorical (moral) imperatives have "an automatic reason-giving force" only because he also assumed a strong version of the principle that "ought implies can." That version is not, I have argued, a necessary part of the priority of the right.

We are faced, therefore, with a dilemma. We are too aware of the variety of forms of self-fulfillment to believe, with Aristotle – or, since his own allegiance to a truly universal morality is unclear, with the Stoics and medieval Aristotelians – that a core morality applicable to all can be based on a good that all desire. Yet the idea that this core morality is binding upon all, whatever their interests, is intelligible only if we can fix a source for this moral legislation – and only the notion of God, which we are disinclined to invoke, seems adequate to this task. From this dilemma stem some of the deepest uncertainties in our present moral thought. We need, but lack, a general understanding of the nature of morality that could replace both the ancient perspective and the Judeo-Christian perspective, which, in often hidden ways, has shaped so much of modern ethics.

There is, I believe, but one possible escape from this dilemma. If the idea of a core morality applicable to all does indeed figure among our most settled convictions, and if it cannot be understood in terms of the priority of the good, then at the heart of our moral convictions lies a belief in the priority of the right. Why can these convictions not stand on their own? If we place at the center of our moral thought the fact that these are convictions from which we will not budge, then there will be something we can adduce as the source of these categorical duties: not God, nor practical reason, but rather the way of life expressed in these convictions. There will no longer be any positive reason to doubt the authority of conscience when it speaks of duties that are unconditionally ours, once it is taken to be no more than the voice of the way of life to which we hold. This understanding of imperative morality would put us beyond the dilemma at which we have arrived. But whether it is not so meager an understanding as to be none at all is a problem I explore in the next chapter.

2

BEYOND RELIGION AND
ENLIGHTENMENT

1. The Modern World and Religion

God is so great he does not have to exist. Thus might we describe the essence of the process of secularization that has so profoundly shaped modern society. The repudiation of idols, the respect for God's transcendence, is what has led to relieving God from the task of being the ultimate explanation for the order of nature and the course of history. To explain something in terms of divine action or Providence always amounts to placing God among the finite causes we have already found or can imagine discovering. Once we have resolved to let God be God, we can no longer use God for our own cognitive ends. A similar unburdening of God seems appropriate in the domain of morality. When the validity of a moral demand is understood in terms of being God's command, the motive of the moral life becomes the desire to please God, as though we could help him or should fear him. Such a conception of God must appear as an all-too-human projection, if we assume that God must transcend such human needs and passions. We respect God as God when we learn to value the moral life for itself without appeal to God's purposes (though we may still believe that God loves what is good and right).

This view of the modern process of secularization has two important implications. The first is that the process is rooted in Judeo-Christian

monotheism itself. The God of the Bible is a jealous God: at the head
of the Decalogue stands the prohibition of idols. It was thus God's fate,
slowly worked out through the centuries, to be freed from the human
tasks of this world, from our need to explain nature and to found
morality. Thus, secularization does not consist in the illegitimate ex-
propriation of the divine attributes and in their Promethean transfer-
ence to man. On this point Hans Blumenberg, the great advocate of
the legitimacy of the modern age, is certainly right. But Blumenberg
seems to me wrong to lay such emphasis on the idea that secularization
has freed us from an incoherent theology that dealt in questions (such
as how an omnipotent God could create a world in which there is evil)
that could not be answered.[1] The alternative view I propose is that
secularization is instead the inner logic of Judeo-Christian monotheism.

This view builds on, yet goes beyond, Max Weber's famous thesis
that certain currents of monotheism (particularly the Calvinist sects
that tied the doctrine of justification by faith alone to the need for
works as proof of election) led to the "innerworldly asceticism" that
created the modern world. I am aiming at a generalization of Weber's
results: God's transcendence has led to his withdrawal from the world
and thus to the autonomy of the world, even where (as in morality)
the world has not become, as Weber thought, the object of rational
domination. In a recent work, *Le désenchantement du monde*, Marcel

Gauchet has developed this view in a very persuasive way. He has shown
that Christian monotheism has been "the religion for leaving religion
behind," a way of eliminating the sacred within the world *ad majorem
gloriam Dei*. "Plus les dieux sont grands," he writes, "plus les hommes
sont libres."[2] The same idea can be found in the famous letters Dietrich Bonhoeffer wrote to Eberhard Bethge, in which Bonhoeffer
sought to distinguish true faith in God from "religion," which he saw
as an expression of human weakness.[3]

In putting forward this conception, I do not want to suggest that the
Judeo-Christian tradition has tended uniformly toward secularization.

1 Hans Blumenberg, *Säkularisierung und Selbstbehauptung* (Frankfurt: Suhrkamp, 1974),
   pp. 44, 134, 201, 208–9.
2 Marcel Gauchet, *Le désenchantement du monde* (Paris: Gallimard, 1985), pp. II, 53. See
   also Peter Berger, *The Sacred Canopy* (New York: Doubleday, 1967), chapter 5.
3 Dietrich Bonhoeffer, *Widerstand und Ergebung: Briefe und Aufzeichnungen aus der Haft*
   (Munich: Kaiser Verlag, 1970), letters of 30 April, 8 June, 8 July, and especially 16
   July 1944.

Catholic thought, by stressing the need for mediation between the individual conscience and God (through the Church, the sacraments, and the saints), has certainly been less favorable to this tendency than Protestant or Jewish thought. In addition, the Christian doctrine of the Incarnation can easily be seen as reintroducing the sacred into the world. It can also, however, be understood as the divine affirmation of the intrinsic value of the world, and in this form it has indeed been an essential element in the process of secularization I have described. The "Judeo-Christian" tradition is obviously not all of a piece. What I wish to maintain is that God's transcendence, if thought through consistently to the end, must lead to secularization.

From this point of view there is no deep opposition between monotheism and modernity. Or at least this is so insofar as monotheism heeds God's transcendence and insofar as modernity requires the purely naturalistic explanation of nature as well as a purely human understanding of morality. Modernity has been a way of fulfilling Judeo-Christian monotheism. By this I do not mean that the two are the same, that every exponent of modernity is, at least implicitly, a believer in the One God. Rather, the point is not only that the two are largely compatible, but also that monotheism paved the way for the successes of modernity. Only thus can we explain why a society that had defined itself by religious ideals for centuries could with such relative ease welcome the autonomy of science and of morality.

The second important implication of this theory of secularization is that the autonomy of science and of morality does not imply that faith must disappear. Otherwise, the theory would scarcely be plausible, for faith is far from dying out. What it asserts instead is that religion can no longer fulfill certain functions that belonged to it in premodern societies. We can no longer expect religion to provide ultimate explanations of nature or ultimate justifications of morality. Or at least, such religious explanations are no longer ones of which the moral life or scientific inquiry recognizes any need. It is in this development that the so-called death of God consists. But such an outcome does not exclude the possibility that we may still find in God an irreplaceable source of meaning for our lives. Indeed, it is possible to affirm, with Jean-Luc Marion, that "la mort de Dieu [est] le visage *moderne* de son insistante et éternelle fidélité."[4] Religious experience, prayer, and

4 Jean-Luc Marion, *L'idole et la distance* (Paris: Grasset, 1977), p. 11.

commitment may still remain important, and perhaps acquire their true significance only when we no longer suppose God serves to justify or fulfill our own purposes. Perhaps faith really stems from the conviction that there is more to life than our purposes can ever grasp. Perhaps also faith responds to those other problems of human existence that understanding the course of the world and the moral rules for living together cannot solve – the problems of coming to terms with the evil we can never punish, the hidden virtue we can never honor, the past suffering we can never redeem.

So when at the beginning I described modern secularization as the realization that God is so great he does not have to exist, I did not mean that God does not exist or that his nonexistence is implied by the secularizing outlook of modernity. I meant that he does not *need* to exist, though it may well be true that he exists. We no longer need God to explain the world and to ground the rules of our common life. Si Dieu n'existait pas, il ne faudrait plus l'inventer. This means a liberation of man. It also means a liberation of God. If we follow Karl Barth and Dietrich Bonhoeffer, as I propose to do, and identify the idea of "religion," in a restricted sense, with the use of God for cosmological and moral purposes, distinguishing it from faith, then we can say that modern society is beyond religion.

2. The Enlightenment Project

So much for what seems already settled. Now we come to the problems that are still with us. Are the leading ideas of the Enlightenment, in which the outlook of modernity has so often found expression, able to take over the role from which God has been discharged? From the fact that God cannot perform these functions it does not follow that man, his heir, must be equal to them. Thus, in the domain of the sciences, there arises the following question: in what sense can we speak of the *truth* of theories that we may well have good reason to *accept,* if we lack a divine guarantee that our reason (that is, our capacity to recognize the validity of reasons) is adequate to the world? In the domain of morality, there is an analogous question: what *authority* can moral demands have to govern our conduct once we have given up the perspective in which they are seen as the commandments of a superior being?

The question about the truth of the sciences does not seem particularly urgent, at least for the sciences themselves, though things may be otherwise for philosophy. Modern (natural) science has learned how to proceed according to internal criteria that can in principle be satisfied on the basis of experimental evidence that must itself conform to scientific standards. In this way progress, the reasoned preference for one scientific claim over others, becomes possible. The scientist can dispense with the external, purely philosophical question about the relation between this process of inquiry and the world itself. There is no need to ask whether a theory that is supported and favored by good experimental evidence therefore corresponds to reality, that is, whether it is "true."

The situation appears very different in the domain of morality. Or at least it clearly does so if we share the distinctive outlook of modern ethics. This has been an *imperative* conception of morality according to which we are subject to certain moral duties whatever our given interests or conception of the good life. Such duties are "categorical," as Kant would say, though in a sense that transcends the peculiarities of Kantian ethics. Even "consequentialist" (e.g., utilitarian) views of morality rely on a categorical "ought." For the obligation to do that action which brings about the most good overall is held by consequentialists to be binding on us whatever our other interests. As I indicated in Chapter 1, this conception of morality draws its rationale from the modern experience that reasonable people differ about the nature of the human good, and from the conviction that they can nonetheless agree upon a core morality binding unconditionally on all. No doubt, this core morality of categorical duties need not make up the whole of our moral self-understanding. But in modern thought it has certainly played a central role.

The imperative conception of morality looks at moral rules as being constraints or laws. Quite possibly we can be accustomed to seeing ourselves as subject to these moral laws without having some notion of their source, some image of a legislator. But this frame of mind is by its nature unstable. The very idea of law impels us to look for its legislator. If we cannot determine its source, we cannot continue to believe that there exists such a thing as moral law. In this regard, therefore, making sense of the foundations of morality is not a purely philosophical matter. It belongs to the survival conditions of morality itself, at least as it has been characteristically understood in modern times.

In the preceding chapter we began to see, however, just how difficult it is to arrive at a convincing view of the basis of the imperative conception. What is the authoritative source of these supposedly categorical moral rules? The modern process of secularization I have been describing shows why, in the light of our monotheistic traditions themselves, the answer cannot really be sought in God. The question now is whether our Enlightenment inheritance can provide an adequate account of the authority of this modern ethic. I am aware, of course, of the danger in assuming a definition of a movement so complex as the Enlightenment. Still, I believe that we may rightly consider as one of its important legacies the project of locating the source of moral norms no longer in God but in the nature of man.

Within the Enlightenment, from the late seventeenth century until today, there have obviously been significant points of disagreement about how this project is to be carried out. One of them has concerned the way in which human nature is supposed to serve as the source of morality. Do moral norms derive their very existence from human nature, or do they consist in independent truths whose authority human nature on its own, without appeal to God, is able to recognize? There has also been the disagreement about which aspect of human nature is supposed to be decisive – sentiment or reason. The sentimentalist alternative showed early on its basic flaw. Feelings of approval and disapproval are too variable from person to person, situation to situation, and culture to culture, to serve as the basis of a universal morality, that is, to ground a morality of duties and rights valid for everyone. This is the conclusion to which Diderot came in *Le Neveu de Rameau,* giving up his first enthusiasm for the sentimentalist ethics he found in Shaftesbury and Hutcheson. If feelings play a role in a universal morality, then they do so only to the extent that they are corrected and guided by reflection. And this seems to lead to the second, rationalist alternative.

In the rationalist view, practical reason itself serves as the source of moral laws. As I have suggested, this view can take two forms.[5] One is that practical reason is able by itself to construct the laws that make up the domain of morality, as in Kant's ethics. The other is that practical reason is able by itself to recognize (by "intuition" or reflection) the authority of independently existing moral principles, as in the early

---

5 For an important discussion of the differences between these two versions, see John Rawls, "Themes in Kant's Moral Philosophy," pp. 95–102 in E. Förster (ed.), *Kant's Transcendental Deductions* (Stanford, Calif.: Stanford University Press, 1989).

eighteenth-century ethics of Samuel Clarke. It is in one or the other of these two forms of moral rationalism that the Enlightenment outlook continues to inspire the dominant currents of contemporary ethics. On the "constructivist" wing, there are today such (otherwise diverse) figures as Alan Gewirth, David Gauthier, and Jürgen Habermas; and more in the "intuitionist" camp, Thomas Nagel. Their common conviction, as I observed in the preceding chapter, is that simply by virtue of being rational agents we must come to accept certain recognizably moral norms of conduct.

To be sure, this kind of rationalism generally supposes that practical reason leads to morality only in light of certain fundamental, nonmoral features of the human condition. These givens are what Hume called the "circumstances of justice" – the relative scarcity of what people want, and the rough physical and mental equality among them. Nonetheless, it does make reason the *source* of morality in that it claims that reason is able to justify our basic moral obligations from a standpoint prior to morality itself, that is, without appeal to any antecedently given moral norms. This is what is essential to the idea of reason as the "source" of morality and not, I should add, the view that there exists a realm of moral facts of which we can gain knowledge by intuition or reflection. The latter view is one I believe to be correct (as I explain in Chapter 5). But it falls short of making reason the source of morality, since it may be true, as indeed I think it is, that reflection can yield moral knowledge only by building upon existing moral commitments.

But here I anticipate what I will have to say in criticism of the rationalist conception. Let us first consider, as we did in the preceding chapter, the fundamental argument underlying the Enlightenment idea that a categorically binding morality has its source in practical reason itself. It will be helpful to have it before our eyes. The argument lies at a very abstract level, so abstract that those who assume it rarely formulate it explicitly. But it is no less essential, and indeed questionable, for that. The argument is as follows:

(1) To act rationally, one must act for what one believes to be good reasons.

(2) One must then also believe that all other rational agents would agree that they are good reasons. Even in cases of instrumental rationality, where one believes a certain action is the reasonable way to satisfy some given interest, one must also believe that all

rational agents would agree that it is reasonable given that interest (which they may or may not share).

(3) If the rationality of some action must be an object of agreement among all rational agents, it seems impossible for it to depend essentially upon normative beliefs (i.e., accepted norms of thought and action) that some rational agents may share but others not.

(4) The rationality of the action must instead be ascertainable from a position of completely detached reflection, in which one stands back from all one's present norms of thought and action except the commitment to reason itself, in order to appraise the merits of the action.

(5) Thus, rational action is such that all rational agents must unconditionally acknowledge its rationality, whatever their other normative beliefs might be. Of course, they need not therefore have good reason to perform such an action, since its rationality, which they must recognize, may consist in its best satisfying some given interest, which they may not share. But the hypothetical imperative ("Given goal G, do action A"), which in this case enjoins the action, implies a categorical imperative ("Either do A or abandon G"). And the rationality of this latter unconditional demand, so it is concluded, must derive from the very nature of practical reason.

As the concept of rationality acquires more specific content, the unconditional or categorical claims on conduct that practical reason is thought to make will supposedly come to resemble what we ordinarily understand by moral obligations. The Enlightenment idea that a categorical morality has its source in practical reason itself has therefore two key components. First, it holds that rational action is, in general, action the rationality of which all rational agents must acknowledge. And second, it supposes that these categorical claims that reason places on conduct amount in effect to what we can recognize as morality.

Both of these components seem wrong to me. Not only must there remain an unbridgeable gap between (5) and what we usually understand as morality, if (5) is true. But the principle (2), which leads to (5) – and which asserts that the rationality of any action must be such as to be acknowledged by all rational agents – is also mistaken. That is the gist of the criticism I sketched in the preceding chapter, claiming that reason cannot be expected to serve as the source of morality. In more or less articulate form, this claim lies at the heart of the disenchantment with the Enlightenment that is so widespread today.

We must now examine, in more detail, why this disenchantment is justified.

3. The Crisis of the Enlightenment

At bottom, the mistake of the Enlightenment project is the failure to see that rationality is as such an abstract capacity. Its rules are abstract ones, such as that contradictions are to be avoided or (perhaps) that one should pursue what one believes to be good and avoid what one believes to be bad.[6] Such rules are at best a necessary, not a sufficient basis for determining (in conjunction with nonmoral information about the world) the validity of any moral norms.

Perhaps the best general way to prove this point is to observe that rationality is not anything like a Platonic essence, its contours fixed independently of what we might choose them to be. I do not mean that we should think a norm is valid or rational just because we have decided that it is so; that would certainly be wrong. But the rationality of a norm differs from the idea of a norm of rationality. Of the norms of thought and action we hold to be valid it is we who decide which (naturally not all!) will also count as norms of rationality. We should do so, however, with an eye to two things we want from a concept of rationality. First, norms of rationality should be highly formal, indifferent to subject matter. Second, they should be as indisputable as possible, readily acceptable to all no matter what else they may believe; for norms about which there are or can be doubts or disagreement are precisely those that we want to be able to show that it is *rational* to accept or reject. (A notion of rationality is rather pointless if we can say about someone who does not share some norm of ours only that he is not being "rational.") How unlikely must it then be that norms of thought and action selected precisely for their formal, indisputable character should be sufficient (along with nonmoral information about the world) to derive anything so substantial as the universalist morality with which we are familiar! In any case, what can be clearly shown is how particular attempts at such a derivation fail: either the

---

6 I add the qualification "perhaps" with regard to the second rule because some philosophers (some Thomists, for example) have understood it to imply directly the famous doctrine of double effect. Without thinking that this doctrine must be invalid, I am sure that it is far too controversial to be drawn simply from what may count as the nature of practical rationality.

norms assigned to the idea of rationality do not really suffice, or they do so only because they go beyond the indisputable and are already substantial moral norms in disguise.[7]

As an example of the first sort of failure, consider David Gauthier's *Morals by Agreement,* the most carefully and broadly argued version of an approach to morality that goes back to Hobbes. Its aim is to show that "morality . . . can be generated as a rational constraint from the non-moral premises of rational choice" – in other words, that agents committed to maximizing their expected utility will have reason, given the fundamentals of the human condition, to constrain their pursuit of individual advantage, thereby prospering more in the long run, if they adhere to certain rules of cooperation founded upon mutual advantage. The difficulty with this account is not just that the outcome of Gauthier's derivation bears only a partial resemblance to ordinary morality, confirming Locke's verdict that "an Hobbist will not easily admit a great many plain duties of morality." That is, one would have thought the hallmark of the moral point of view lies in respecting those who may not, and indeed those (the immature, the weak, the handicapped) who cannot benefit us in some way, but whom Gauthier himself must put beyond the pale of (his) morality.[8] The problem is also that rational agents as Gauthier understands them, their rationality consisting in maximizing expected utility, really have as such (that is, without any antecedent moral commitments) no sufficient reason to prefer being cooperative to seeming cooperative but being ready, when the time is ripe, to take advantage of those who do wish to cooperate.[9] There is no road that leads from prudence to morality.

The opposite sort of failure infects Kant's account of how morality arises from rationality. At the heart of moral thinking, Kant believed, lies a universalization criterion ("Act only according to those maxims

---

7 A similar conclusion emerges from Thomas Nagel's illuminating critique of R. M. Hare's attempt to draw a substantial morality from the formal features of "moral language." See his "Foundations of Impartiality," pp. 101–12 in D. Seanor and N. Fotion (eds.), *Hare and Critics* (Oxford University Press, 1988), an essay all the more striking in that it seems at odds with the considerable sympathy for the rationalist project evident in Nagel's *View from Nowhere.*

8 Gauthier, *Morals by Agreement,* pp. 4, 268.

9 For arguments showing that Gauthier fails to prove that rational agents, as he conceives them, have good reason to be cooperative, "constrained" maximizers, see the essays by Geoffrey Sayre-McCord, David Copp, and Holly Smith in Peter Vallentyne (ed.), *Contractarianism and Rational Choice* (Cambridge University Press, 1991).

which you can at the same time will that they become universal laws"), which can plausibly account for many, if not all, of the duties of ordinary morality. But, contrary to Kant, this criterion goes well beyond what can be drawn from the idea of practical rationality as such. To see this, note that it involves more than the requirement to avoid contradictory maxims. It makes the demand that not just under certain conditions (e.g., where all parties are committed to acting morally), but *always* we judge the morality of our maxim of action, not according to what will ensue if we, perhaps alone, act on the maxim, but according to what would ensue if everyone were to act on it. In other words, it forbids us to determine what we morally ought to do by reference to how others are likely to use our actions for their own, perhaps immoral purposes. Whether correct or not, this sort of outlook (which Max Weber called "the ethics of conviction") is surely too controversial to be drawn from the mere notion of practical rationality.

Rationality as such constitutes, then, too slender a basis for establishing the validity of any moral obligation. In saying this, I do not wish to deny that we can justify the validity of certain moral obligations. But we can do so only by relying upon the presumed validity of other moral obligations. Practical reason cannot therefore be the source of morality. On the contrary, reason becomes capable of moral argumentation only within an already existing morality. Not by ascending to an absolutely detached point of view, but only through belonging to a moral tradition, or to a variety of moral traditions and practices, can we find our moral bearings. When we try to rise above our historical situation, reason loses its substance and becomes mute.

This conclusion points to the fact that the rationalist argument I sketched earlier suffers from not just one, but two fundamental mistakes. Not only does there lie an insuperable gap between whatever norms of conduct the bare notion of practical rationality can establish and even the most basic moral obligations we recognize, but also the principle (2) on which this argument relies is incorrect. That is, conduct that is rational for one agent in a given situation need not be so for another. Whether it is rational depends generally on what else he happens to believe, and such background convictions may well differ from person to person, belonging as they may to different moral traditions.

It is by pursuing the connection between moral rationality and tradition, I shall argue, that we can find our way out of the crisis of Enlightenment ethics. But before pushing farther down that path, we must look at what many consider the strongest argument for thinking the authority of morality *must* be sought outside existing practice and in the nature of reason itself. Is it not a basic principle of practical rationality, independent of morality, that an agent ought to maximize his expected utility – that is, seek to satisfy his given preferences in the most efficient manner possible? And is not this principle one we see as unconditionally binding on our conduct, forming the basis on which we should adopt all our other rules of conduct? Whatever may be the defects in Gauthier's own construction, must we not continue to seek a derivation of morality from this basic form of rationality, if morality is really to have any authority for us? Is not maximization indeed the basis on which we can see that certain prevalent forms of moral thinking (particularly "deontological" ones) are really without rational warrant?[10]

This line of thought rests, however, on a confusion. In some senses of the term, "maximization" is a far from incontestable commitment. If it is supposed to imply, for example, that means can always be traded off against ends, so that an action that is in itself unacceptable should be done if it leads to something of greater good, then some people will reasonably reject it as a rule of conduct. They will not hold the substantive belief that there exists a single kind of ultimate value that means and ends variously promote or express. Maximization cannot count as a fundamental norm of practical reason if it amounts to but an eminently controversial view about the nature of value. To serve that role, it must instead be understood in a sense that does not presuppose the validity of consequentialist forms of reasoning. Indeed, the only plausible sense in which the maximization of expected utility can be deemed a fundamental commitment of ours is that by itself it implies no substantive beliefs about the nature of value. It must be construed broadly enough to allow that the deontologist "maximizes," too, when he seeks to conform *as best he can* to the moral principle he holds supreme, namely, that one is to respect certain rights, whatever the consequences, even for the extent to which others may then respect these rights.

10 This objection, made to a view resembling the moral contextualism I shall go on to defend, occurs in David Gauthier, "Why Contractarianism?" pp. 18–22 in Vallentyne (ed.), *Contractarianism and Rational Choice*. For the view that there is an elective affinity between maximizing rationality and consequentialism, see Samuel Scheffler, "Agent-Centered Restrictions, Rationality, and the Virtues," pp. 251–2 in Scheffler (ed.), *Consequentialism and Its Critics* (Oxford University Press, 1988).

In this suitably abstract sense, maximization of expected utility means simply that it is rational to do the best we can. What "the best" is, however, will be determined by our substantive beliefs about the way in which different things are good, being commensurable forms of a single value or instead reflecting heterogeneous values that can be ranked, if at all, only in order of importance (a "lexical ordering").[11] If practical reason is essentially maximizing, this entails only that we are to do the best we can in the light of whatever we already believe about what is good. It is in such beliefs, and not on the principle of maximization, that there is disagreement between those who accept deontological norms and those who do not. Clearly too, nothing in this idea of maximization requires that moral norms, to have authority for our conduct, must be derived from the maximizing pursuit of nonmoral aims. Reason as maximization does not of itself imply that such a derivation is necessary, nor does it lend any support to the notion that reason must prove to be the source of morality. To do the best we can is a principle we observe no less when we deliberate within an existing morality, and within one that may not be simply consequentialist. The view that morality has its source in reason really comes from elsewhere – not from any formal principles of rationality, but rather, as we shall see later, from a metaphysical conception of the aims of reason.

4. Two Illusory Solutions

The disenchantment with the Enlightenment is therefore justified. A rationalist ethics cannot succeed. Reason cannot take over the function of grounding morality, now that God has been dispensed from the task. There are a number of possible responses to this situation.

One would be to conclude that the imperative conception of moral-ity – the idea of a morality binding on all, whatever their interests – makes sense only within the theological perspective of God as moral legislator, and that we should look for a new moral conception in which the notions of law and legislator do not play so central a role.[12] Following this line of thought, we might easily conclude that such an

---

11 See Chapter 7, this volume.
12 This was already the view of Hume (*Enquiry Concerning the Principles of Morals,* appendix 4) and of Schopenhauer (*Über das Fundament der Moral,* §4). See Chapter 1, this volume.

ethic has in fact been available for some time. It is the ethics of
Aristotle, according to which morality, far from consisting in categorical duties, forms part of the self-realization to which all human beings
are drawn by their nature. It is not by accident that neo-Aristotelianism
has come to appeal to so many thinkers today, in America as well as in
Europe.[13] The different forms it has taken agree upon one essential
point: morality must be viewed as an *attractive*, not an *imperative* ideal,
as an element of the flourishing life we naturally desire and not as a
set of norms imposed on our self-fulfillment from without. The recent
resurgence of interest in this outlook testifies to the crisis of the
imperative conception of morality.

Nonetheless, neo-Aristotelianism betrays a profound blindness
about the modern condition. A characteristic theme of modern
thought is that rational agreement about the nature of the good life is
improbable. The more we talk about the meaning of life, the more
likely it is that we will disagree. This experience is one of the principal
reasons Aristotelian ethics lost so much of its prestige in the first
centuries of the modern era. Aristotle had assumed that the meaning
of life or the nature of self-realization could be the object of rational
consensus, and so had explained in these terms the worth of the
virtues. But Aristotle's trust in the eventual unanimity of reasonable
people has shown itself to be far too sanguine. That is why early
modern moral philosophy, beginning with Grotius (the true father of
modern ethics), sought to circumscribe a core morality, valid for all, as
independent as possible of controversial views of the human good.[14]
The imperative conception of morality to which this line of thought
led has its roots in one of the distinctive experiences of modernity.

In an important sense, therefore, neo-Aristotelianism founders on
the same difficulty as Enlightenment ethics. Man's essence does not
provide any firm point of reasonable agreement on which a universal
ethics can be established. This is indeed the heart of our contemporary

13 I am thinking, for example, of G. E. M. Anscombe ("Modern Moral Philosophy"
   [1958], reprinted in her *Collected Philosophical Papers*, vol. 3 [Minneapolis: University
   of Minnesota Press, 1981]); Alasdair MacIntyre (*After Virtue* and more recently *Three
   Rival Versions of Moral Inquiry* [Notre Dame, Ind.: University of Notre Dame Press,
   1991], pp. 154, 193); Robert Spaemann (*Basic Moral Concepts*, German original
   1982 [London: Routledge, 1989]; and Michel Villey (*La formation de la pensée
   juridique moderne* [Paris: Montchrestien, 1975]).
14 See Grotius, Prolegomena to the *De jure belli et pacis*, sections 39, 11; and also
   Pufendorf, *Specimen controversiarum circa jus naturale ipsi nuper motarum* (Uppsala,
   1678), p. 9.

crisis of ethics – a crisis that is not a secret of the academy, but very much a part of the public culture. Although the foundations of the sciences are in fact in no more obviously solid a state than those of morality, the sciences have developed internal criteria permitting them not only to increase their technological potential, but also to view the status of their foundations as a purely philosophical problem. For this reason, their cultural prestige has not declined. Morality, by contrast, cannot so easily immunize itself against fundamental questions of self-understanding.

This crisis of ethics might lead one, of course, to think the best solution is a return to the religious perspective. This nostalgia for the sacred is as old as an awareness of the problem itself. Some years ago, Daniel Bell, for example, wrote a powerful plea for just such a return.[15] He proclaimed that in an age of antinomian hedonism (so he described the culture this moral crisis has produced) it is more and more urgent to recognize that there must be limits to the cult of self-expression. Bell went on to identify these limits with the sacred. "Only a God can save us," Martin Heidegger's famous and similarly motivated declaration from the Black Forest, might also have been voiced by Bell on the urban East Coast of the United States.

But my remarks at the beginning of this chapter show why this solution will not work, either. A return to a religious ethic, even if impelled by a belief in its truth and not just in its utility (which is unlikely), is shortsighted. Bell does not ask why such an ethic was abandoned in the first place. If the secularization of morality had been an illegitimate coup d'état, or if it had originally been just a promising alternative to a religious ethic that seemed in difficulty, there would be good reasons to consider going back to the point of departure. But secularization has instead been the inner logic of Judeo-Christian monotheism, so a return must be pointless. It would lead in the end only to where we are already.

5. Universality and Tradition

Our only hope, I am convinced, is to keep our moral thinking in touch with the conditions of modernity. We must not yearn for lost certainties. Nor, I might add, should we rush to embrace the empty

---

15 Daniel Bell, "The Return of the Sacred?" pp. 324–54 in his *The Winding Passage* (New York: Basic, 1980).

promises of "postmodernism." For at least in the hands of thinkers such as J.-F. Lyotard, the idea of postmodernism ends up confusing the rejection of philosophical rationalism with the abandonment of reason itself. Lyotard is right, that is, to reject that "modern" view of history that sees it as the unfolding of reason and moral progress. This myth of history, dubious in itself, only builds on the Enlightenment myth that morality has its source in reason. But from this healthy – postmodern, as he calls it – distrust of simplifying myths, or *méta-récits*, Lyotard infers that moral thinking must therefore be combative and rhetorical rather than reasoned.[16] This is a non sequitur and fails to escape the terms of the rationalistic idea of reason it attacks.

The crisis of the Enlightenment, I believe, does not call for the desperate remedies of deserting reason, categorical duty, or the secular point of view. The proper solution lies instead in building on the connection between moral rationality and tradition to which I alluded earlier.

This solution is best laid out in two stages. The first consists in getting clearer about the form a secular ethics, without religious foundations, must take. One possibility has been explored by what I have been calling the Enlightenment project. It aims to show how the demands of morality – or at least of that core morality to which we hold everyone accountable – are based on practical reason as such, that is, on our ability to stand back critically from all that history has made of us and to determine from there what our duties are. But a "humanist" ethics can also take another, and I believe more plausible, form. We can regard our moral convictions as necessarily rooted not in reason as such, but rather in one or several traditions of moral thought and practice that are historically contingent (i.e., not necessary given the nature of practical rationality as such), and that we can elaborate and even change in part, but never completely leave behind, on pain of losing our moral bearings. In this conception, too, the authority of morality would not involve reference to God's majesty or purposes. But just as important, it would not be assumed that man possesses an essence, unsullied by contingency and sufficient to ground

---

16 Jean-François Lyotard, *La condition postmoderne* (Paris: Editions du Minuit, 1979) and *Le différend* (Paris: Editions du Minuit, 1983). It is the same fallacy that, on the aesthetic level, leads "postmodern" thinkers to reject "modernism" as a whole when their target is really the ideology of the avant-garde. On the difference between aesthetic modernism and avant-gardism, see Antoine Compagnon, *Les cinq paradoxes de la modernité* (Paris: Seuil, 1990), especially p. 163.

a morality. On the contrary, this image of the moral life views man as a being whose reason can be exercised only within a body of existing belief and whose moral sense is always historically conditioned.

What exactly would this outlook consider to be the source from which morality, and again in particular a core morality of categorical duties, draws its authority? Not, of course, reason as such, either as the capacity to construct such obligations or as the ability to recognize their authority. The source of their authority would instead be *our form of life*, insofar as it embodies this universal morality. The idea is that this form of life is authoritative for our conduct if, however historically contingent it may be, it has made us what we are, and if we identify with it and reason within its terms about what we ought to do.

To appreciate the import of this outlook, it is necessary to distinguish two claims that are usually combined in the concept of a universal morality: (1) that there is a set of (categorical) duties that obligate each person with regard to all other persons as such; and (2) that this system of duties is such that each person, simply by virtue of being rational, has good reason to accept them as his duties. The failure to keep distinct these two ideas has been important in making ethical rationalism seem so appealing. It has also in turn led antirationalists (such as Bernard Williams), who find no way that reason could be the source of morality, to dismiss the very idea of a categorical morality as a "peculiar institution."[17]

I propose, however, that we reject the idea of *universal justifiability* (2), while keeping that of a *universalist content* (1). That is, why can we not affirm a set of duties binding on all without supposing they must be justifiable to all? (Though one of these duties may well be that we should do our best, if need be, to justify to others the duties to which we hold them subject.) To do this, it is true, we must give up the familiar principle that someone can be said to have a categorical moral obligation only if his present beliefs are such that he could be rationally convinced of its validity. Yet this principle – which is effectively a version of " 'ought' implies 'can' " – is far from evident. It has indeed been an essential ingredient in the modern forms of ethical rationalism. But the point I urged in the preceding chapter against Kant's use

---

17 See Bernard Williams, *Ethics and the Limits of Philosophy* (Cambridge, Mass.: Harvard University Press, 1985), chapter 10, and my criticisms in *Patterns of Moral Complexity*, p. 87, and in "Les limites de la reflexion en ethique," pp. 199–214 in *L'age de la science, vol. 1: Ethique et philosophie politique* (Paris: Jacob, 1988).

of the principle applies here, too. The plausible view about "ought" and "can" is that someone can have a moral obligation if he can come to acknowledge it either by rational argument or by some morally permissible mode of training or socialization. Thus, a person need not be able to grasp what justifies a moral obligation for it to apply to him nonetheless. As I have just suggested, moreover, our ability to reason about the elements of a categorical morality is itself rooted in our allegiance to a form of life. If people are able to see the value of what they unconditionally ought to do, that is in general a social achievement rather than a necessary truth.

Understanding the authority of the imperative conception of morality means, therefore, that we recognize the form of life to which we belong and acknowledge the moral traditions we share and see as sustaining a set of duties categorically binding on all (even on those who do not participate in this form of life). This historical-sociological view of universal morality was introduced by Hegel, in the theory of modern *Sittlichkeit* he opposed to Kant's moral philosophy, and it became a central theme in the classics of modern sociology.[18] It cannot be denied, of course, that our moral thinking continues to be riddled by important disagreements about what, exactly, our duties to others are, as in the amount of assistance we owe the poor or in whether to admit a right to abortion. But these controversies should not blind us to the broad consensus about a range of core duties from promise keeping to respect for bodily integrity, nor to the shared belief that these duties are binding on us all whatever our interests or conceptions of the good. Often we need reminding, it seems, that ours is a form of life which, permeated by the modern experience of reasonable disagreement about the human good, rests on the conviction that we can nonetheless agree upon a core morality.

If I am right that the Enlightenment program of moral rationalism will not succeed, then it cannot be simply by virtue of being reasonable – that is, by applying our general capacities of reason to the givens of the human condition – that we share a commitment to such a core morality. Our allegiance to it must instead be understood as our belonging to a form of life in terms of whose moral traditions we

18 See E. Durkheim, *De la division du travail social* (1893; Paris: Presses Universitaires de France, 1960), book I, chapter 7; book II, chapter 3; conclusion; *L'éducation morale* (1925; Paris: Presses Universitaires de France, 1963), first part; Talcott Parsons, *The Evolution of Societies* (Englewood Cliffs, N.J.: Prentice-Hall, 1977), chapter 9.

reason as we do. This appeal to "tradition," I should observe, does not entail disowning that very expectation of reasonable disagreement about the good life that gave rise to the need for a core, categorical morality. The traditions of belief and practice to which I refer do not involve some substantial, controversial idea of the ultimate meaning of life. Regrettably, many thinkers who have seen the link between moral rationality and tradition have made this into an indictment of modern thought. They have forgotten that commitment to a universal (if minimal) morality has itself become an essential part of our way of life.

This alternative moral self-understanding is one I have so far only described, not justified. What recommends it is the second part of the solution I propose to the crisis of the Enlightenment. This is an epistemology that moves beyond the usual dichotomy between reason and historical contingency. It shows why (despite appearances, perhaps) I am far from advocating some sort of ethnocentric relativism.

6. Reason and History

I have observed before how the justification of moral beliefs (particularly those concerning categorical duties) loses its problematic character once we no longer suppose we must reason from an absolutely detached point of view but rely instead upon the presumed validity of our other moral beliefs. What I propose now is a theory of rational belief that makes this contextual form of justification appear no longer deficient, but normal. It is not applicable solely to the realm of ethics, and indeed draws on some ideas of American pragmatism. But since in recent years the term "pragmatism" has been appropriated (by Richard Rorty) for ends that are not the same as mine, I shall not make much of this historical connection.

Essentially, this theory of rational belief builds on a rather obvious fact, as well as on two cognitive norms that are as important as they have been neglected. The *fact* is that we are always in possession of a great many beliefs. To this fact are added the following *principles:* (1) We need a good reason to open our mind just as we need one to close it. More precisely, just as to adopt a belief we do not yet have we must have positive, specific reasons to believe it is true, so to put in doubt a belief we already have, we must have good reasons to believe it is doubtful, that is, that it may be false. (Doubting a proposition means, of course, believing neither it nor its opposite, but suspending judgment.) (2) To justify a proposition is not simply to give some true premises from which the proposition follows, but instead to give reasons that dispel a doubt to the effect that the proposition may be false. The first principle rests on a demand for symmetry in the conditions under which we may rightly begin or cease to believe. The second assumes that justification is a problem-solving activity, and in particular one geared to the twin goals of acquiring truths and avoiding falsehoods. Together these two principles have the important consequence that we need to justify a belief we already have only if we have first found reasons to believe it is doubtful. Not belief itself, but rather change of belief, forms the proper object of justification.

It is this consequence that brings out the novelty of the two principles. Usually it is assumed that all of our existing beliefs ought to be justified. Reason, it is supposed, requires that at least once in our life we stand back from the beliefs we already have and examine their credentials. So in particular it is held that beliefs serving to justify other beliefs must themselves be justified. This assumption that belief as such requires justification has become so routine, so unthinking, that its original motives have been lost from sight. It has its source, in fact, not so much in reason as in the metaphysical aspiration to view the world *sub specie aeternitatis,* an aspiration animating most of Enlightenment thought as well. The demand that each of our beliefs be justified is the demand that we undo the weight of historical circumstance and re-think our commitments on the basis of reason alone. This conception of when belief must be justified grows out of a very different purpose than the view that justification is a response to doubt (or at least this is so as long as the world of becoming is not taken to be the world of illusion).

The decisive question is thus whether we want epistemology to be a guide to eternity or a code for problem solving. If we give up that metaphysical aspiration and take as our rule that we must have positive reasons for thinking some belief of ours may be mistaken if we are to put the belief in doubt and so demand its justification, the idea that all our beliefs must be justified will fall away. The mere fact that we already have a belief, and that we have it because of our historical context, is not a good reason to think it may be false, and so not a good reason to demand that it be justified. Moreover, if we indeed find positive reasons for putting a belief of ours in doubt, we must continue to rely on our other existing beliefs, not only to find a solution to this doubt, but also, even before that, to discover the positive reasons that give rise to our doubt. There is in this view, therefore, no opposition between historical rootedness and rationality.

To be sure, this sketch of a theory of rational belief needs filling in. But there is one classical sort of elaboration of which it does not admit. The standards of belief to which we appeal in justifying some problematic claim figure among our given beliefs, and no more than any other such beliefs do they as such require legitimation. We need to justify them only if they become problematic, and then – here, too – we determine their worth by arguing on the basis of other beliefs and standards that are not then in doubt. We cannot therefore hope to establish once and for all, and independently of a given view of the world, the correct standards of acceptable belief, at least beyond the elementary rules of logic. The classical idea of epistemology as providing timelessly valid and purely formal rules of belief acquisition must thus be abandoned. But this does not mean the end of reason or a surrender to relativism.

Without supposing that I have answered every question that might be raised about this approach, I do want to make two further remarks to prevent misunderstanding. First, I must emphasize that despite rejecting the metaphysical conception of reason, I urge no general hostility toward metaphysics. On the contrary, in Chapter 5 I point out the need to assume the existence not only of physical and psychological facts, but of normative facts as well. Such a view of the world may certainly count as "metaphysical." All this is consistent, however, since there is a crucial difference between the nature of the world and the nature of our access to it. We may coherently hold, as I believe we should, that there exists a normative dimension of reality, irreducible to physical and psychological fact, that we apprehend by reflection; but we do so – at least in the case of morality and other matters that similarly go beyond the absolutely incontrovertible – only by thinking within our historical context, building on what we already happen to believe.

Second, the conception of justification I am defending is obviously not what is called "foundationalist." But neither is it "coherentist," as this common alternative is usually conceived.[19] Both of these views of justification share the assumption that all our beliefs are to be justified.

19 A good example of the common use of this dichotomy is the excellent book by Jonathan Dancy, *Introduction to Contemporary Epistemology* (Oxford: Blackwell, 1985). See also David O. Brink, *Moral Realism and the Foundations of Ethics* (Cambridge University Press, 1989), pp. 101–4, 123. The contextualist view of justification I propose is in many ways akin to what Rawls has called the method of "reflective equilibrium," though many discussions of this method do not distinguish clearly between contextualism and coherentism.

They differ only in whether this is to be in terms of their relation to some foundational set of beliefs or in terms of the "coherence" relations of mutual support among our beliefs. Just this shared assumption is what I believe must be rejected. As I have noted, the *contextualist* view of justification proposed here can be described as claiming that not our beliefs but rather changes in them are the proper object of justification. In deciding whether to adopt a new belief, therefore, we are to ask not whether the belief set comprising our existing beliefs plus the new one is justified by its coherence, but instead whether adding the new belief is justified by what we already believe. (Note that the coherentist must be in some difficulty about the status of his criteria of coherence, since they surely figure among his existing beliefs. Are they supposed to be at once part of what is justified and also what serves to justify?)

Now, to return to the domain of morality, an implication of this contextualist position is that our existing moral convictions do not as such call for justification. We may rely upon them in determining what new moral views to adopt without having to make sure that they are themselves justified. In the misleading terminology sometimes favored today, they are the "intuitions" against which we check a moral view we do not yet accept. (To call them "intuitions" can suggest that we arrived at them in some immediate, untheoretical way, when in reality the important thing about them is that they make up our existing body of moral belief, which itself may be the product of extensive theorizing.) To argue, as some have done,[20] that appeal to existing moral beliefs is illegitimate, it being necessary to show that they are not just believed but also credible, is to remain immured in that metaphysical conception of reason that I have urged we outgrow. Naturally, there are circumstances in which we are indeed obliged to reexamine our moral beliefs. But such situations occur when we have uncovered some positive reason to suspect that those beliefs may be mistaken. We do not have to justify them just because we have them.

It follows that if we already believe in a set of universalist duties, duties binding on every person whatever his or her interests, they are authoritative for our conduct. Where we find reason to change some of these convictions or to elaborate them further, it will be on the basis of other such convictions that remain fixed. And if we ask for the

---

20 See, e.g., R. B. Brandt, *A Theory of the Good and the Right* (Oxford University Press, 1979), pp. 16–23.

source of these moral laws, it will be the form of life that sustains them – a distinctively modern one that is shaped by the expectation of reasonable disagreement about the good life and the conviction that we can nonetheless agree upon a core morality binding upon all. This conception of morality is then, as I indicated, one in which reason and historical contingency no longer stand opposed.

In saying that the source of authority of this categorical morality is our form of life, I mean that it is what, in complying with this ethic, we ultimately aim to heed. That is, to the question why we should conduct our lives in this fashion, we can answer in the end only that this is the way of life we hold to, this is where our conscience feels at home. By its source of authority I do not mean as well what may serve to justify this ethic. The source of morality's authority will combine both of these elements only when it is assumed, as in philosophies that make reason the source of morality, that all our moral beliefs must be justified to be authoritative for our conduct. This assumption I reject. That is why it would be a mistake to object that I am begging the question about the authority of this universal morality. I am not arguing that this morality is justified because we have an allegiance to it. On the contrary, if we have such an allegiance, the question of justification does not arise. It does not do so until we come upon a good reason to doubt whether this morality is correct.

And here I should note that, according to the principles of rational belief I have presented, a good reason for doubting an existing belief is not the mere fact that we come upon somebody with grounds to reject it. A good reason for us to doubt, and so to raise the question of justification, must be one that is good by our own light, for it must be supported by other beliefs of ours. I hope that by laying out the weaknesses of the alternatives to this categorical morality, and by show-ing how we may conceive of it without extravagant expectations about the powers of reason as such (which have inspired the ongoing efforts of Enlightenment rationalism), I have dispelled any supposed grounds for doubting its validity.

Perhaps some readers will have objected for some time now that talk of "the universal morality we share" is disingenuous, our "existing moral convictions" coming to very little in each of us and to even less in what is common. Just who, they will ask, is this "we"? But I suspect that this ready skepticism is itself disingenuous, or at least distracted by immediate disputes from seeing a more abiding reality. The genuine controversies that occupy our moral attention can easily blind us to the moral convictions that go without question and that form indeed the common ground on which such disagreements draw. We miss something important about modern society if we fail to acknowledge, for all the differences about the good and the right that divide us, the moral "we" that we continue to be.

Still, convinced though I am of the correctness of the moral epistemology I have laid out, I want to admit to a nagging worry: even if the metaphysical aspiration to eternity is to have no role in a proper conception of reason, could it still have been a necessary element in the historical formation of those universalist moral traditions that are ours today? Could we have gotten to where we are now only if we had not reasoned as I am urging we now should, only if instead we had imagined this morality was the voice of reason itself? A positive answer would neither refute the epistemological principles I have defended nor discredit our inherited moral beliefs. But it ought to make us wonder whether we should not be grateful that people have not always reasoned as we think they should.

These remarks about the nature of rational belief will not resolve all problems of justification in the domain of morality. Many vital questions will remain as difficult as before. Much depends on the nature of the moral traditions we can continue to acknowledge after several centuries of legitimate criticism, but also of reckless attack. But I believe we can still recognize in our form of life a commitment to a universal ethic of categorical duties. By reasoning *within* this form of life, we are not doing less than reason demands. In reality, no doubt, a great deal of moral argument already proceeds along these lines. What needs to be changed is our self-understanding. In this way we can avoid the chief failure of Enlightenment ethics, yet continue to affirm the moral outlook of modernity. We can rely upon a conception of reason that is equal to our unprecedented intellectual situation – a situation that is beyond religion and Enlightenment.

3

THE SECRET PHILOSOPHY
OF LEO STRAUSS

1. A Weimar Intellectual

"What is it about Strauss' writings that continues to shatter respectable intellectual categories and rules, thereby arousing so much fascination and so much hatred?" This is the question with which Thomas Pangle introduced a recent collection of essays by Leo Strauss.[1] It is not easy to answer. Certainly Strauss was a controversial figure in political philosophy, not least since his death in 1973. His former students, the most famous having been Allan Bloom, guard his memory and his teaching vigilantly. His opponents not only disagree with particular points of his scholarship, but often suggest some dangerous flaw in the character of his mind. Again, why? What prejudices, or what certainties, did he assail?

At the heart of Strauss's thinking, as Pangle went on to observe, lay the conviction that there is such a thing as moral truth. In itself, however, this is surely an unlikely spark for the passionate debates that swirl around him. The opposite view, namely that morality is but the expression of group ideology or individual preference, has indeed become a common routine of thought. But Strauss was hardly alone in

---

1 Leo Strauss, *The Rebirth of Classical Political Rationalism,* Thomas Pangle (ed.) (University of Chicago Press, 1989), p. vii.

this century in the defense of the possibility of moral knowledge, and the other champions of "moral cognitivism," as it is called, have not provoked such extreme reactions. The reasons for Strauss's power to enthrall and repel must lie elsewhere.

The key, I think, is the peculiar urgency and direction of Strauss's search for moral truth. That search was connected with a root-and-branch critique of modernity. Modern thought seemed to Strauss morally disastrous from beginning to end. His message was that only a return to the ancients can save us. As we know from similar arguments in our own day, total critiques of modernity are likely to breed both enthusiasm and irritation.

But another factor is involved, too. Strauss was loyal to what I have called in previous chapters the metaphysical conception of reason, that is, the conviction that to be rational is to reflect upon the validity of our commitments from a standpoint above what historical contingency has made of us. This notion of reason was scarcely peculiar to Strauss. But the wholesale repudiation of modern thought led him to heed it in a far more single-minded and thorough fashion than many others who have favored it. The result was the famously elusive nature of his own positive moral philosophy. For some, Strauss's art of evasion creates a captivating mystique. For others, it means no more than it seems – his ultimate lack of substance. My own judgment agrees with the second reaction, but I find in the ultimate sterility of Strauss's thought a greater philosophical importance than others in this camp are disposed to see. By virtue of completely disowning the thought of his own time, Strauss turned into a striking illustration of just where the metaphysical conception of reason, if consistently followed as it seldom is, must lead. To understand how Strauss thus ended up in silence, however, we must retrace the development of his thought.

Strauss was born in 1899 in Kirchhain, Germany. Raised an Orthodox Jew, he developed a considerable interest in medieval Jewish thought and in Spinoza. He studied philosophy at a number of German universities and worked at the Academy of Jewish Research in Berlin. After leaving Germany in 1932, Strauss spent most of the rest of his life teaching political philosophy in U.S. universities. As a result, his renown is largely confined to North America, though there are now signs of interest in France. The roots of his thought go back, however, to the period before his emigration.

The best account of his deepest concerns remains the intellectual autobiography he composed in 1965 as a preface to the English translation of his book *Spinoza's Critique of Religion*.[2] In this piece he described his plight as a Jewish intellectual in Weimar Germany. The liberal ideals of the Enlightenment seemed to him, as to many Germans of the time, hollow or unjustified. The doctrine of moral progress, championed at the turn of the century by Hermann Cohen, the great neo-Kantian philosopher and the intellectual leader of the German Jewish community, seemed decisively refuted by World War I and the rise of fascism. Moreover, the influential irrationalism that he and others associated with Nietzsche and Heidegger seemed the inevitable outcome of modern thought. Once the source of value was no longer thought to lie in the cosmos or in God, but was cast instead into the flux of history, the question of how we ought to live, Strauss supposed, could be a matter only of human will, not of human reason.

Strauss studied with Heidegger for a year in the 1920s, and was immensely impressed by the passion and profundity with which Heidegger criticized modern conceptions of reason. Later Strauss called him "the only great thinker in our time."[3] But he never accepted Heidegger's ugly political conclusions. Liberal values of freedom and equality, even if they appeared baseless philosophically, still seemed to Strauss clearly preferable to the totalitarian movements with which the new irrationalism naturally allied itself. Strauss's fundamental question was: how is one to escape the dilemma in which modern philosophy points in one direction and common decency in another?

Strauss's book on Spinoza, published in Germany in 1930, offered one solution. The Enlightenment's attack on the idea of divine revelation was misconceived, he argued, since reason cannot show the invalidity of a form of thought that itself limits the authority of reason. If the Bible is indeed the word of God, then miracles have occurred. Reason cannot prove that they have not occurred, since rational forms of argument all assume that the course of the world is orderly, never miraculous.[4] Strauss, however, did not pursue this line of thought, and did not trade modern thought for religious orthodoxy. Another way out of the dilemma drew his attention.

This other solution was first glimpsed, Strauss reports,[5] as he was reviewing a book by Carl Schmitt, the German constitutional theorist

2 Leo Strauss, *Spinoza's Critique of Religion* (New York: Schocken, 1965).
3 Strauss, *Rebirth of Classical Political Rationalism*, p. 28.
4 Strauss, *Spinoza's Critique of Religion*, pp. 9, 28–9, 146, 192, 216.
5 Ibid., p. 31.

who soon became a chief intellectual apologist for the Nazi coup
d'état. From Schmitt he drew the idea that it was Hobbes who held the
key to modern moral thought. (Whether Schmitt is a helpful guide to
modernity is a question I take up later, not only in this chapter, but in
a subsequent one devoted to Schmitt himself.) In 1936, then in exile,
Strauss published his famous book on Hobbes.[6] His principal claim
was that Hobbes had departed from Plato and Aristotle by deliberately
lowering his sights. Instead of appealing to ancient standards of virtue,
Hobbes proposed to understand what social life is and ought to be
solely in terms of passions and interests. His aim was thereby to replace
utopia with efficiency. If standards were lowered, success would be
more likely. An important theme of Strauss's book was thus that
Hobbes's enthusiasm for the new science, far from being what led to
his new conception of political life, was itself fueled by this drive for
efficiency, for mastering the human condition.

The crucial point for Strauss, increasingly stressed in his subsequent
writings, was that in lowering moral standards, Hobbes had made a
choice. In other words, the opposite choice was also possible, then and
now. The modern drive for mastery, and the sacrifice of common
morality to which it eventually led, could be overcome, he concluded,
by a return to the high ancient models that modern thought had
chosen to reject.[7]

One apparent obstacle to such a return, however, was the extent to
which historical circumstances shaped the content of ancient moral
philosophy. This fact seemed readily explained by what Strauss called
"historicism," the view that no moral thought can be truly objective
since it expresses only the conventions of its age. Strauss could obviously not be happy with this sort of outlook. Its relativism was at odds
with his cherished idea of moral truth. During the 1940s he devised an
alternate explanation according to which the historically conditioned
character of Greek ethical philosophy was, in fact, intentional. Wishing
to protect themselves, recognizing that their ideals were not perfectly
realizable, Plato and Aristotle (and their medieval followers as well)
often concealed their own thought by accommodating themselves to
the opinions of their contemporaries. What they wrote was not pre-

6 Leo Strauss, *The Political Philosophy of Hobbes* (University of Chicago Press, 1952).
7 Leo Strauss, *What Is Political Philosophy?* (University of Chicago Press, 1988), pp. 49–
51; idem, "The Three Waves of Modernity," pp. 81–98 in *Political Philosophy: Six Essays
by Leo Strauss* (Indianapolis: Bobbs-Merrill, 1975).

cisely what they thought. Self-concealment also characterized the writ-ings of early modern thinkers, Strauss added, but for the opposite reason. The moderns wished to hide their apostasy from ancient ideals. The modern pursuit of attainable goals was meant to make the old technique of caution, "the art of writing," ultimately unnecessary.

Thus was born Strauss's famous doctrine of "esoteric teaching," his conviction that philosophical texts can contain hidden meanings reserved for an elite readership that knows truly how to read.[8] Such a doctrine is easily abused, of course. Strauss himself often indulged in questionable, even preposterous, "reading between the lines," as when he claimed that *The Prince* contains twenty-six, or twice thirteen, chap-ters because Machiavelli believed that God was no different than luck; or that Locke was a closet Hobbesian, worshiping like Hobbes at the altar of power.[9] For such fantastic claims Strauss has been justly ridi-culed.

The doctrine also raises the unnerving question of its applicability to Strauss's own writings. How much of what he wrote represents merely accommodation to existing opinion, and not his own "hidden teaching"? Is indeed his talk about recovering the idea of moral truth but one such mask, concealing a far bleaker view of the human condi-tion? Strauss's elusiveness can seem to call for just this approach, and some very interesting interpretations have been devised along these lines.[10] For better or worse, I have chosen not to follow their example. In part, this is because I am unsure what standards of evidence "read-ing between the lines" can accept and where it will end. But also, I believe that an illuminating explanation of Strauss's evasions arises from what he did manifestly say. I have decided to take Strauss at his word, particularly in his declarations about the possibility of moral knowledge, because taking them seriously has been an essential ele-ment in the positive reputation he has enjoyed, and because his way of pursuing that goal embodies an important philosophical lesson.

I take, therefore, Strauss's doctrine of esoteric teaching as chiefly an expression of the philosophical purpose in the name of which he introduced it: the attempt to defuse the appeal of historicism and to

---

8 Leo Strauss, *Persecution and the Art of Writing* (University of Chicago Press, 1988).

9 Leo Strauss, "Niccolò Machiavelli," p. 311 in *History of Political Philosophy,* L. Strauss and J. Cropsey (eds.) (University of Chicago Press, 1987); idem, *What Is Political Philosophy?* p. 49.

10 A fine example appears in Stephen Holmes, *The Anatomy of Illiberalism* (Cambridge, Mass.: Harvard University Press, 1993), chapter 3.

rescue the idea of moral truth by a return to the ancients. This fight against historicism was not, we should note, a rejection of historical understanding and its reconstruction of the problem context to which a past thinker was responding. What Strauss vigorously opposed was the idea that this sort of historical study could ever render the truth or falsity of past theories an idle question.

Plato and Aristotle had believed that there is a moral truth discoverable by reason. This classical rationalism was the route Strauss chose out of the corrupt modernity he saw around him. A stark antithesis between ancient virtue and modern freedom, by which he meant the mere absence of constraint or license, became the pivot of his thought.[11] Yet Strauss also never lost his respect for the authority of revelation. Indeed, he was fond of insisting that the deepest of philosophical problems lies in the conflict between Athens and Jerusalem.[12] By this he meant to underscore not just the intractability of the conflict, but also what classical reason and revelation have in common. Together they stand opposed to the view that there exist no moral standards outside the welter of passions and interests. They are both, according to Strauss, antimodern.

Strauss's preface to his book on Spinoza reveals a great deal about the historical context of his thought. Like many Weimar intellectuals, Strauss assumed that the moral irrationalism of Nietzsche and Heidegger was not a local aberration, but the inner destiny of modern philosophy.[13] (The suspicion that it was, instead, a symptom of a Germany unable and unwilling to accept modern liberal and democratic ideals seems never to have crossed his mind.) There were many at the time who supposed that the total success of modern science, plus the utter failure of modern philosophy, had created extraordinarily powerful means unchecked by any rational ends. With Max Horkheimer, Theodor Adorno, Hannah Arendt, and Heidegger himself after 1934, Strauss shared the bleak conclusion that modernity was the reign of "instrumental reason," technically inefficient and morally irresponsible. For all these thinkers, the history of modern thought was one of moral decline and the unbridled will to power.

---

11 Strauss, *Rebirth of Classical Political Rationalism*, p. 244; idem, *Liberalism Ancient and Modern* (Ithaca, N.Y.: Cornell University Press, 1989), p. 12.
12 Strauss, *Rebirth of Classical Political Rationalism*, p. 206.
13 Strauss, *Spinoza's Critique of Religion*, p. 30–1.

2. A Flawed History of Modern Ethics

Strauss's view of the problem of ethics was typical of Weimar. His originality lay in the solution he pursued. He did not share the later Heidegger's notion that the seeds of modern decadence had already been planted by Plato. Nor did he believe, with Horkheimer and Adorno, that a return to classical rationalism was intellectually impossible. For Strauss, "classical natural right" stood in total opposition to modern thought and offered a viable alternative to it, since it testified to reason's ability to rise above historical circumstance and discover moral truth.[14]

Thus, Strauss harbored none of Arendt's nostalgia for the Greek polis. In his eyes, Plato and Aristotle were not paradigms of moral philosophy because of what they said about the polis, which was merely one historical form of political life among others. Their eminence derived instead from their search for a timeless morality. That is why Strauss's criticism of modern liberalism differs radically from a form of antiliberalism popular today: he felt little attraction to the Romantic concern for tradition and community, which many contemporary thinkers have made into a stick with which to beat "liberal individualism." Strauss was no communitarian. The essential ambition of classical thought, he always argued, was to transcend the sense of belonging, to reason *sub specie aeternitatis*. For him, Romanticism was part of the modern disease of capitulating to history.[15]

Strauss repeatedly professed allegiance to modern liberal democracy. Some of the bitter opposition to Strauss supposes that he rejected such values, that (like Schmitt) he scorned the idea of international justice and longed for the closed society.[16] But this is a misconception (at least about Strauss himself, if not perhaps about some of his disciples). Strauss did have an acute sense of the disparity between the ideal and the real, and he stressed the need for moderation. But he never

---

14 Leo Strauss, *Natural Right and History* (University of Chicago Press, 1953), pp. 15, 89.
15 Strauss, *Natural Right and History*, pp. 13–15, 319.
16 In an article that otherwise contains many telling criticisms of Strauss, "Sphinx without a Secret" (*New York Review of Books*, 30 May 1985, pp. 30–6), Myles Burnyeat seems to fall prey to this misconception. For Strauss's acceptance of liberal democracy, see his *Rebirth of Classical Political Rationalism*, p. 6; idem, *Liberalism Ancient and Modern*, p. 15.

abandoned the belief that political life must be brought as far as possible into accord with morality, not with raison d'état. As a political form liberal democracy seemed to him a good approximation to the ideal, something like the "mixed regime" favored by the ancients. What he attacked was chiefly the liberal theory of such arrangements. In his view, modern ethics, unlike ancient thought, cannot provide a viable defense of liberal democracy, since it turns by nature into the glorification of power. It can find no norm loftier than expediency.

Much of Strauss's fascination, for his followers, springs from his repudiation of modern thought. There is a secret thrill in belonging to a lonely band of prophets. But just how plausible is the Straussian critique? At great length in *Natural Right and History* (1953), Strauss charged that the key feature of modern ethics, which ultimately condemns it to irrationalism, is "the shift of emphasis from natural duties or obligations to natural rights." Premodern thought made duties primary; the individual's rights were derived from the duties others owed him. To make rights primary, Strauss argued, is tantamount to making morality serve preexisting passions and interests.[17] For a right, if it is unchecked by a notion of duty, is just a demand to have some desire satisfied. Such a right comes without a persuasive claim that there is moral value in the satisfaction of that desire. In short, the modern view, in Strauss's account, is that one has a right to something simply because one wants it a lot: rights are but the expression of strong preferences. Although individuals may restrain their wants for the sake of civil peace, such compromises will be inherently unstable, and no moral blame can attach to the "superman" who casts social decency aside in order to indulge his exorbitant desires. The modern primacy of individual rights, Strauss insisted, leads straight to Nietzsche.

This conception of morality does fit some modern thinkers (particularly Hobbes, being but a distillate of his thought), but it by no means fits all. Indeed, the primacy of duties over rights, which Strauss extolled as "premodern," was itself a principle first formulated clearly by Samuel Pufendorf in the seventeenth century.[18] And Pufendorf was not the only modern to hold that morality is more than just an arrangement by which competing individuals can most efficiently satisfy their various

17 Strauss, *Natural Right and History*, pp. 182–3, 227, 248.
18 See Pufendorf, *De jure naturae et gentium* (1688), III.v.1–5 (where on this score he is criticizing Hobbes).

desires. Many modern moral philosophers have taught that the value of morality lies, more deeply, in telling us which forms of life make us more fully human. Kant is the premier example. Although Strauss often made a point of spurning Hermann Cohen's neo-Kantian faith in moral progress, he had little to say about the heart of Kant's own ethical theory. In *Natural Right and History*, for example, he noted simply that in one passage Kant asked why moral philosophy is called the doctrine of duties and not the doctrine of rights; the suggestion was that Kant could find no reason not to make rights primary. Strauss failed to mention, however, that *in the very next sentence* Kant used the basic terms of his own theory to defend the traditional view, arguing that we can believe we are free and therefore entitled to rights only because we understand ourselves to be bound unconditionally by moral duty.[19] Misleading quotations of this sort are unfortunately not rare in Strauss's writings. And surely an account of modern ethics that does not give a central place to Kant, and irresponsibly distorts his thought as well, ought to have little claim on our conviction.

Equally defective is Strauss's picture of the underlying motivation of modern ethical thought. For him, modern ethics rested on a mere choice, an abrupt decision to lower standards for the sake of practical success. That is why, in his more fanciful moments, he could imagine that modernity was an option of which ancient thinkers were already aware and that they wisely declined to embrace.[20] Missing from Strauss's outlook is the sense that earlier forms of thought had given rise to problems that modern thinkers were aiming to solve. From Strauss's account one would never suspect that there were fundamental philosophical and religious inadequacies in premodern thought that the characteristic features of modern ethics were seen to remedy. Yet that is precisely what occurred. A century of bloody religious wars, and the growing realization that reasonable people are likely to differ and disagree about the nature of the good life, led to the search for a core morality that all could affirm despite these sectarian and cultural differences. In a sense, this search did express a lowering of sights. Glorious but controversial views of the good life would have to be transferred from the domain of common morality, the ideals a society as a whole is to affirm, to the private sphere, where like-minded people

19 Strauss, *Natural Right and History*, p. 182. The passage from Kant is in *Metaphysik der Sitten* (Berlin: Akademieausgabe, 1902–), VI, p. 239.
20 Strauss, *What Is Political Philosophy?* pp. 36, 43, 96.

may pursue together their special vision. In the hands of many, however, this core morality remained a code of duty, not a scheme for
license. It was viewed as a dimension of intrinsic value, part of what
makes us truly human. It was certainly not motivated by an arrogant
plan to master the world, as Strauss maintained. The appeal of this
core morality lay instead in the conviction that deep disagreements
about the good life make it increasingly imperative to focus on the
moral bonds that can still tie us together. A sensible assumption would
be that this strand of modern ethics, like any current of thought, has
its share of weaknesses and mistakes, but Strauss gave us no sound idea
of what they are.

3. An Elusive Teaching

By itself, Strauss's failure as a historian does not invalidate his effort to
arrive at an objective morality. When we turn to his writing about this
philosophical topic, however, we find a curious change of tone. He was
no longer bold. He was coy. He had very little to say about the overall
shape or content of moral truth.

Sometimes he remarked intriguingly that this objective morality
ought to be called "natural right," not "natural law," since it may not
be fully expressible in the form of rules.[21] Sometimes he conceded
that it need not have its source in God or the cosmos, though he never
budged from the belief that the knowledge of it involves rising above
our historical context.[22] Sometimes he asserted that some moral truths
(he did not say which ones) are so evident that they cannot be coherently doubted.[23] But generally he viewed moral truth as the remote
object of an ongoing quest. Indeed, he often associated his outlook
with Socrates' "philosophical skepticism" – convinced that there is an
objective moral truth but not claiming to be in possession of it.[24]

Strauss did little to explain how this skepticism, this primacy of the
journey itself, can fill the moral vacuum supposedly left by modern
thought. In the past, moral skeptics have urged conformity to existing
custom. But for Strauss this attitude would only play into the hands of
"modern historicism." Moreover, it is true, as Strauss declared, that
moral skeptics might not deliberately harm anyone, but it is unclear

21 Strauss, *Natural Right and History,* p. 162.
22 Ibid., p. 94.
23 Ibid., p. 32.
24 Strauss, *What Is Political Philosophy?* pp. 11, 116, 121.

on what basis (other than conformity to current practice) they could aim to do good for others.

The really important question is why Strauss ended up with so little to say. My hypothesis is that he fatally disarmed himself. Historical and philosophical commitments conspired to keep him mute. His wholesale condemnation of modern thought reinforced another, more strictly philosophical *parti pris*. This was his conviction that reason requires us to transcend our historical circumstances and to look at the world, as best we can, from a standpoint of complete detachment. The result was that he was without resources for coming to any conclusions about moral truth. Strauss stood back from so much he had nothing left to go on. This "metaphysical" conception of reason is, of course, a far less peculiar notion than the bankruptcy of modernity. Many philosophers through the ages have supposed that thought becomes objective only when we peel off what history has made us and look at the world from the standpoint of eternity. Still, this ambition, however widespread, is extravagant. History and reason are not like oil and water. Irrationalism and transcendence are not the sole alternatives.

On the contrary, we can show in general that some idea is true only by relying upon our other beliefs, including our accepted norms of thought and action, which we have in large part received from earlier thought, and that we have found (so far) no positive reason to doubt. That does not mean that the historical context of beliefs from which we reason holds any guarantee that we will reach the truth: the compatibility of history and reason, as I see it, is distinct from notions of historical providence. Nor do I mean that for the sake of argument we merely decide to assume these background beliefs without thinking them to be true. The point is not historicism, not a surrender to convention. The moral is rather, as Wittgenstein once observed, that we should begin at the beginning and not earlier.[25] We always reason on the basis of a great many beliefs we already possess. Just as we need a good reason to adopt a belief we do not yet have, so we need a good reason to question a belief we already hold – that is, to examine its credentials and seek its justification. The mere fact that we hold a belief because of our place in history is not a reason to think it might be false. So nothing in the idea of reason implies that we should aim to rise above what history has made us. The demands of reason concern rather how we are to go on in the light of what we have become. I expounded this view at length in the preceding chapter.

25 Wittgenstein, *Über die Gewissheit*, § 471.

Strauss himself deployed a number of sound arguments against some of the usual "positivist" ways of denying the possibility of moral knowledge.[26] He argued (1) that the mere fact that people disagree about what is morally correct does not entail that there is no truth of the matter; (2) that occasionally irresolvable conflict between some moral values does not mean that all of morality is impervious to reasonable agreement; and (3) that the fact that no "ought" can be derived from an "is" does not rule out reasoning about values directly. Yet none of these negative arguments proves that the only way to acquire moral knowledge is to stand back altogether from our moment in history. The development of scientific knowledge is nothing like that. It consists in building on what we have inherited rather than in beginning from scratch. Strauss, by contrast, made demands of moral thought that go beyond what science, surely our paradigm of knowledge (though Strauss himself, looking down on modern science as but "instrumental reason," would not have agreed), can satisfy. It is no wonder he came up empty-handed.

If earlier moral thinkers, aspiring like Strauss to transcendence, did arrive at what they considered moral truths, that is because – as historical studies show – they complied with that ideal far less consistently than he did. They relied, even if implicitly, on a battery of inherited moral beliefs. That was something Strauss felt he could not possibly do. His hatred of modernity propelled him to adhere ruthlessly to the call of transcendence. Thereby he made himself into the purest example of where the metaphysical conception of reason must lead. It is not incidental that this conception of reason has also fostered much of the moral nihilism that he himself so vigorously denounced. Despite his intentions, Strauss's thought could not but resemble the nihilist philosophy he loathed.

Strauss was a thinker of great learning and conviction, but his vision, historical and philosophical, was fundamentally flawed. The school of thought he founded, and which shows no signs of extinction, draws its inspiration, of course, more directly from the historical than the philosophical component of his thought. The metaphysical conception of reason, however well illustrated by Strauss, is a more general phenomenon. No doubt Strauss will continue to have faithful followers as long as the vogue of modernity bashing persists. They, too, will promise much and deliver little.

26 Strauss, *Natural Right and History*, chapter 1.

II

BEYOND NATURALISM

4

NIETZSCHE'S LEGACY

Toward the end of 1888, a few months before he collapsed in a Turin square tearfully embracing a mistreated horse, Friedrich Nietzsche undertook to assure the world he was to be a destiny, "no mere man, but dynamite."[1] One day, so he announced in *Ecce Homo,* his name would be associated with the memory of something tremendous. Yet in explaining what his world-historical importance would be, Nietzsche stopped again and again to ask, uneasily, "Have I been understood?" And indeed has he? It seems that he was right to worry. Over the past hundred years, Nietzsche has meant all things to all people.

Not a movement – social, political, intellectual, artistic – has been without members who championed him as a guiding genius. There have been Nietzscheans of the Left and the Right. There have been Nietzschean vegetarians, sexual liberationists, Zionists, and socialists – also, of course, Nietzschean National Socialists. Undeterred by Nietzsche's well-known swipes at feminism and Christian "slave morality," there have even been Nietzschean feminists and Nietzschean Christians. "Let woman rediscover her own cruelty, turn on the beaten and mutilate them," cried Valentine de Saint-Point in imitation of the

---

1 Friedrich Nietzsche, *Ecce Homo,* "Warum ich ein Schicksal bin," § 1, in idem, *Werke in drei Bänden,* K. Schlechta (ed.) (Munich: Hanser, 1966), II, 1152.

master. "Nietzsche was an extraordinary phenomenon," Ernst Bertram
explained in 1918, "within the history of Nordic Christianity."[2]

In Germany, World War I forms a watershed in this flood of
Nietzsche interpretation. Before the war, Nietzsche's appeal extended
across the German political spectrum and throughout the avant-garde,
from radical expressionism to the conservative Stefan Georg circle;
only the traditional Right of Church, Kaiser, and Nobility closed its
doors to his influence. But with the war and its aftermath of disorder,
the cosmopolitan Nietzsche began to fade in Germany, and the nation-
alist, *völkisch* Nietzsche came to the fore.

Nietzsche the German patriot was an image that his sister Elisabeth
had been hawking ever since his madness and death in 1900. Her
Nietzsche Archives in Weimar supervised the publication (often bowd-
lerized) of his writings and sponsored the sale of little Nietzsche statues
and similar trinkets. This image caught on, once the Right lost its
moorings in tradition and turned radical. Nietzsche himself detested
patriotic sentiment and loathed his sister's anti-Semitism. For the Germans he felt chiefly disgust. "It is with Germans," he charged, "as it is
with women: one never fathoms their depths; they don't have any, that
is all. . . . This German race has no fingers for nuances, no *esprit* in its
feet and does not even know how to walk. The Germans ultimately
have no feet at all, only legs."[3] But in 1933 *Thus Spake Zarathustra* was
placed along with *Mein Kampf* in the vault of the Tannenberg Memorial
that commemorated Germany's victory over Russia in World War I.
Only very slowly has this conception of Nietzsche as the prophet of
Nazism and the architect of the "conservative revolution" begun to
wear off in post-1945 Germany. Signs are emerging of the more aesthetic sort of Nietzsche interpretation that has gone on unchecked
elsewhere, particularly in France, but also in the United States.

In general, there has scarcely been a limit to the causes, in Germany
or elsewhere, that have claimed Nietzsche for their own. Recently, a
new Nietzsche has joined the list – Nietzsche the herald of "postmodernism."[4] It is natural to view Nietzsche's sprawling posterity as largely

2 Steven E. Aschheim, *The Nietzsche Legacy in Germany, 1890–1990* (Berkeley and Los
   Angeles: University of California Press, 1992), pp. 62, 211. An earlier version of this
   essay appeared as a review of Aschheim's book in *The New Republic*, 17 May 1993.
3 Nietzsche, *Ecce Homo*, "Der Fall Wagner," §§ 3, 4, in *Werke*, II, 1149, 1150.
4 See some of the essays collected in David Allison (ed), *The New Nietzsche* (New York:
   Dell, 1977) and Sylviane Agacinski et al. (eds.), *Nietzsche aujourd'hui?* 2 vols. (Paris:
   Union générale d'édition, 1973).

a mass of misappropriation, from which the message of the real
Nietzsche must be distinguished and recovered. But this view, I believe,
is mistaken.[5] The welter of Nietzsche interpretation is not so much a
betrayal of the "real Nietzsche" as it is the expression of the very nature
of his thought. Almost every one of these interpretations is as good as
the others, except insofar as it claims to be the right one. Only when
we have grasped this will we have understood Nietzsche's true legacy.

What is it about Nietzsche's thought that gives it this remarkable,
proliferating power? "Perspective," Nietzsche wrote in 1866 in *Beyond
Good and Evil,* "is the fundamental condition of life."[6] Properly understood, this perspectivism forms the core – indeed the sole substance –
of Nietzsche's philosophy. It is the formula that Nietzsche's many
apostles have all imbibed (though rarely held consistently) as they have
gone on to make "Nietzscheanism" so many different things. It is the
one thing the "real Nietzsche" did essentially stand for, Nietzsche's
other opinions really being but the first in the long line of optional
interpretations it produced. To see why perspectivism could beget such
a varied progeny, it pays to look at its philosophical character closely.[7]

Perspectivism was the premise on which Nietzsche hammered away
at the explicit and implicit Platonism of previous philosophy, and at
the "Platonism for the masses" that was Christianity. The basic idea was
not simply that whenever we think or act, we do so from some particular standpoint, shaped by our biology, our history, and our interests.
This is probably true, but it is not very newsworthy. Nietzsche's criticism
of Plato went deeper: there is also, he proclaimed, no "true world"
beyond these perspectives against which they are to be measured.
"There are no facts, only interpretations."[8]

This notorious statement from Nietzsche's *Nachlass* (the writings
published posthumously under the title *The Will to Power*) is itself
easy to misinterpret, though clearly perspectivism, whatever it means
exactly, must have some trouble with the very idea of "misinterpreta-

5 The special merit of Aschheim's *Nietzsche Legacy* is that, in addition to being a
   fascinating chronicle of Nietzsche's reception, it exposes the error of this view (pp.
   3, 7–8).
6 Friedrich Nietzsche, *Jenseits von Gut und Böse* (*Beyond Good and Evil*), "Vorrede" in
   Werke, II, 566.
7 Arthur Danto's *Nietzsche as Philosopher* (New York: Columbia University Press, 1965),
   chapter 3, offers an excellent account of Nietzsche's perspectivism, though I would
   wish to emphasize the importance of value in this doctrine more than he does.
8 Friedrich Nietzsche, *Aus dem Nachlass der Achtzigerjahre* in *Werke,* III, 903.

tion." It is clear what Nietzsche did not mean. His point was not the banality that every statement of fact involves interpretation, depending as it does on various assumptions and expectations. Though this is sometimes said to be Nietzsche's great insight, it is in reality neither particularly novel nor terribly damaging to the ambitions of previous philosophy. The omnipresence of interpretation does not by itself imply that some interpretations are not better than others, and that some get the facts right while others miss their mark. And indeed, Nietzsche's maxim "There are no facts, only interpretations" cuts deeper than just this kind of false dichotomy between fact and interpretation.

Nor was Nietzsche a Berkeleyan idealist, denying the existence of a world distinct from minds and the perspectives they project. As he immediately cautioned, the idealist claim that "everything is subjective," that the key to an interpretation is the interpreter behind it, is itself but one more interpretation, and so a view that we do not have to embrace. And neither did he hold, as Michel Foucault and Jacques Derrida later would, that it is a view we should not adopt, and that there are no authors, only texts.

Nietzsche's perspectivism is at bottom a doctrine not so much about the nature of what is as about the nature of what ought to be. What a perspective does is to lay down, to establish (as opposed to discovering) what will count as right and good and what will not. The thesis that there is no true world independent of perspective means that there is no way we ought to think and act apart from how we choose to do so. The world itself contains no directions about how we are to think and act, no objective values that we should acknowledge. The only values are the ones we create. Of course, this view can carry implications about the nature of what exists. If norms of good evidence are, like all values, something we invent rather than discover; and if we also assume (as so-called metaphysical realists may not, but Nietzsche certainly did) that "facts" are whatever we have good evidence for; then there can be no facts independent of perspective, no way the world can be said to be apart from how we choose (and could just as well have chosen otherwise) to view it. There are only optional interpretations.

Still, we get the right slant on Nietzsche's perspectivism if we see it as primarily a view about the nature of value. That is how Nietzsche himself understood it. In its light, other basic themes of his thought fall into place. Nihilism, for example, is just the negative half of perspectivism. It is the realization that there are no objective values, yet without the positive affirmation of ourselves as all along the creators of value. Nihilism breeds despair only because it grasps but half the truth. "The question of nihilism, 'What for?', arises from the habit of thinking that the goal must be posited, given, demanded *from the outside* – through some *superhuman authority*."[9]

Nietzsche traced the advent of nihilism to the fact that, as the Madman famously announces in *The Gay Science* (1882), man has killed God.[10] He understood the death of God in part as others, such as Feuerbach, had before him: God is but an externalization of human aspirations that man is now learning to reclaim for himself. But Nietzsche also meant something much more radical than Feuerbach ever imagined. Man has created not only God, but also the values of goodness, love, and pity of which he made God the paradigm and sponsor. So, as man now comes into his own, he is free to set up different, contrary values in their stead. Thus, for George Eliot, the translator of Feuerbach's *The Essence of Christianity* (1841), Nietzsche had nothing but contempt: her declaration that although God is inconceivable and immortality unbelievable, duty is peremptory and absolute put her among that uncomprehending multitude about whom the Madman remarked, "I come too soon. They do not yet know the deed they have done."[11]

Without the Christian God, Christian values become problematic, optional. But the acid of nihilism, Nietzsche insisted, cannot remain bottled up in the moral realm. It must envelop value wherever it is, even the values (logical coherence, explanatory power) by which science operates and the value of knowledge itself. In a later preface, written in 1886, Nietzsche looked back on the book that had launched his philosophical career in 1871 and argued that *The Birth of Tragedy* was in reality concerned with "the *problem of science,* science grasped for the first time as problematic, as questionable."[12] The values of science, that is, of systematic knowledge in general, are themselves in no way objective. They, too, are values we create and could create differently.

Nietzsche believed that his contemporaries vastly overrated the value of knowledge. Not only did positivists wrongly suppose that the life of

9 Ibid., 554.
10 Friedrich Nietzsche, *Die fröhliche Wissenschaft* (*The Gay Science*), §125, in *Werke*, II, 126–8.
11 See Nietzsche's biting diatribe against G. Eliot in *Götzendämmerung* (*Twilight of the Idols*), "Streifzüge eines Unzeitgemässen," § 5, in *Werke*, II, 993.
12 Friedrich Nietzsche, *Die Geburt der Tragödie* (*The Birth of Tragedy*), "Versuch einer Selbstkritik," § 2, in *Werke*, I, 10.

science was a safe refuge from troubling questions about the objectivity of value, but the widespread devotion to a historical knowledge that sees everything as a predictable part of its historical context was also paralyzing creative energy. Action requires forgetting, he countered in *The Use and Abuse of History* (1874); the new comes to be only by ignoring the old.[13] We must be bold enough to ask, "Why not rather untruth?" Here, then, was the reason that Nietzsche assigned art a greater dignity than science. Knowledge is in the service of the creative will, and it must not be allowed to turn against it. "My book," he wrote in the preface to *The Birth of Tragedy*, "was the first to view science through the optics of the artist."[14]

Clearly nihilism for Nietzsche was not the end, but the beginning, of wisdom. Realizing that there are no objective values is not a cause for despair. It leads instead to the self-affirmation of the *Übermensch*. Even today, the usual translation of this Nietzschean term as the super-man is likely to make one giggle or take alarm. Yet the idea is clear enough. The superman is not a different species or a higher race. It is man himself – once he learns to affirm who he really is. We are to celebrate what we always have been and always will be: the creators of value, beings whose nature is fundamentally *will*, the "will to power" that fashions its own rules of thought and action. We are to make ourselves into works of art, self-created, not answerable to any higher authority.[15] Saying yes to what we really are cannot be for Nietzsche, of course, something we objectively ought to do. We might just as well deny what we are, subjecting ourselves to some supposedly pre-given values. Strictly speaking, Nietzsche could say against such "Platonism" only that self-affirmation is what he chose to will. That is just what he does when he has Zarathustra correct himself in mid-teaching, "The Superman is the meaning of the earth. Let your will say: the Superman *shall be* the meaning of the earth."[16]

Not always, however, was Nietzsche so consistent. Under the banner of his perspectivism, he assembled a rather specific ethic, which he treated not simply as one he willed for himself but as the right one for

---

13 Friedrich Nietzsche, *Unzeitgemässe Betrachtungen* (*Untimely Meditations*), II, "Vom Nut-zen und Nachteil der Historie," § 1, in *Werke*, I, 213. For the challenge "Why Not Rather Untruth?" see idem, *Jenseits von Gut und Böse*, § 1, in *Werke*, II, 567.

14 Nietzsche, *Die Geburt der Tragödie*, "Versuch einer Selbstkritik," § 2, in *Werke*, I, 11.

15 Alexander Nehamas, *Nietzsche: Life as Literature* (Cambridge, Mass.: Harvard University Press, 1985), is an excellent meditation on this theme.

16 Friedrich Nietzsche, *Also Sprach Zarathustra*, "Vorrede," § 3, in *Werke*, II, 280.

a perspectivist to hold. It embodied, first of all, the intellectual honesty that he admired in Schopenhauer – the refusal to flinch before the disappointments and horrors of the world.[17] Attractive as it is, however, this fearless pessimism is not a virtue that perspectivism need recommend. Just as possible is the aestheticism that flees the real world for the world of art – art now being understood not just as the creation of value, but more specifically as *illusion* – and lives by Nietzsche's own observation that "we have art that we may not perish of truth."[18]

Nietzsche's ethic also contained some rather nasty values. One was war. "You say that it is the good cause that hallows even war?" Zarathustra asks. "I say unto you: it is the good war that hallows any cause."[19] Another was pitiless cruelty. "Weaklings and failures should perish," he urged in *The Antichrist,* "that is the first principle of *our* humanity. They should even be helped to perish."[20] This heartless code was, however, no more an essential element of his perspectivism than the humanitarian and democratic sentiments he so violently scorned. Nietzsche seems to have supposed that once the objectivity of Christian values had been dispelled, only the opposite of those values could be affirmed. But this is a non sequitur. Even if he was also right that these Christian values express simply the resentment that the weak feel for the strong,[21] perspectivism cannot require that we ought to affirm rather than deny our nature. As Nietzsche could himself wonder, "Why not rather untruth?"

Nietzsche's assimilation of perspectivism to an ethic of war and cruelty was abetted by the magical aura with which he endowed the idea of life. Life was supposed to be the source of all perspectives, the ultimate vantage point from which the *Umwertung aller Werte,* the revaluation of all values, was to proceed. "Science is to be viewed through the optics of the artist, and art itself through the optics of life."[22] Yet such an Archimedean point is impossible. Values cannot be revalued except on the basis of already accepted values. Nietzsche's idea of life is itself a value term. "Cruel and implacable against all that

17 Nietzsche, *Die Geburt der Tragödie,* § 20, in *Werke,* I, 113; *Menschliches, Allzumenschliches* (*Human, All Too Human*), "Vorrede," § 4, in *Werke,* I, 740.
18 Nietzsche, *Aus dem Nachlass der Achtzigerjahre,* in *Werke,* III, 832. Also III, 691–3.
19 Nietzsche, *Also Sprach Zarathustra,* I, "Vom Krieg und Kriegsvolke," in *Werke,* II, 312.
20 Friedrich Nietzsche, *Der Antichrist,* § 2, in *Werke,* II, 1166.
21 Friedrich Nietzsche, *Zur Genealogie der Moral,* I, § 10, in *Werke,* II, 782.
22 Nietzsche, *Die Geburt der Tragödie,* "Versuch einer Selbstkritik," § 2 in *Werke,* I, 11.

is weak and old in us, and not only in us":[23] though trumpeted in Darwinian terms, his valorization of life went necessarily beyond what biology could establish. After all, an ethics can just as well undertake to correct nature as to follow it.

Once we see Nietzsche's perspectivism for what it is, and distinguish it from his ethics, we can better appreciate the history of Nietzschean-ism that I have summarized. Nietzsche has remained a contemporary for so many since the 1890s because our iconoclastic century has found mirrored in his perspectivism its own aspiration to throw off the weight of the past and to bring forth new values. Yet each of the forms taken by Nietzsche's protean legacy, almost without exception, has dressed up its own revolutionary values – sexual, dietetic, political, aesthetic – as the message of "the real Nietzsche." This confuses the license to create value with the specific values one chooses to create (and can seem to give those values a special authority they cannot really possess). There is no such real Nietzsche. Each of these Nietzsche-inspired dispensations is as authentic as the other, their very multiplicity testi-fying to the unlimited horizons that Nietzsche's perspectivism opens up. Indeed, Nietzsche was himself the first to make the mistake. Long before his sister Elisabeth got her hands on his estate and his reputa-tion, he supposed he knew the values the real Nietzsche stood for.

Perspectivism, the one thing we may identify with the real Nietzsche, is also where Nietzsche's real importance lies. In itself a dizzy doctrine, perspectivism can be made manageable by being cast in a cut-rate version that focuses only on moral value. Then it resembles the cozy view of many Anglo-American philosophers today, for whom moral judgments are but expressions of preference, unlike the statements of fact typical of science. This kind of moral "subjectivism" or "non-cognitivism" seems, however, far less consistent than Nietzsche's own position. As science worshipers of just the sort Nietzsche dismissed, do not such philosophers fail to realize that if moral values cannot be more than expressions of preference, then neither can the values of science, or indeed of all reasoning? If, as their "naturalism" supposes, there are no objective moral values because only the material world and states of mind – the objects of modern natural science – truly exist, then by the same token must not the way we ought to think be no less something we make up than how we ought to act? Must not all value, moral or cognitive, share the same fate?

---

23 Nietzsche, *Die fröhliche Wissenschaft,* "Was heisst Leben?" § 26, in *Werke,* II, 59.

This conclusion, which is Nietzsche's own, is the one to which contemporary philosophical naturalism, however much its proponents might wish to keep clear of Nietzsche's company, seems ultimately to reduce. Far from being cozy, such an outlook boggles the mind. Imagine thinking that even so basic a rule of reasoning as the avoidance of contradiction has no more authority than what we choose to give it. Imagine thinking that we could just as well have willed the opposite, seeking out contradictions and believing each and every one. Has anyone the slightest idea of what it would be like really to believe this?

To be sure, bizarre theories may be true. But it seems safe to say that more often they spring from error. Perhaps we should think twice about the naturalism that Nietzsche, and much of present-day philosophy as well, have been at one in assuming rather than in examining. Maybe the world consists not just of matter in motion plus our thought and actions in response to it. Maybe it consists of value as well. For are we not beings whose nature is to reflect, and is not reflection the attempt to discover what indeed we ought to think and to do? These are the thoughts that led Plato, Nietzsche's opposite, to conclude that the objective world we seek to understand contains not just matter and mind, but value too. For one of the central functions Plato assigned the forms was to serve as the objective norms against which we may measure our actions and our own conceptions.

No doubt some of the value we find in the world is there only because we put it there, conferring value on things in the light of our own desires and interests. But if Plato is right, this cannot be the whole story. Must we not also believe that some values, cognitive as well as moral, exist independent of our will? Are not some of our values ones we do not simply prefer, but believe that we ought to prefer? And when we do bestow value on things, do we not often suppose that there is a right and wrong way to do this? If so, then our lives cannot be ones of limitless self-creation – and not just because we are shaped by forces we cannot fully control.[24] Our lives must instead rest on respect for the claims that the world makes upon us.

Probably the most powerful obstacle to accepting this conclusion is

24 The "blind impress of chance" is the only limit that so radical an anti-Platonist as Richard Rorty, for example, places on his espousal of Nietzschean self-creation. See his *Contingency, Irony, and Solidarity* (Cambridge University Press, 1989), p. 43. I have discussed somewhat further the limits to self-creation in "Une théorie du moi, de son instabilité et de la liberté d'esprit," pp. 127–45 in Henri Grivois and Jean-Pierre Dupuy (eds.), *Mécanismes mentaux, mécanismes sociaux* (Paris: La Découverte, 1995).

not simply the idea that it is unintelligible, but also the conviction that it is pernicious. For a broad current of modern philosophy, the belief that there exist norms independent of our will forms the very essence of alienation; it betrays a fear of acknowledging our own creative freedom. To respect something as being greater than we are is supposedly to think less of ourselves. Nietzsche himself certainly shared this widespread conviction. His exemplary importance consists in the fact that he gave it its most radical expression. But seeing where this led him, we should also feel moved to question his guiding assumptions. In reality, the debate between Nietzsche and Plato is far from over. I show in the next chapter why we ought indeed to adopt the antinaturalist vision of the world Plato represents.

5

MORAL KNOWLEDGE

Naturalism is the view that the world, as the totality of what is, consists solely of the physical and psychological phenomena that are the object of the modern natural sciences. The world is but matter in motion, along with the thoughts and feelings we have in regard to it. In its more radical forms, this view of the world portrays, of course, the mind itself as but a complex system of matter in motion. But naturalism, even broadly conceived, is, I believe, one of the great prejudices of our age. It is widely shared and explicitly affirmed. It is used as a standard for acceptable belief, and its consequences are drawn out systematically. But naturalism is far more often assumed and deployed for various purposes than examined in its own right and supported by argument. It faces, in fact, grave philosophical difficulties so serious and so obvious that only dogmatic precommitment can account for why they are rarely even acknowledged.

One of the perennial manifestations of naturalism has been the denial of the possibility of moral knowledge. Philosophical naturalists have argued that morality can involve only the expression of attitudes, not the possession of truths, there being nothing in the world itself of which moral judgments could be true. The only facts there supposedly are concern the way things are and how we do think and act, but not how we ought to do so. These "anticognitivist" arguments are to my mind rather poor. Bringing out their defects is obviously important for

moral philosophy. I am persuaded, however, that this has the extra
benefit of pointing to what is fundamentally wrong in naturalism itself.
In this chapter my primary aim is to establish that, contrary to these
naturalistic arguments, moral knowledge is indeed possible. But I want
also to show why we must open ourselves to a metaphysically broader
conception of the world.

In modern times, naturalism has been so appealing an outlook
because of the great success and prestige of the natural sciences. Yet
modern science is by no means so hospitable to the naturalist spirit.
On the contrary, the belief that the achievements of modern science
ought to command our assent is precisely what puts us beyond naturalism. For this belief makes reference to a truth about what we ought to
believe. It forces us therefore to accept the basic tenet of Platonism
(the rest we may set aside) – namely, that the world must be large
enough to admit, not only of physical and psychological truths, but of
normative truths as well. If we can know that there are things we ought
to believe, the way is then clear to recognizing that we can also have
knowledge of what we ought to do. This is the way I argue that there
can be such a thing as moral knowledge. In earlier chapters I had
much to say about the inadequacy of ancient ethics to the modern
world. But in one regard (though it is not the one most popular
today), I believe we should follow the ancients, or Plato at least. We
should give up the naturalism that has come to dominate so much of
modern philosophy.

1. Truth and Moral Judgment

Philosophical naturalism has used two sorts of argument to show that
morality cannot be a form of knowledge. They share the common
strategy of reaching such a conclusion by way of demonstrating that,
properly speaking, moral claims cannot even count as expressing beliefs. The first argument denies that the idea of truth applies to moral
claims. The second holds that moral claims have an inherent motivational force that beliefs as such cannot possess. Both arguments
founder, however, on the same fundamental dilemma. They remain
coherent only at the price of implying that there can also be no
knowledge of what we ought to believe – a conclusion that leaves
problematic why we should believe such a conception of morality. Let
us examine the two arguments in turn.

The first anticognitivist argument is that the idea of moral claims being true is unnecessary or even incoherent, since the notion of moral truth has or could have no explanatory function. It is not, supposedly, a notion that helps or could help to account for what would remain otherwise unexplained. The conclusion generally drawn from this argument is that moral claims must thus be conceived not as true or false, but rather as expressing the preferences, or a certain ("impartial" or "universalizable") class of preferences, that those making such claims have about how they or others should act. One might instead conclude that moral claims, though indeed descriptive in meaning, are nonetheless all false. In either version, the key point is that the idea of moral truth having no explanatory role and so no raison d'être, moral knowledge does not exist.

Obviously, the argument assumes that our claims about the natural world, about physical and psychological reality, are not in the same situation. Why does it hold that in their case the notion of truth is explanatorily essential and that such claims do constitute genuine beliefs? The basic idea is that truth can play a role in accounting for the very existence of these beliefs. The natural world, it is supposed, shapes the sense experience by virtue of which we arrive at our beliefs about that world. Though sense experience may always have to take on some conceptualized form, there is also no sense experience that is not causally dependent on the world, and no beliefs about the natural world arise independently of sense experience. Thus, the origin of beliefs about the natural world is best explained by reference, not just to the person's other beliefs and conceptual resources, but also to this world itself. Here, be it noted, the natural world is understood as involving an independent order of facts ("natural facts" we could call them) of which the beliefs are true or false, an order "independent" in the sense that the facts would obtain even if the beliefs about them did not.

Indeed, so the argument continues, sometimes the fact that figures in the best explanation of a belief about the natural world will be the very fact that makes it true. Its best explanation will turn on its truth. Such will be the case, if besides being true, the belief would not be held unless it were true. This is what it is for the belief to constitute *knowledge*. A belief counts as knowledge only if the truth of the belief belongs to the best explanation of the belief itself. A special case of this idea occurs when the belief is an inferred belief, a "theory" (in the lax sense of the term favored today), that we hold because of certain observational evidence. Since the theory will not count as knowledge unless its truth belongs to the best explanation of our belief in it, we may adopt the theory as being confirmed by the evidence only if the truth of the theory belongs to the best explanation of the evidence. It is often in terms of this principle, called "inference to the best explanation," that the explanatory importance of the idea of truth for our beliefs about the natural world is formulated.

Now the anticognitivist argument we are considering holds that moral claims need not or indeed cannot be similarly explained by reference to some independent order of "moral facts." That is why they cannot be considered as possibly true, and why the idea of moral knowledge is misconceived. Here is how Gilbert Harman, for example, presents the argument (invoking the principle of inference to the best explanation):

> Observation plays a role in science that it does not seem to play in ethics. The difference is that you need to make assumptions about certain physical facts to explain the occurrence of the observations that support a scientific theory, but you do not need to make assumptions about any moral facts to explain the occurrence of the so-called moral observations [as when we say that we "see" that an action is morally wrong. – C.L.] . . . In the moral case, it would seem that you need only make assumptions about the psychology or moral sensibility of the person making the moral observation.[1]

Harman's view is that a more economical explanation of our moral judgments is available than one that appeals to an independent order of moral facts. Our moral judgments (or more exactly, the specifically moral component of such judgments) can be adequately explained, he claims, by purely psychological facts, by the "more or less well articulated moral principles that are reflected in the judgments you make, based on your moral sensibility."

The late J. L. Mackie presented a stronger version of the argument. We can make no sense, he claimed, of how anything so metaphysically "queer" as objective moral values could play a role in bringing about our moral judgments.[2] Presumably, Mackie believed that we are able to grasp how physical phenomena can be causally responsible for

---

1 Gilbert Harman, *The Nature of Morality* (New York: Oxford University Press, 1977), p. 6. See, too, Allan Gibbard, *Wise Choices, Apt Feelings* (Cambridge, Mass.: Harvard University Press, 1990), pp. 121–2.

2 J. L. Mackie, *Ethics: Inventing Right and Wrong* (Harmondsworth: Penguin, 1977), pp. 38–41.

beliefs about the physical world. Even though the precise way in which physical causes produce mental phenomena remains largely a mystery, his thought must have been that it is always through some physical process that the world acts on the mind. Since moral qualities, if they existed objectively, would have to be very different from the physical qualities involved in psychophysical causation, Mackie inferred that no sense could be made of how they can affect the mind, and so of how we can come to know moral facts. In the end, appeal can be made only to some occult faculty of "intuition."

Mackie's reasons for the explanatory impotence of moral facts aim to establish a stronger conclusion than Harman's. Postulating the existence of objective moral values, he believed, is not so much uneconomical as incoherent. It should also be noted that the two philosophers differ in their conception of the real nature of moral claims. Mackie believed that moral judgments are indeed descriptive in meaning, that in making them we mean to be answerable to an independent moral reality; so for him they are necessarily false. This was his "error theory" of moral judgment. Harman's conception is more representative of the view of morality noncognitivists tend to take. Moral claims, far from being descriptive in intent, are simply expressions of an impartial kind of preference – in Harman's own account, one that is nonetheless based on social conventions.[3] This latter difference is not, however, so important as what Harman and Mackie have in common and share with other noncognitivists who find this first argument, in either of its two versions, convincing. They all assume that a naturalistic vision of the world, according to which there exist only physical and psychological facts, leaves nothing unexplained about our moral judgments.

2. The Indispensability of Normative Truths

The first thing we must examine in this anticognitivist argument is the notion of truth it employs. In holding that truth has an explanatory role to play, the argument supposes, even more fundamentally, that a belief is true or false in virtue of an independent order of facts. The "independence" here is causal, the idea being that the facts would supposedly obtain even if the beliefs about them did not. Truth is assumed to be a relation between a belief – or, more exactly, between the proposition expressed by a belief (i.e., *what* is believed) and the

3 Harman, *Nature of Morality*, pp. 12, 90.

way the world is independently of that belief being expressed. A first important question about this argument is whether such a conception of truth is too restrictive. Might there not be a broader conception that does not imply that propositions are true or false by virtue of the way the world is? If so, moral judgments could then be deemed capable of truth without the world itself having to contain some dimension of moral value.

This line of thought does not seem promising to me. If there were such an innocent notion of truth it would surely be found in the so-called disquotational theory, which aims to take a deflationary attitude toward this hallowed subject. Yet even this theory cannot get around the fact that truth involves a relation to the way the world is (causally) independent of the proposition that is true or false.

According to the disquotational theory, the statement that a proposition is true says no more than the proposition itself: " 'snow is white' is true" means no more than "snow is white." The utility of the truth-predicate consists in allowing us to assent to propositions we cannot or choose not to articulate ("the Schrödinger equation is true").[4] This theory must assume, however, that the subject of the truth-predicate, the proposition in question (e.g., "snow is white"), is an *affirmation* about the way things are. It need not be an affirmation that is actually asserted; it may even be the object of a question or a possibility that is just being entertained. But whether or not it is the object of some propositional attitude or other, the proposition must be understood as affirming something to be the case; it must be expressed by a *declarative* sentence. And though the notion of truth may in itself be rather trivial, the idea of an affirmation is not, and so ultimately the idea of truth is not, either. I am not alluding to the fact that propositions, if taken to exist in their own right, are philosophically controversial entities. We may set aside that question and look simply at beliefs. My point is that what is believed (the so-called proposition) must be understood as an

---

4 For this theory of truth, see W. V. O. Quine, *Pursuit of Truth* (Cambridge, Mass.: Harvard University Press, 1993), pp. 80–2, and Paul Horwich, *Truth* (Oxford: Blackwell, 1990). Horwich is one who believes that such a deflationary theory would allow the noncognitivist to attribute truth to moral claims ("Gibbard's Theory of Norms," *Philosophy and Public Affairs* [Winter 1993], pp. 67–8). But as I go on to argue, this view misses the implications of the fact that the disquotational theory is one of truth for propositions, that is, affirmations. Not by accident, in other words, do noncognitivists regard moral judgments as expressing not affirmations that something is the case, but rather preferences of some sort or other.

affirmation that something is the case, and this implies that whether it is the case or not is independent of the belief itself being held. The idea of truth thus presupposes the existence of a way the world is that is causally independent of our beliefs about it and that is that by virtue of which our beliefs are true or false. Not even the disquotational theory of truth can avoid this implication. So the first anticognitivist argument cannot be defused by the objection that truth is too innocuous a notion for its purposes.

But though its idea of truth is unobjectionable, this argument does harbor a number of mistakes, and fatal ones, since they produce the conclusion that there can be no moral knowledge. First, in the weaker version, which asserts that there is no need to explain the formation of moral claims by reference to an order of moral facts, the argument seems to be circular. Suppose it is true that our moral claims can be explained in terms of our "more or less well articulated moral principles." This sort of explanation would show that there need be no moral facts by virtue of which the claims are true or false, only if it is assumed that the background principles are themselves not true or false by virtue of an independent order of moral facts. This assumption is what is at issue. More generally, the ability to account for moral claims in terms of the "psychology or moral sensibility" of those who make them does not settle the question. The existence of moral facts can be shown to be an unnecessary assumption only if the psychological categories thus invoked do not imply the existence of moral truths. Like other proponents of this version of the argument, Harman does not prove this to be so.

In ordinary life, we often explain moral claims in terms of psychological factors that imply the existence of moral truths. Is this not what we are doing when we say that someone concluded he should lie because, looking hard at the situation, instead of blindly following a rule, he *recognized* that it required him to lie? We do not ordinarily understand our moral convictions, or at least our deepest ones, as merely the expression of our preferences or as commitments we simply decide to adopt. The difference between moral good and bad is not something we naturally think of ourselves as *creating*, but rather something to which we *respond*. We do not suppose that something is morally right because we prefer it; we think that it is because something is morally correct that we should prefer it. We assume that the difference between moral right and wrong is independent of our preferences. This ordinary understanding may be wrong. Naturalism, in its dominant form, must hold that it is an error – that in reality moral value is but a projection, a way we color the world in the light of our own desires.[5] But surely the burden of proof lies with those who claim that the idea of moral response is a mistake. They must show that it is one, and not just assert that it is one in the light of their own naturalistic outlook.

At this point, the stronger version of the argument may seem the better line of thought for the noncognitivist to take. Instead of actually having to produce a more economical way of accounting for moral beliefs, can he not just point out that explaining their existence in terms of an independent order of moral facts is incoherent? How could the supposedly moral qualities of things play a causal role in the formation of belief in anything like the way we understand psychophysical causation (the causal dependence of belief upon the physical qualities of things) to take place?

This reasoning, too, should fail to convince. Among other things, it makes the assumption, common with proponents of both versions of the first anticognitivist argument, that if there were moral facts, they would have to be like physical and psychological facts in being available to perception or observation; otherwise, they could be assigned only to some mysterious faculty of "intuition." Given this assumption, it must indeed be unfathomable how the elements of such facts can play a role in psychophysical causation. But moral facts are in reality not like this at all. Instead of involving an additional feature of the world we perceive, they are best viewed as facts containing *reasons:* "*A* ought morally to do X" is the same as "*A* has a moral reason to do X." Moral facts thus figure among the whole range of facts that involve justificatory reasons for belief and action – reasons, moreover, we recognize not by perception and not by some obscure faculty of "intuition," but by *reflection*.[6] Moral knowledge is therefore best understood as one species of the reflective knowledge of reasons rather than as a kind of perceptual knowledge. As we shall see, a number of things favor this view. One immediate advantage is that it lets us avoid having to make sense of how the supposedly moral qualities of otherwise physical and psychological entities play a causal role in the formation of moral beliefs.

5 The "projectivism" of the naturalist outlook may hold that the error infects only this common understanding of morality and not morality itself, moral claims not being in themselves descriptive statements (though in many ways they function like them). This is Simon Blackburn's "quasi-realism"; see his *Spreading the Word* (Oxford University Press, 1984), chapter 6.
6 See the similar view in Nagel, *View from Nowhere,* pp. 144, 148.

We might even agree with the noncognitivist that the moral qualities we may seem to perceive in the world are but moral distinctions we "project" onto it. But the moral distinctions themselves will not, therefore, be our own creation. They will consist in an order of reasons, the authority of which for our conduct we recognize on reflection, and to which we thus understand ourselves as responding.

This conception of moral truth may still seem not to answer the question of how moral truth can help to explain the formation of moral beliefs. Even when the moral facts in virtue of which moral beliefs are true or false are taken to involve reasons, it may seem obscure how such reasons – as opposed to beliefs about these reasons – can explain causally the formation of beliefs. A reason is not a physical state of affairs. (Sometimes we cite, for example, the weather as a reason, but strictly speaking the reason to take an umbrella is the *bearing* the rain has on our possibilities of action.) Nor is a reason a psychological state (for a reason can obtain, even if no one recognizes it), but rather the possible object of one. A reason is an abstract object. How then can reasons play any causal role in the formation of belief?

The present question has in fact a generality that takes it beyond the realm of morality. How is reflection, as a form of knowledge in which we discover reasons for belief and action, even possible? Since philosophy itself proceeds by reflection, not perception, the problem concerns at bottom whether philosophy can indeed be a form of knowledge. Viewing the problem in this more general light, we can at least note that moral cognitivism need not resort to an obscure faculty of "intuition," and we may also surmise that anticognitivists, at least of the sort we have been considering, must be in some difficulty about the cognitive status of their own philosophical position. I will come back to this point.

But as for the causal role of reasons in belief formation, this problem might seem less alarming if while we agree that helping to explain some part of experience is the standard for judging that something is real, we also observe that causal explanation is not the only kind of explanation there is. "Normative explanation" exists, too, in which we explain some belief or action, not by giving the causal factors that produced it, but by giving the reasons that justify it. The explanatory criterion of reality must be broad enough to encompass both sorts of explanation. Thomas Nagel is one who has put forward this view.[7] It is

7 Ibid., pp. 144–6.

unclear, however, that the distinction between causal and normative explanation, valid though it may be, is enough to remove the difficulty. As Nagel himself recognizes, the second sort of explanation is often used in conjunction with the first. Many times we explain causally the origin of someone's belief by saying that it followed from other beliefs of his, and not just by saying that he believed that it followed from them, for we think he had this latter belief only because it is in fact true. Perhaps the normative elements in such causal explanations of belief are really dispensable.[8] But to the extent that they are not, the problem remains of how reasons (as opposed to beliefs about reasons) can produce belief. There is a further weakness in Nagel's use of the distinction between causal and normative explanation to dismiss the force of the anticognitivist argument. By itself, the distinction does not suffice to make normative explanation, too, a criterion of reality. The distinction is compatible with the idea that only what serves in the causal explanation of experience should be said to be real.

The conception of moral knowledge as a knowledge of reasons faces, then, an important difficulty. Even so, this first anticognitivist argument remains unacceptable for the fundamental reason that in the end it undermines itself. As I have already suggested, the noncognitivist's rejection of moral facts, understood as involving one class of reasons, must entail the rejection of normative facts generally, that is, of all facts involving what one ought to believe or do. No special feature of moral reasons – distinguishing them from all other sorts of reasons – has so far been given for thinking that they alone do not form an independent order of facts in virtue of which moral beliefs are true or false. If moral claims cannot be understood as being true or false, it would seem that normative claims in general must lack truth-value as well.

Mackie, for example, argued that since moral claims are "inherently action-guiding" – by which he meant that they necessarily move the will of those who make them – the idea that there exist objective values in virtue of which such claims could be true is metaphysically and epistemologically queer.[9] The world itself would have to be such that knowledge of it would have a necessary influence on the will, the ascertainment of fact being (in this case unlike elsewhere) at the same time the impetus to act. I shall later express some doubts about the

8 So Harman believes; *Nature of Morality*, p. 130.   9 Mackie, *Ethics*, pp. 38–41.

notion of inherent action-guidingness. But for now let us note that to the extent that the recognition of moral reasons does necessarily move the will, the acceptance of reasons for belief about any domain does so, too. To accept that we ought to avoid contradiction entails, in the main, that we will be moved to change our set of beliefs once we find an inconsistency. Thus, the allegedly "magnetic" import of moral claims cannot keep moral values from being objective except on pain of implying the same for cognitive ones.

The key point is that if there cannot be objective moral reasons – in virtue of which moral beliefs are true or false – because their causal efficacy is unintelligible, then equally there cannot be objective reasons in virtue of which beliefs about what ought to be believed about the physical and psychological worlds are true or false. The notion of moral truth is no more dubious than the idea of there being a truth or falsity to any claim that something ought to be believed – at least so far as this first anticognitivist argument is concerned. The consistent noncognitivist should deny to all normative beliefs the capacity of being true or false. He should deny that there can be knowledge of any sort about what we ought to believe or do.

This outcome is not just unwelcome in itself. It also appears inconsistent with the naturalist's normative claim that only what serves in the causal explanation of experience should be said to be real. For that claim seems to express a normative *belief,* that is, to be a claim taken to be true. Does it not purport to *describe* the basis on which we ought to form our beliefs about the nature of reality? Generally, moral noncognitivists have proceeded as though it does. They have assumed it expresses a true belief about the correct criterion of reality. But that assumption manifestly conflicts with their implicit denial that normative claims can be true, that they are, properly speaking, beliefs at all. So long as noncognitivism views itself as the true doctrine of what is to be believed and commits itself to the present argument, it undermines itself.[10]

As a rule, moral noncognitivists find their position easy to accept, indeed obviously true, because they never look at normative judgments concerning belief and fail to recognize what their position implies about them. They focus solely on (moral) judgments about what is to

---

10 Cf. Hilary Putnam, *Reason, Truth and History* (Cambridge University Press, 1981), pp. 206–11.

be done. Harman is an exception, since he does observe[11] that reasons in general, and not just moral facts, stand in the way of his naturalism. But he fails to appreciate the difficulty of his position. He seems to think it sufficient to remark that reasons could be naturalistically understood in terms of "acceptable reasoning," if the latter were in turn understood as "reasoning that an ideally functioning reasoner might reason, an ideally functioning reasoner being anyone whose reasoning is not distorted or misfunctioning in one way or another."[12] But this remark is not sufficient. It expresses instead the vain attempt to get rid of the irreducibly normative by in fact explaining one normative notion in terms of another. Reasons are here explained by reference to "acceptable reasoning," "acceptable reasoning" by appeal to "ideal functioning," and "ideal functioning" in terms of the absence of "distortion" or "misfunctioning." One is no nearer a naturalistic explanation of the normative at the end than at the beginning. Harman seems unable or unwilling to face the fact that his naturalism would destroy the very idea of rationality.

Chastened by these remarks, the moral noncognitivist might agree that his naturalism cannot be total, and that he must accept the truth of certain normative propositions concerning the formation of belief. Could he not still deny that specifically moral claims can possibly be true? He could indeed. But what would be the rationale for such a position? Since the considerations given so far against the possibility of moral truth, if they hold at all, tell against normative truth in general, this seminaturalism seems unable to justify its exclusion of moral truth.

One way moral noncognitivism could prove acceptable, therefore, would be to succeed in uncovering some such basis for distinguishing between moral claims and normative claims about belief. I have no a priori argument to show this cannot be done. But it is fair to say that philosophers who embrace some version of the first anticognitivist argument have not generally acknowledged that such should be their task. Nor is it clear what form this discrimination would take. One ready idea might be that moral claims must look "queer," if taken to be true, because they are categorical in character, whereas normative claims about belief involve merely hypothetical imperatives (i.e., they apply to us only given that we want to pursue truth and avoid error), and so can count as being true or false without implying the existence of normative facts. But this way of contrasting the two kinds of norms

11 Harman, *Nature of Morality*, p. 125.   12 Ibid., pp. 129–30.

is doubly dubious. First, norms about belief seem generally as categorical as moral norms. When it comes to deciding what to believe, are we not supposed to pursue the goals these norms promote, to seek truth and shun error, whether we want to or not? (Of course, they need not be our goals when we are engaged in things other than the formation of belief.) And second, normative claims that are indeed hypothetical in form cannot, if regarded as true, escape whatever non-naturalistic implications would beset categorical ones, similarly construed. For any hypothetical imperative, "If you seek X, you ought to do Y," implies an imperative of the form "Either do not pursue X or do Y," which, though perhaps not "moral," is certainly categorical, binding whatever the agent may happen to want. The prospects for "seminaturalism" seem, therefore, not very promising.

There is, I believe, but one other form a consistent moral noncognitivism might take. Instead of seeking to find some special feature of moral claims, one could turn around and embrace the idea that all normative claims, even those concerning what we should believe, are neither true or false. One would then concede that, strictly speaking, it is not true that we should abide by the most elementary rules of reasoning, these being but rules we simply prefer to operate by. One would even have to admit that this is not itself the true view of what we should believe about the world, but merely the view its adherents prefer. If others take a contrary view of reality and consider some normative claims to be true, then they will not be making a mistake so much as doing what noncognitivists prefer they would not do. Such an outlook is indeed consistent. But in what way is it attractive? Who can really regard how one ought to think as but a matter of preference?

Some philosophers believe that this sweeping noncognitivism can actually accommodate the thought that fundamental normative distinctions, including the difference between moral right and wrong, are independent of our preferences.[13] When we say that a certain norm would be valid even if we did not accept it, such a statement, they argue, makes sense without having to imply that there exists an independent normative fact. Instead, the statement simply expresses acceptance of a second-order norm to the effect that we should accept the given norm even if we do not want to. No doubt, the statement does

13 For example, Gibbard, *Wise Choices, Apt Feelings*, pp. 164–70; also Blackburn, *Spreading the Word*, pp. 217–20. Neither author is perfectly clear about recognizing that his noncognitivism must extend to normative claims in general.

express acceptance of this second-order norm. The moral cognitivist need not disagree. But is that all the statement involves? The crucial question is *why* someone would think he should accept a given norm whether or not he might want to do so. The natural answer would be that the person thinks it indeed true that he ought to do or believe what the norm commands. The moral noncognitivist we are now considering cannot, of course, accept this answer. But what sort of answer can he supply? Only, it seems, that if the person thinks he ought to accept the norm whether he wants to or not, this is simply because he prefers to do so. (Such is the preference of which, according to him, the second-order normative claim is but the expression.)

This analysis is far less accommodating than its proponents suggest. The realization that moral right and wrong is independent of our preferences just insofar as we prefer that it be so, that the rules of reasoning are independent of what we may want only insofar as we want them to be so, seems destined to sap any confidence we may have in the objectivity of these norms. The distinction between first-order and second-order preferences will not obviate the fact that the validity of norms, both of thought and of action, will be but a matter of our preferences. If this is what we believe, then nothing forbids our choosing to observe whatever norms we please. It is best to call this position by its proper name, which is irrationalism. Such an outlook is not without precedent. As we saw in the previous chapter, the heart of Nietzsche's philosophy was the announcement that all values – moral, aesthetic, and scientific – are something we simply create. I doubt that Anglo-American philosophers of the naturalist persuasion would be keen to place themselves under Nietzsche's banner. But that, it seems, is where they belong.

3. The Unity of Theoretical and Practical Reason

The second important argument in the arsenal of the moral noncognitivist has been the one Hume made famous. " 'Tis impossible," Hume wrote, "that the distinction betwixt moral good and evil, can be made by reason; since that distinction has an influence upon our actions, of which reason alone is incapable."[14]

14 Hume, *A Treatise of Human Nature*, L. A. Selby-Bigge (ed.) (Oxford University Press, 1975), p. 462. The argument goes back, in fact, to Francis Hutcheson, *Illustrations on the Moral Sense* (Cambridge, Mass.: Harvard University Press, 1971), pp. 120–2.

There are two premises in the argument, each of which merits careful formulation. Hume's first, major premise is that reason – by which he meant reasoning – is itself motivationally inert. The premise should in fact be more broadly expressed as holding that belief is motivationally inert. By "belief" I mean a psychological state in which one holds something to be true or false, a state that could in principle be shown by reasoning to constitute knowledge. The first premise asserts, then, that believing that something is the case cannot by itself move us to act one way or another. It can have an influence on action, according to Hume, only in conjunction with a "passion" or desire, with an affective state, which is something quite different from a belief.

The second, minor premise is that moral claims are not motivationally inert: to think that some course of action, for example, is morally good or bad is by itself to be moved to pursue or avoid it, or to be moved to recommend or condemn it to others, though of course contrary motives may nonetheless prevail. The conclusion is thus that moral claims should not be understood as beliefs. They are incapable of constituting knowledge. The argument points directly, therefore, to an expressivist conception of moral claims: unable really to describe anything, they can only express the preferences of those who make them. The Humean argument still commands the assent of many noncognitivists today.[15]

But this anticognitivist argument, too, is not really so persuasive as it may seem. Much can be said against each of its premises. Let us begin with the minor premise. Is it so clear that moral claims have a necessary influence on the will, so obvious that they are "inherently action-guiding"? This view is generally called *internalism*. Is internalism so evidently true? I do not think so. It seems quite possible to believe that a certain course of action is morally correct without feeling at all inclined to pursue it ourselves (or to recommend it to others). It is not that we would then believe simply that others think the action morally correct. On the contrary, we could agree that from the standpoint of morality we ought really to do the action, and yet not conduct from

---

15 See C. L. Stevenson, "The Emotive Meaning of Ethical Terms" (1937), reprinted on pp. 415–29 in W. Sellars and J. Hospers (eds.), *Readings in Ethical Theory* (New York: Appleton-Century-Crofts, 1952); R. M. Hare, *The Language of Morals* (Oxford University Press, 1952), p. 29.; J. L. Mackie, *Hume's Moral Theory* (London: Routledge & Kegan Paul, 1980), pp. 54–5 and idem, *Ethics*, pp. 23, 40; Blackburn, *Spreading the Word*, pp. 187–8.

that standpoint our own deliberations about what to do. In such a case, we would have no "allegiance" to morality – by which I mean (as I shall explain later), not that we would fail to desire to act morally, but that we would not believe we ought to do so. We would believe that certain things are required of us morally while believing that we ought to deliberate in accord with some different sort of standards. The amoralist is just as capable of determining what is morally correct as the boor is of determining what is required by etiquette.

Moreover, moral claims about events or persons in the past, which thus refer to no open possibilities of action, also seem often to have no necessary influence on the will. To think that calling Brutus noble or Nero vicious must move the will in some way, that it must involve a resolve to guide our own conduct by their example or a similar recommendation to others, is to substitute for experience a preconceived theory. It may well be true that we could not simply appraise the past in this way unless we first understood how to use such terms of appraisal to guide our present and future conduct. But this point will not save the premise in question. However derivative the ability to make them, moral claims about the past really are often such as to involve no necessary movement of the will. This is also why it will not do to object that while for the amoralist moral claims will not be inherently action-guiding, his own evaluations of conduct, whatever they may be, will be so – in other words, that Hume's premise, properly formulated, is that our own practical evaluations, moral or otherwise, must move our will. For the amoralist, too, can employ his standards in mere commentary on the past. When, therefore, our moral appraisals do not leave our will to action indifferent, this is not a fact about the nature of moral claims as such. It is a reflection of our allegiance to morality as a guide to action, and of our belief that the object of appraisal involves a possibility of action open to us or to those we are addressing.

No doubt, many philosophers committed to the possibility of moral knowledge have also supposed that moral beliefs necessarily move the will. Such was the view of Samuel Clarke, who was Hume's principal target.[16] But that is no reason that moral cognitivists should continue to embrace internalism, and so have it turned against them by Hu-

16 See Clarke's *Discourse of Natural Religion*, vol. 1, pp. 198–9 in D. D. Raphael (ed.), *British Moralists* (Oxford University Press, 1969).

means.[17] The sensible view is that moral discourse is sometimes merely descriptive in intent and sometimes also action-guiding, depending on the purposes of those who engage in it.[18] If this view may be called *externalism*, then externalism seems the correct account of the relation between moral claims and motivation. It should not be assumed, however, as it often is, that if for externalism moral judgments are not inherently action-guiding, they can then motivate only in conjunction with a desire. As I have suggested, the extra element necessary for the will to be moved may instead consist in further beliefs.

The major premise of the Humean argument, namely that reasoning alone (or more broadly, belief alone) cannot move us to act, is in no sounder a condition. Hume's own grounds for espousing it are unconvincing, since they must also imply that reasoning alone (or belief alone) cannot move us to believe anything. Reasoning alone cannot move us to act, Hume averred, because the deliverances of reason are "representative," capable of being true or false, whereas actions are not. But believing or coming to believe, as opposed to the content of belief, cannot be true or false either. So the first premise, as Hume understood it, would also mean that reason cannot be argumentative, cannot convince, cannot produce belief.[19]

It is hard to see how any other understanding of the major premise (I shall limit the discussion to the motivational import of reason, but the results can be easily extended to the motivational import of belief) can avoid what must surely be this unwelcome consequence. Hume himself may have been prepared to accept it in light of his general skepticism about the powers of reason. But such is not the framework in which the Humean argument continues to gather its adherents today. They are not disposed to accept that reason is incapable of producing belief. For if that were true, then there could be no such thing as reasoning or coming to believe one thing by inference from others.

17 To a similar observation by Jonathan Harrison, *Hume's Moral Epistemology* (Oxford University Press, 1976), pp. 13–15, 54, Mackie could reply only that Harrison was abandoning a core element of the cognitivist position; see his *Hume's Moral Theory*, p. 55.
18 For a similar view, see G. J. Warnock, *The Object of Morality* (London: Methuen, 1971), pp. 125–38.
19 See R. Edgley, "Practical Reason," pp. 18–32 in J. Raz (ed.), *Practical Reasoning* (Oxford University Press, 1978).

Now if reason can produce belief, the Humean argument seems unable to show that it cannot equally produce action (or the will to action). Of course, it is possible that having reasoned to the conclusion that some action should be done, we feel no inclination to do it. But however we may analyze this well-known sort of malfunction in practical reasoning, the crucial fact is that there corresponds to it an exactly similar failure of theoretical reasoning: it is equally possible that having reasoned to the conclusion that some belief should be adopted, we feel no inclination to do so. Practical reasoning is in itself no more inert than theoretical reasoning.

True, often our reasoning that a certain action should be done leads us to do it only in virtue of some affective state or desire that we think the action will best satisfy. Reasoning about how to get what we want can then move us to act only because it is in the service of our wanting something. It is also true that we do not reason, or more exactly we think we ought not to reason, that something is to be believed because the belief will best satisfy some desire. Nothing should be believed just because believing it will get us something we happen to want. On the contrary, we think that beliefs should be formed in order to satisfy cognitive standards and goals we believe we ought to uphold.

So here is a point at which theoretical reason and practical reason can diverge. But what argument will show that they must always thus diverge? Why can we not reason about what to do, with the aim not of getting what we happen to want, but simply of complying with our beliefs about how we ought to act? Why can practical reason not sometimes move us as theoretical reason does, without the influence of some given affective state? We suppose it can, of course, when we assume we are able to comply with moral norms that are "categorical" – which is what, as a matter of fact, theoretical norms present themselves to be. We believe, in this case, that there are moral demands we can and should fulfill because we ought to do so, and not because we can thereby satisfy some desire. Doubts have been raised about the intelligibility of categorical moral norms.[20] But one might well wonder whether in the end they do not put the usual understanding of theoretical norms into question as well. Certainly, Hume's argument for his major premise cannot be used to promote such doubts, except on pain of denying that reason alone can move us to believe.

Some will object that, to move us to act, the conclusion that some

20 See the first two chapters in this book.

action is our categorical duty must work together, if not with some ulterior desire, then with the desire to fulfill our categorical duty. The only basis, however, for postulating such a desire is the wish to hold on to the Humean theory at all costs. Why must we not only believe we ought to do our categorical duty, but also desire to do it, in order for us to be moved to act by our conclusion that some action is our categorical duty? Though we must have, as mentioned before, an allegiance to this categorical morality, if we are to be moved to comply with it (and not just apply it as the amoralist would), why must such an allegiance consist in a desire rather than in the belief that we ought to comply with it? This allegiance may indeed be best understood as rooted not in the very nature of practical rationality, but in our training in a form of life (see Chapters 1 and 2); but surely socialization can produce beliefs as well as desires. To suppose our allegiance to this morality must involve a desire to observe it is in the end no better than the view that we must not only believe we should be rational in adopting beliefs, but also desire to be rational in adopting them, if the conclusion that a certain belief would be rational is to move us to believe it. And that would again be to deny that reasoning alone can move us to believe – a conclusion that can only attract those few who (perhaps like Hume himself) espouse a general skepticism about the power of reasoning.

The Humean argument as a whole holds that moral claims – or more generally practical claims about what ought to be done – have a motivational force that is absent from reason as such, or more broadly, from belief as such. It maintains that moral claims are therefore not really beliefs at all and so cannot constitute knowledge. My objections to its first premise show that the Humean argument (if it is not meant to express a general skepticism about reason) relies in effect on an untenable dualism of theory and practice. Under normal conditions, reasoning about what to believe moves us indeed to believe. Reason, in the conduct of the understanding, is not motivationally inert. The normative beliefs that guide such reasoning, beliefs about how we should decide what to believe, have therefore a necessary influence on the will. In this regard, they are no different from the moral claims that figure in our deliberations about how to act. (Here I am excluding from consideration moral claims that do not concern open possibilities of action or that do not command our allegiance, just as I am excluding claims about the proper conduct of the understanding that do not belong to our own deliberations about what to believe; for in such

cases there is no necessary influence on the will.) Likewise, the distur-
bances of the will that can make us indifferent to doing what we
believe we ought to do are not dissimilar to those that can render us
indifferent to believing what we believe we ought to believe. Finally,
there seems no way of showing that to move us to act, reasoning about
what to do must – not just sometimes, but always – serve some given
desire, except by implying that reasoning about what to believe can by
itself never move us to believe. Agreeing, as we should, that reasoning
alone can move us to believe, we have then no basis for denying that
reasoning alone can move us to act. Here lies the basic mistake of
the Humean argument. In motivational import, there is no necessary
difference between theoretical and practical reasoning, between the
conduct of the understanding and the conduct of action. Their difference need be one only of content.

In virtue of its dualism of theory and practice, the Humean argument denies the cognitive status of moral claims in a way that would
refuse it to normative claims generally. In reality, normative judgments
about what we should believe are no more nor less "inherently motiva-
ting," no more nor less formative of the will, than normative judgments
about what we should do. The Humean argument bears, therefore, the
same fundamental flaw as the first anticognitivist argument I considered. It, too, implies that the proper conduct of the understanding
cannot be an object of knowledge. Failing to discriminate between
moral claims and normative claims in general, Humean noncognitivism is thus faced with the same dilemma. If it understands itself as the
correct view about how we ought to think about moral claims, it
contradicts itself. If instead it boldly accepts the conclusion that there
can be no correct answer to how we ought to think, then it avoids self-
contradiction only at the price of embracing irrationalism. Those who
find this price too high have no choice but to acknowledge that moral
claims can constitute a form of knowledge, one whose domain is a
certain class of reasons for action.

4. The Perceptual Model of Moral Knowledge

So far it has been to dissolve the cogency of anticognitivist arguments
that I have insisted upon the principle that moral claims belong among
normative claims in general. This principle also has another, more
positive use. It points to the form a proper account of the nature of
moral knowledge should take. Moral knowledge should be seen as one

kind, among others, of normative knowledge – knowledge, that is, of what we ought to believe and to do. Moral cognitivists seem to me to have violated this principle almost as often as noncognitivists. For by its light, two very influential models of moral knowledge must appear misconceived.[21]

The first of them is the *perceptual* model of moral knowledge. Its most distinguished proponent was John McDowell, in a number of writings published in the 1980s. (Since then, apparently for reasons I would applaud, he seems to have left this view behind, as I shall explain.) McDowell's aim was to underscore the similarity between the experience of moral value and the perception of secondary qualities.[22] Phenomenal colors and other so-called secondary qualities are certainly subjective in the sense that an adequate understanding of what it is for something to possess them must refer to the perceptual capacities we have. Thus, an object's being red just is its being such as to look red under normal conditions. Despite this mind dependence, however, secondary qualities are not simply subjective, a mere figment of the imagination. There is a real, other than solely conventional, distinction between correctly and incorrectly perceiving the color of a thing. Correct color perception is a response to the way the world is, and in this regard it is objective, for an object that looks red under normal conditions really is different from one that looks green.

Our moral experience, so McDowell argued at this time, should be viewed as having a similar structure. The way things are morally is not

21 One important view of the status of moral claims I shall not examine closely is "moral constructivism." While holding that morality is an object of reason, this position denies that there are any moral facts independent of a conception of ourselves as setting down fair rules of interaction. Moral reasons are but rules that we construct and impose on ourselves. This position seems to have been Kant's and that of many who have followed him. Its ultimate coherence, however, is doubtful. Surely a constructed rule is reasonable not simply because we have constructed it, but because the rule is one we ought to construct for ourselves, one that it is fair or right to adopt. It follows that there must be normative truths independent of our self-legislative activity. Moreover, it seems improbable that they would not have to include specifically moral truths. (On this point, see Chapter 2, this volume.) Of course, this conclusion allows that *some* of our moral commitments may be understood as being constructed by us.

22 John McDowell, "Non-Cognitivism and Rule-Following," pp. 154–7 in S. Holtzman and C. Leach (eds.), *Wittgenstein: To Follow a Rule* (London: Routledge & Kegan Paul, 1981); and idem, "Values and Secondary Qualities," pp. 112–17 in T. Honderich (ed.), *Morality and Objectivity* (London: Routledge & Kegan Paul, 1985). For an earlier version of the same approach see C. I. Lewis, *Values and Imperatives* (Stanford, Calif.: Stanford University Press, 1969), pp. 53–4.

a notion we can grasp apart from referring to how things look to a person having some degree of moral sensitivity. There are no moral facts, he then claimed, independent of the specific sorts of interests that make up the moral point of view. But again, McDowell insisted, this mind dependence does not imply that in viewing some action or quality as morally good or bad we are not responding to something in the action or quality itself. It can still be true that an action that looks bad from the moral point of view really differs from one that looks good. Moral distinctions, though subjective in one way, are not simply projections we cast upon the world. They also have their own sort of objectivity.[23] McDowell's general thesis was that we must abandon the habitual opposition between something being "subjective," that is, mind-dependent, and its being "objective," forming part of the world. Then we will conceive how there can be such a thing as moral knowledge. It is at bottom moral perception.[24]

The fundamental flaw in this conception, however, is that it cannot account for the normative content of moral knowledge. We may, of course, properly speak of "seeing" that some action is morally bad. Something of its moral character is there to be perceived. We may see that it is bad because we see that it is cruel, and we can see that it is cruel because we see that it involves deliberately hurting someone's feelings. But it makes no sense to say we "see" the action's being something that *ought not to be;* that is, there is no sense in saying we *perceive the reason* why the action should not be done. The notion of perception seems unduly inflated, leaving no room for any other kind of knowledge at all, if it is possible to speak in something other than a *façon de parler* of perceiving reasons. Who would think of saying we perceive the reasons for accepting some scientific theory?

In the end, the question of what can rightly be called an object of perception is perhaps not very important. It may just be an issue of nomenclature. What does matter, and deserves to be put at the center of attention, is the formal similarity between moral judgments and normative judgments in general. From the beginning, McDowell was moved, in fact, to add that moral perception presents itself as a *"merited"* response to value: to recognize something as morally good is to

---

23 McDowell, "Values and Secondary Qualities," pp. 112–17; idem, "Non-Cognitivism and Rule-Following," pp. 142, 156–7; idem, "Are Moral Requirements Hypothetical Imperatives?" *Aristotelian Society,* [suppl. vol.] 52 (1978), pp. 16–17.
24 McDowell, "Moral Requirements," p. 23; also David McNaughton, *Moral Vision* (Oxford: Blackwell, 1988), chapters 3–4.

acknowledge that we *ought* to approve of it.[25] This remark beckons toward the normative element of moral judgment, though at the same time it fits ill with the analogy of perception. In his more recent writings he seems to have come to appreciate this point. The discussion of moral knowledge in his Lindley Lecture of 1987 leaves behind the perceptual analogy and wisely turns to a moral epistemology that "centres on the notion of susceptibility to reasons."[26] And the idea that normative thought in general is engaged in attending to a "space of reasons," which "are there whether we know it or not," forms the heart of McDowell's 1991 Locke Lectures, *Mind and World.*[27] This conception of moral knowledge is on the right track.

5. Cognitivist Naturalism

Given the usual aims of philosophical naturalism, one might not have expected that another recent and important model of moral knowledge has been explicitly naturalist in conception. This new *cognitivist naturalism,* developed by such philosophers as Richard Boyd, Nicholas Sturgeon, Peter Railton, and David Brink, testifies in fact to how inescapable the naturalist outlook has come to seem.[28] The distinctive feature of this model is the way it seeks to elude G. E. Moore's famous critique of the "naturalistic fallacy." Moore held that a moral property cannot be defined in terms of natural (i.e., physical and psychological)

---

25 McDowell, "Values and Secondary Qualities," p. 118.
26 John McDowell, "Projection and Truth in Ethics," Lindley Lecture 1987 (University of Kansas Press, 1987), p. 9. One argument sometimes offered for the perceptual model is that it makes sense of the fact that our moral sensitivity to a given situation is not explicable simply in terms of the application of moral principles to the situation; often we must be able just to see the moral facts involved. This is the view, for example, in McNaughton, *Moral Vision*, pp. 62, 192. I agree that moral sensitivity can involve more than the application of principle, namely the exercise of judgment. But moral judgment is best understood as recognizing moral reasons that go beyond the reasons given by accepted principles themselves. See my *Patterns of Moral Complexity,* pp. 7–9.
27 John McDowell, *Mind and World* (Cambridge, Mass.: Harvard University Press, 1994). The specific discussion of moral judgment as a response to reasons is limited to pp. 78–84.
28 See, e.g., Richard Boyd, "How to Be a Moral Realist," pp. 181–228 in G. Sayre-McCord (ed.), *Essays on Moral Realism* (Ithaca, N.Y.: Cornell University Press, 1988); N. Sturgeon, "Moral Explanations," pp. 229–55 in ibid.; Peter Railton, "Moral Realism," *Philosophical Review* 95, no. 2 (April 1986), pp. 163–207; and most of all David O. Brink, *Moral Realism and the Foundations of Ethics* (Cambridge University Press, 1989).

properties, in the sense that the terms referring to natural properties would be synonymous or identical in meaning with the term referring to the moral property. So far, it is argued, Moore was right, but he erred in concluding that if moral knowledge is possible, it must be knowledge of "non-natural" properties. Despite absence of synonymy, a moral property, according to this new ethical naturalism, can still *be* some set or interconnection of natural properties, either by being identical with it or by consisting in it. The moral property may in fact be the very same property as the set of natural properties, in the way water just is H_2O, or it may be realized or constituted by the natural properties without being identical with them, in the way mental states may consist in brain states while also being realizable in principle by other ("functionally equivalent") material systems. Moral knowledge is possible, it is claimed, as knowledge of what are at bottom natural facts.

Moore rejected the naturalist thesis that moral properties are in fact natural properties because he thought one could always intelligibly treat as an "open question" whether any given natural quality is indeed morally good or bad.[29] According to the new cognitivist naturalism, the intelligibility of such an open question rules out synonymy between moral and natural terms, but it does not exclude the possibility that moral properties are in fact natural properties. After all, one can intelligibly ask whether water is indeed H_2O (in a way one cannot ask intelligibly whether water is indeed an aqueous substance), without it failing to be the case that water is identical with H_2O. Similarly, it remains true that one cannot deduce moral facts from natural facts alone. The new ethical naturalism does not deny the underivability of the (moral) "ought" from the "is." But so, too, one cannot derive the visible features of the things of ordinary life (such as water) simply from their molecular composition, though this does not imply that the ordinary substance water is not just H_2O. The point is that one can establish this identity, one can derive the qualities of ordinary substances from their molecular composition, if one appeals to "bridge principles" expressing laws that connect the two domains. That is supposedly the case, too, with moral facts and natural facts. We can show that moral facts just are natural facts (by being either identical with them or constituted by them) if we can rely upon knowledge of the lawlike connections between them.[30]

29 G. E. Moore, *Principia Ethica* (Cambridge University Press, 1903), p. 15.
30 See Brink, *Moral Realism*, pp. 151–63.

According to this view, therefore, the injustice of some social institution, for example, will be identical with, or consist in, various natural (physical, psychological) facts about the institution and its relation to other natural facts – the fact, let us say, that it assigns certain liberties to some of its members while denying them to others. One might be tempted to suppose that the notion of there being moral facts (and so moral knowledge) must then be superfluous, since we could make do just with referring to the underlying natural facts themselves. But this, it is claimed, would be shortsighted. Even if the moral facts are actually identical with natural facts, we might find it difficult to identify the relevant natural facts except under a moral description. And if the moral facts instead consist in natural facts, the moral characterization of these facts may prove indispensable. For if different arrays of natural facts constitute the same moral fact (if, for example, different social arrangements amount to the same sort of injustice), we may have no way of grouping these natural structures together, no way of regarding them as all of a kind, except from a moral point of view. If we gave up referring to moral facts, we might lose information.[31]

Despite the ingenuity of its construction and the validity of its objection to the "open question" argument, this naturalist model of moral knowledge seems to me unacceptable, failing indeed for the same reasons as the perceptual model. It does not account for the specifically *normative* character of moral beliefs. What could be the naturalistic substance of the fact, for example, that being unjust, the institution *ought* not to exist, that there is a reason to change it? Reasons may indeed arise from the natural facts being as they are. Thus, that the institution ought not to exist follows from its involving an unequal assignment of fundamental liberties. So normative judgments may be derivable from statements of natural facts in the same way that statements about ordinary substances are derivable from statements about molecular composition – that is, by appeal to "bridge principles" (say, a theory of justice). But this supervenience of the "ought" upon the "is" falls short of establishing that facts involving reasons consist in, or are identical with, natural facts.[32]

The new cognitivist naturalism has said, in fact, nothing to show that facts involving reasons consist in natural facts. Nor is it at all clear what such an account would look like. The claim that nonsynonymous terms may actually refer to the same thing, true as it is, does nothing to

31 Ibid., pp. 192–6.   32 As Brink recognizes, p. 160.

indicate just how this may also be the case for normative and natural terms. Normative facts (which involve reasons) and natural facts seem altogether different things, if only because we discover them in such different ways. Natural facts we ascertain by observation and experiment. Reasons we discern by reflection.

6. Morality and Reflection

By this point, many readers will probably feel that the moral "ought" to which I have been referring is something thoroughly mysterious. Some will conclude, if they have not thought so all along, that if moral facts must look like this, it surely is best to give up the idea that they can exist. Others will continue to hold that, though there can be moral knowledge, it must somehow amount to knowledge of the natural world. But there is a mystery here only for those who assume a naturalistic view of the world. What needs to be done is to abandon an uncritical, pious attachment to naturalism. For such is the sort of allegiance it generally commands.[33] We must open our mind to the real possibility that the world is a more complex place.

The best way to remove the mystery is to observe that the moral "ought" is not alone in its challenge to the naturalistic worldview. Moreover, this broader challenge does not stem, as commonly supposed, from the fact that mathematics, too, purports to be about something other than the natural world. We need to attend not to how moral judgments bear some *analogy* to mathematical ones, but rather to the fact that moral judgments form one *species* among others of normative judgment in general. Whether rejecting or defending the possibility of moral knowledge, philosophical naturalists have said

---

33 Thus, in *Wise Choices, Apt Feelings,* p. 154, Allan Gibbard declares confidently, "It might be thought that ordinary conceptions of rationality are Platonistic or intuitionistic. On the Platonistic picture, among the facts of the world are facts of what is rational and what is not. . . . If this is what anyone seriously believes, then I simply want to debunk it. Nothing in a plausible, naturalistic picture of our place in the universe requires these non-natural facts. . . ." At no point in his book does he offer a defense of his naturalistic starting point, only an elaboration of it. (Nor, for that matter, does he plainly recognize its ultimate consequences for the understanding of what it is to think as one should.) The simple precommitment to naturalism is explicit also in G. Harman, "Is There a Single True Morality?" and N. Sturgeon, "Moral Explanations," pp. 29–30 and 58, respectively, in David Copp and David Zimmerman (eds.), *Morality, Reason and Truth* (Totowa, N.J.: Rowman & Allanheld, 1985).

nothing about morality that must not equally apply to other normative forms of thought. And what they have said fails to make sense of the idea that there are correct answers to how we ought to determine what beliefs to accept – that there is such a thing as the proper conduct of the understanding. The inadequacy of naturalism is in the end its inability to account for normative truth in general. Thus, the minute we suppose it is true that we ought to believe something, we have broken with the naturalistic perspective. Acknowledging that there are indeed reasons for belief and action is enough to dispel the mystery.

The organ of normative knowledge, the means by which we come to discern reasons for belief and action, is, as I have said, reflection. There is nothing more essential, not just to the objectivity of morality, but even to the very possibility of philosophy as a form of knowledge, than reflection, and yet at the same time there is nothing more difficult to analyze. I cannot offer here even the outline of a general theory of this cognitive capacity.

But I can note, in passing, that this notion of reflection as the faculty of moral knowledge coheres with the historically situated character of moral knowledge that I have advocated in earlier chapters. To say that we discover reasons for belief and action by reflection does not by itself prejudge what resources reflection must have at its disposal to carry out this task. In fact, reflection is not, I believe, so much a "source" of normative knowledge as it is the means by which, on the basis of our existing convictions (including our present standards of belief and action), we determine what further, often what more specific, reasons for belief and action to accept, or what already accepted ones to reject. Reflection is always situated. As such, it finds its place within the reconciliation I proposed earlier in this book between reason and history.

It will be recalled that this conception implies, in essence, that the question of justification arises with respect to *changes* in belief, and not with respect to belief per se. We can reason only in a context of given belief, which as such does not call for justification, but on the contrary gives us the means for considering possible changes of belief, a context that is ours in virtue of our place in history. Historical context is not something reason must transcend, but rather a condition of its possibility. The evident failure of the rationalist project of drawing fundamental moral obligations from a notion of practical reason as such does not therefore mean, I have argued, that morality cannot be a form of knowledge. We must instead apply to the domain of morality

the historical epistemology I have just summarized, recognizing that
moral argumentation properly proceeds from the moral convictions
that historically are already ours. This entails giving up a *metaphysical
conception of reason,* understood as involving the search for a vision of
the world, and of the moral universe, *sub specie aeternitatis.* But if the
argument of the present chapter is correct, this cannot also mean
avoiding *a metaphysical conception of the objects* of moral knowledge.[34] Or
at least such is the case if a non-naturalistic conception of the world
must count as "metaphysical." It should not be supposed that "metaphysics," which today functions mostly as a term of abuse anyway, is all
of a piece.

There remain, of course, great difficulties in this conception of
normative knowledge, particularly in understanding how reasons, as
something non-natural, can become the object of reflection (which is
a psychological, natural process). But this problem must be weighed
against the even greater difficulties naturalism itself presents. As is so
often the case in philosophy, no position is without its drawbacks.
Philosophical judgment consists in making out where the weightier
considerations lie. By leaving no room for there being reasons for
belief, naturalism contradicts itself. Or it does so as long as it presents
itself as the truth regarding what we ought to believe about the world
rather than simply a point of view its proponents prefer. And if it is
merely their preference, why *should* we believe what they do?

Basically, Plato was right. Either we must admit that the world is
more than the natural world and that it comprises not only physical
and psychological reality, but normative reality as well, or, like the
Sophists, we must abandon reason for persuasion. Philosophy itself can
then only pretend to be a form of knowledge. To choose reason is thus

34 In *Mind and World,* where he has come to regard normative judgment as responsive
    to a "space of reasons" (see Section 4, this chapter), John McDowell maintains that
    such judgment expresses a "second nature" of ours that is essentially dependent on
    tradition (pp. 88, 95, 125–6). This view certainly resembles the idea of reflection I
    advocate here. But McDowell also believes it keeps him from a "rampant platonism"
    about this space of reasons (pp. 77–8, 83, 88, 178). I cannot really tell whether here
    he and I part ways, though many will find my platonistic (that is, non-naturalistic)
    conception of reasons "rampant" enough. The trouble is that McDowell says too
    little about what this term of abuse means. His own view of reasons is supposed
    instead to be "naturalistic" (pp. 78, 88), but he has deliberately expanded the idea
    of nature beyond the domain of modern natural science to include whatever reasons
    might prove to be, apparently provided that they can be grasped by our "second
    nature." So far as these remarks go, which are too indefinite to be of much help,
    there need be no difference between us.

to embrace the view of Moore, and of Sidgwick before him, that moral value is something real and non-natural.[35] But it is not to adopt their way of defending this view. Unlike Plato, Moore and Sidgwick failed to see the matter in its true generality. We should not focus, as they did, on moral thought specifically (much less should we rely upon the invalid "open question" argument). Our concern should be with the possibility of normative truth in general.[36]

---

35 "The fundamental notion represented by the word 'ought' or 'right' [is] essentially different from all notions representing facts of physical or psychical experience"; Sidgwick, *Methods of Ethics*, p. 25.
36 Husserl's *Philosophie als strenge Wissenschaft* (1911) does deal with the question in its proper generality, and in a way that is for the most part detachable from the peculiarities of his "phenomenology."

III

LIBERALISM AND MODERNITY

6

POLITICAL LIBERALISM

The business of laws is not to provide for the truth of opinions, but for the safety and security of the commonwealth, and of every particular man's goods and person.

John Locke

1. The Idea of Neutrality

Like any tradition of thought, liberalism is marked by disputes among its adherents as well as by disagreements with its adversaries. Here as elsewhere, one of the continuing objects of internal dispute has been precisely the way this form of political thought should be distinguished from its rivals. There is thus a limited value in trying to discern the "essence" or "guiding spirit" of liberalism. Still, it is not an entirely worthless project. The best approach lies in keeping in mind the basic *problems* that liberal thought has sought to solve. Some versions of liberalism will then appear more appropriate than others in that they take the problems seriously and construct liberal principles around them. In this perspective, viable forms of liberalism cannot be ones that themselves give rise to these problems.

Since its rise in the sixteenth century, liberal thought has followed those earlier currents of political philosophy that have sought to place the powers of government in the service of moral principle. In contrast

to the proponents of *raison d'état,* therefore, liberal thinkers have argued that there are things governments ought to be prohibited from
doing. The nature of these limits has not been simply prudential, as
though they merely involved rules of conduct by means of which rulers
may continue in power or states remain strong. Instead, the idea has
been that there is a common good, which government ought to respect, to promote if need be, but never to violate.

But liberalism has also taken to heart one of the cardinal experiences of modernity. It is the increasing awareness that reasonable
people tend naturally to differ and disagree about the nature of the
good life. A century of bloody religious wars was a fact no early liberal
thinker could ignore. But this phenomenon is not only a religious one.
Over the past four centuries, the nature of the good life in a great
many of its aspects has come to seem a topic on which disagreement
among reasonable people is not accidental, but to be expected. Being
reasonable – that is, thinking and conversing in good faith and
applying, as best as one can, the general capacities of reason that
belong to every domain of inquiry – has ceased to seem a guarantee of
unanimity. On these matters of supreme importance, the more we talk
with one another, the more we disagree.

The many different forms of experience and strands of thought
contributing to this conclusion are too numerous to recount here. But
some initial clarifications are necessary. In referring to reasonable
disagreement about the good life, I am not appealing to the doctrine
often called "pluralism," which asserts that there are many valid forms
of human self-realization. This doctrine is itself an affirmation about
the ultimate nature of the human good. The expectation of reasonable
disagreement has rather to do with the fact that positive views about
the nature of the good life, be they "pluralistic" or "monistic," have
come to seem eminently controversial. (I pursue this distinction in
the next chapter.) Equally important is the point that acknowledging
reasonable disagreement about the good life need not lead to skepticism. That is, we may still believe that we have sound reasons for
certain views about what makes life worth living. We may thus be
entitled to claim that people who reject them are in error. The crux is
that, all the same, we would be foolish not to expect our views to meet
with controversy in a calm and careful discussion.

In the light of this experience, the decisive question for liberal
theory has therefore been the terms under which people can nonetheless live together in political association. Greek and medieval thinkers

generally agreed that moral principle must shape the powers of government. But they entertained very sanguine prospects about the possibility of reasonable agreement about the good life.[1] For them, it was axiomatic that here, too, reason tends naturally toward single solutions. The result was that, in their different ways, Greek and medieval thinkers usually assigned to the state the task of protecting and fostering substantial conceptions of the good life. The proper ends of government must look very different to liberal thinkers for whom unanimity about the good life is more likely to be the fruit of coercion than of reason.

To avoid the oppressive use of state power, the liberal goal has therefore been to define the common good of political association by means of a *minimal moral conception*. Political life has continued to be viewed as an undertaking guided by moral principle. But the terms of political association must now be less comprehensive than the views of the good life about which reasonable people disagree. More precisely, fundamental political principles must express a moral conception that citizens can affirm together, despite their inevitable differences about the worth of specific ways of life. To call this moral conception "minimal," of course, means only that it serves as a common ground, and not that those who embrace it will live up to it without effort and without exception.

It is in this light that we should understand the traditional liberal concern for the protection of individual liberty. Freedom is not a univocal notion. There are many different ideals of freedom that, not necessarily to the exclusion of one another, we might pursue. The kind of freedom that has mattered for liberalism is, as often said, a "negative" freedom, the freedom from undue government interference. This goal need not be considered by liberals, however, as the only sort of freedom we should value. Perhaps the "positive" freedom of self-determination, or individual autonomy, also forms an ideal we should espouse. But positive conceptions of freedom, specifying as they do the ultimate purposes to which we should put our negative freedom from government interference, tend naturally to be the object of reasonable controversy. That is why liberalism holds that negative freedom is the kind of liberty that is relevant from a political point of view.

The liberal ideal of freedom ought also to be distinguished from the

---

1 The chief exception to this generalization, of course, is the various forms of ancient and medieval skepticism.

view that freedom is merely doing as we please. Liberalism is often accused of regarding every kind of limit to liberty, even the rule of law, as in itself an unwelcome imposition, to be accepted only to prevent a greater loss of liberty. And indeed, some liberals seem to have held just this view, as when J. S. Mill declared that "all restraint, qua restraint, is an evil."

But this is a mistake. Liberalism does not really equate liberty with license and law with burden. Against such an equation stands, for example, Locke's insistence that "the end of law is not to abolish or restrain, but to preserve and enlarge freedom ... where there is no law, there is no freedom."[2] Our preceding reflections, introductory though they are, suggest that Locke is the right guide here. The value of negative freedom, I have said, forms part of a liberal idea of the common good. Though more must be said about the "minimal" moral principles defining this common good, clearly they require respect for the reasonable disagreement people have about the nature of the good life. In other words, the liberal ideal of freedom itself rests upon fundamental moral duties we have to one another. Individuals may do as they please only because and to the extent that that is how they ought to be treated. This means, incidentally, that the common good in liberal thought is not, as sometimes supposed, simply the sum of the different goals individuals pursue on their own. But it also means that the core moral principles constituting this common good must find expression in the rule of law, if the space for reasonable disagreement about the good life is to be guaranteed. That is why law does not simply limit freedom, but rather makes it possible.

The virtue of active citizenship, which the so-called civic republican tradition has so persistently emphasized, plays therefore a necessary role in liberal thought, too.[3] Far from encouraging a wholesale retreat

---

2 J. S. Mill, *On Liberty*, chapter 5, p. 150 in *Utilitarianism, On Liberty, and Considerations on Representative Government* (New York: Dutton, 1976); John Locke, *Second Treatise of Government*, §57. The view expressed by Mill goes back through Bentham to Hobbes; on the relation between law and liberty Hobbes and Locke took diametrically opposite positions.

3 On this republican theme, see Quentin Skinner, "Two Views on the Maintenance of Liberty," pp. 35–58 in Philip Pettit (ed.), *Contemporary Political Theory* (New York: Macmillan, 1991); Philip Pettit, "Liberalism and Republicanism," *Australian Journal of Political Science*, 28 (1993), pp. 162–89; and idem, "Negative Liberty, Liberal and Republican," *European Journal of Philosophy*, 1, no. 1 (1993), pp. 15–38. Both Skinner and Pettit seek (wrongly, I believe) to set up an opposition between liberalism and republicanism on this issue.

to private life (which is yet another frequent misconception), a liberal political order calls on the resolve to preserve the rule of law that is indispensable to liberty. There is not, therefore, the opposition between ancient and modern conceptions of liberty, political participation, and negative freedom that some political thinkers have thought to exist (though Benjamin Constant himself in his famous discourse *De la liberté des anciens comparée à celle des modernes* [1819] certainly did not make this mistake). Still, it remains true that liberalism must distinguish the republican virtue of citizenship from allegiance to any controversial ideal of the good life, and in particular from the idea (which enthusiasts about the ancient Greek polis often express) that political life represents the highest form of human endeavor.

A natural notion to describe the essential character of liberalism is that of *neutrality*. The principles of a liberal political order aim to be "neutral" with respect to controversial ideas of the good. I myself have used this terminology before.[4] But to ward off misunderstanding, I must draw attention to two drawbacks to using the term "neutrality." First, it can wrongly suggest that liberalism is not a moral conception, that it is "neutral with respect to morality." The point is rather that it aims to be neutral with respect to controversial views of the good life. For the liberal pursuit of this neutrality itself expresses the moral commitment to finding terms of political association that can be the object of reasonable agreement.[5] Second, the notion of neutrality can be variously understood. One construal, prevalent in the utilitarian tradition, has been the idea that there is a common denominator of value. Different views of the human good, it is said, can be seen as so many ways of pursuing a common value (pleasure, or the satisfaction of desire), so that the "neutral" way of handling conflicts between those views would be the course of action that, each person counting

---

4 See my *Patterns of Moral Complexity*, chapter 3. I was following the lead of other contemporary liberal thinkers such as Ronald Dworkin in his "Liberalism," pp. 113–43 in Stuart Hampshire (ed.), *Public and Private Morality* (Cambridge University Press, 1978); and Bruce Ackerman, in *Social Justice and the Liberal State* (New Haven, Conn.: Yale University Press, 1980).

5 Naturally, the liberal state need not be neutral, either, with regard to whatever ideas about the good life are a matter of reasonable agreement in the society. Two of the criticisms of the ideal of neutrality in Joseph Raz, *The Morality of Freedom* (Oxford: Clarendon Press, 1986), p. 128, seem to miss this point; his third criticism is that neutrality cannot rule out the use of bargaining to endorse highly unjust principles, but this ignores the point that liberal neutrality is a moral conception, not a matter of bargaining (see Section 2 of this essay).

equally, brings about the greatest amount of the common value overall. This is not, however, the only possible understanding of neutrality – fortunately so, since there does not seem really to be such a common currency of value. A more promising account is that neutral principles are ones we can justify without assuming the validity of those views of the good on which people reasonably disagree. This is the idea of neutrality I propose.[6] It is, as I have noted, itself a moral conception, however minimal, and one that I must now try to develop further.

One point to note immediately is that this requirement of neutrality applies primarily to the fundamental, that is, constitutional, principles of political association, which fix the basic rights and duties of citizens. Such a political order may and generally will assign nonconstitutional decisions to less demanding rules, and notably to majority voting. On such issues the appeal to controversial ideas of the good may in fact be legitimate. In this chapter, however, I shall be concerned only with the liberal understanding of the fundamental principles of political life.

I have already observed that the project of basing such political principles on neutral ground need not be motivated by skepticism. Some liberals have indeed been skeptics about our ability to know the nature of the human good. But skepticism is not the only way of justifying liberal neutrality. Nor is it the best way, such skepticism being itself something on which reasonable people differ. The reason for prescinding from controversial views of the good, in the establishment of political principles, is not that we cannot rightfully believe our own views are better supported by experience and reflection than those of other people. It is not, as Thomas Nagel has proposed, that when we appeal to "a higher standard of objectivity" we find that such disagreements "come down finally to a bare confrontation between incompatible personal points of view."[7] On the contrary, we may be

---

6 Liberal neutrality, so understood, is thus a procedural ideal. Generally, it also involves a "neutrality of aim" requiring that political principles not be intended to favor any controversial view of the good life, since the reasons justifying political principles often concern the aims of state action. But it does not imply a "neutrality of effect" by which political principles have an equal influence on all permissible ways of life, for this is likely to be impossible. See the discussion in John Rawls, *Political Liberalism* (New York: Columbia University Press, 1993), pp. 191–4.

7 See Thomas Nagel, "Moral Conflict and Political Legitimacy," *Philosophy and Public Affairs* (Summer 1987), pp. 215–40 (at 232). Nagel says (p. 229) that his account does not depend on any skepticism, but it certainly assumes that the ideals toward which a liberal state should be neutral are less "objective," less well justified than those that should inform its principles.

able to present others the reasons for our ideal of the good life and even explain in detail what errors prevent them from agreeing with our view. (These are Nagel's two conditions for complying with what he calls the "higher standard of objectivity.") The familiar fact is that nonetheless our views can continue to meet with reasonable disagreement. This can happen because different conceptions of the good life usually involve (to an extent we may not realize at first) rather articulate but different structures of purposes, significances, and activities. On the basis of such structures, one can explain how opposing views go wrong; yet reasonableness alone – that is, good faith and common reason – is too thin a basis for choosing between these rival structures.[8]

I have insisted on the fact that liberal neutrality does not arise from skepticism about the good so that we may better appreciate the importance of this question: moral in character though it is, why should we adopt this principle of neutrality? What reasons can we have for abstracting from disputed views of the human good and seeking terms of political association on which people can reasonably agree? That the liberal principle of neutrality does require justification is plain from its not being the only way we could respond to the fact of reasonable disagreement about the good life. We could instead demand that the state sponsor our view of the good, however controversial, and reply to our opponents that, though they may be reasonable, they are simply mistaken about what makes life worth living. In itself, this position is not illogical, and it is scarcely unknown. What counts against it? The inadequacy of skepticism as an answer to this question suggests that the basis for the ideal of neutrality is not primarily *epistemological*. My view is that it is itself *moral*. Even so, a crucial question concerns the moral commitments that should serve as the basis of political neutrality. Only when we have made this point clear can we fully grasp the minimal moral conception liberalism embodies.

2. The Romantic Critique of Individualism

The difficulty to which I have just alluded lies in the fact that one very influential group of moral justifications stands out as particularly problematic. Kant and Mill sought to justify the principle of political

---

8 For a good development of this idea see Alasdair MacIntyre, *Whose Justice? Which Rationality?* (Notre Dame, Ind.: University of Notre Dame Press, 1988); see also my review of the book in the *Journal of Philosophy* (August 1989), pp. 437–42.

neutrality by appealing to the ideals of autonomy and individuality. By remaining neutral with regard to controversial views of the good life, constitutional principles express, according to them, the supreme value that ought to shape the whole of our life. There are important differences between the two ideals of autonomy and individuality. But they agree in the following demand, which unites Kant and Mill in what I shall call a philosophy of "individualism": we should always maintain a contingent allegiance, revisable on reflection, to any substantial view of the good life, that is, to any concrete way of life involving a specific structure of purposes, significances, and activities (such as a life shaped by certain cultural traditions, or devoted to a particular religion). Such forms of life can be truly valuable, according to Kant and Mill, only if we understand them as ones we choose, or would choose, from a position of critical detachment, in something like an experimental spirit. The source of value, and so the supreme value, is what is expressed in this posture of choice: our freedom to rise above empirical circumstance (Kant), or our need to distinguish ourselves from others (Mill). In words as true of Kant's doctrine as of his own, Mill wrote in *On Liberty* that

> the human faculties of perception, judgment, discriminative feeling, mental activity, and even moral preference are exercised only in making a choice. He who does anything because it is the custom makes no choice. . . . If a person possesses any tolerable amount of common sense and experience, his own mode of laying out his existence is the best, not because it is the best in itself, but because it is his own mode.[9]

Their view was that this sort of individualism offers the best justification of the political principle that the state should not promote one controversial view of the good life at the expense of others. If, in our role as citizens we are to be treated apart from status and ascription, our rights independent of whatever view of the human good we may affirm, that is because our deepest self-understandings ought to involve a distance toward such substantial ideals. For Kant and Mill, *citoyen* and *homme* coincide at heart.

There are a great many liberal thinkers who have justified liberalism on the basis of the ideals of autonomy and individuality. The theories of Kant and Mill stand out only as the versions most widely known and most often emulated. But the problem with this sort of defense of liberalism is that these ideals are far from uncontroversial. Although

---

9 Mill, *On Liberty,* pp. 116, 125. For a discussion of Kant's ideal of autonomy in this context, see my *Patterns of Moral Complexity,* pp. 76–84.

they are not themselves substantial views of the good life, but govern the way in which we are to affirm such views, they are nonetheless objects of reasonable disagreement. One of the central strands of the Romantic movement, continuing on to our own day, has been a powerful critique of individualist ideals.[10] Romantic thinkers from Herder to the so-called communitarians of today (such as Alasdair MacIntyre and Michael Sandel) have stressed the values of belonging and custom. Some ways of life, they have argued, have a value we can appreciate only if we do not think of our allegiance to them as *elective*, as a matter of decision, but regard it instead as *constitutive* of what we hold to be valuable. That is, such ways of life (shared customs, ties of place and language, and religious orthodoxies) shape the sense of value on the basis of which we make whatever choices we do. We understand them as being ours not because we elect them, but rather because they make up the traditions to which we belong. Their value is manifest only if in them we move and have our being. This is not a metaphysical thesis about the conditions of personal identity over time. Nor is it the truism that we have, as a matter of fact, inherited these ways of life from tradition. The idea is rather that the *value* of these inherited forms of life depends on our thinking of them as ones we continue to affirm, not because we choose to do so, or even would choose to accept upon reflection, but because of a sense of belonging.

In calling this current of thought "Romantic," I do not mean to lose sight of the fact that Romanticism itself was so complex a phenomenon as to defy almost any generalization. There were many Romantics who did not share these ideas (pursuing instead, for example, a Promethean individualism). Nor would I deny that present-day "communitarians" also pursue other concerns, and that they do not always formulate even this one very clearly.[11] But a new respect for tradition and belong-

---

10 For more on this Romantic critique, see my *Patterns of Moral Complexity*, chapter 5. For contemporary examples, see Alasdair MacIntyre, *After Virtue* (Notre Dame, Ind., University of Notre Dame Press, 1981); and Michael Sandel, *Liberalism and the Limits of Justice* (Cambridge University Press, 1982).

11 For a good philosophical survey of some of the recent communitarian arguments, see Will Kymlicka, *Liberalism, Community, and Culture* (Oxford: Clarendon Press, 1989), pp. 47–73. I do think Kymlicka fails to grasp the value of belonging (that is, the limits of critical reflection) that I evoke here and explain better, I hope, than in those passages of *Patterns of Moral Complexity* he criticizes. Kymlicka declares that "no matter how deeply implicated we find ourselves in a social practice or tradition, we feel capable of questioning whether the practice is a valuable one" (p. 54). Yet might not certain moral commitments be so much a part of our self-understanding as moral beings that to question them would be to strip ourselves of a moral outlook sufficient to guide any sort of moral evaluation?

ing, along with a rejection of the supposedly shallow and dangerous individualism of the eighteenth century, did figure undeniably among the central concerns of the German Romantics, the French counterrevolutionary theorists (de Maistre and Bonald), and English Romantics such as Wordsworth and Scott. And these convictions have become part of the Romantic inheritance that continues to shape Western culture today.

In its most cogent formulation, this Romantic idea is not that belonging as such is a great value, as though the actual self-understandings and purposes we thereby affirm were merely a secondary matter. Some fairly horrible ways of life can become customary. The point is rather that the ideals of autonomy and individuality effectively blind us to the real merits of many ways of life. Indeed, to many Romantics, the unchecked pursuit of these ideals has seemed bound to destroy the very roots of morality. If autonomy and individuality are supreme values, they must regulate the way we affirm not only our substantial views of the good life, but our most fundamental moral commitments as well (as in fact they do in the moral theories of Kant, Mill, and many other liberal thinkers). Yet these basic commitments, such as keeping our promises or avoiding causing pain to others, seem difficult to understand as objects of decision, at least if we view ourselves as moral beings whose allegiance to morality arises out of something more than expediency. We cannot view these commitments as ones we choose, or would choose, were we to stand back and reflect upon them. They are so integral to our very conception of ourselves as moral beings that to imagine them as objects of choice would be to imagine ourselves as without any guiding sense of morality – and so not only ill-equipped to actually choose them, but also lacking the right sort of identification with them. Such commitments seem better understood as felt convictions, the role of which is to shape whatever choices we do make. Their value is properly grasped when they are seen as the inherited basis of choice, not as the objects of choice. This is the conclusion Wordsworth memorably recorded in *The Prelude:*

> Thus I fared,
> Dragging all passions, notions, shapes of faith,
> Like culprits to the bar; suspiciously
> Calling the mind to establish in plain day
> Her titles and her honours; now believing,
> Now disbelieving; endlessly perplex'd

With impulse, motive, right and wrong, the ground
Of moral obligation, what the rule
And what the sanction; till, demanding *proof,*
And seeking it in everything, I lost
All feeling of conviction, and, in fine,
Sick, wearied out with contrarieties,
Yielded up moral questions in despair.

(1805 version; X.889–901)

Though I have said something in defense of these Romantic ideas in the first two chapters of this book,[12] I do not want to insist here on their validity. For the purposes of political liberalism (in contrast to the full scope of moral philosophy), the important point is that they are views at which reasonable people can arrive. For our question here is the sort of moral justification that liberal theory should seek for the principle of political neutrality. Recall that one of the cardinal problems to which liberal thought has sought a solution is the fact that reasonable people tend to disagree about the nature of the good life. In the liberalism of Kant and Mill, the moral values which were used to justify the principle of political neutrality have turned out to be just as controversial as other views about human fulfillment. The Romantic enthusiasm for custom and belonging has become as permanent and influential a part of Western culture as the contrary ideals of autonomy and individuality to which Kant and Mill appealed. This means that the Kantian and Millian conceptions of liberalism are not adequate solutions to the political problem of reasonable disagreement about the good life. They have themselves become simply another part of the problem. The liberal principle of political neutrality toward disputed ideals may seem a minimal moral conception, but appearances can prove misleading. The principle carries whatever burdens of controversy weigh upon the reasons for affirming it.

Kant's and Mill's shortcomings are very important, for much of liberal thought over the past two centuries has followed their lead of associating liberalism with the ideals of autonomy and individuality. The link has seemed so obvious that many members of the Romantic movement, and many contemporary communitarians inspired by Romantic thought, have been moved to reject liberal political ideals. The

12 See also "Histoire et raison dans la philosophie politique," pp. 221–48 in my *Modernité et morale,* as well as my book *The Romantic Legacy* (New York: Columbia University Press, 1996).

unmasking and repudiation of "individualist" and "atomist" views of man have been a recurring pattern of antiliberal polemic, stretching from Herder and Hegel to MacIntyre and Sandel.

This situation calls for a recasting of liberal theory. An appropriate name for this reformulation is "political liberalism." It has been the goal of a number of recent writings by John Rawls, and also of my book *Patterns of Moral Complexity*. It is the attempt to understand how liberalism can be strictly a political doctrine and not a general "philosophy of man,"[13] not a "comprehensive moral doctrine."[14] In this approach, the principle of political neutrality still has a moral justification, but it is one intended to be far less controversial than the Kantian and Millian ideals of autonomy and individuality. I think that a better model than Kant or Mill for this conception of liberalism is many of the theories of natural law (Grotius and Pufendorf) and toleration (Locke and Bayle) developed in the seventeenth century. They were responding to reasonable disagreement about the nature of the true religion and therefore sought political principles that could be affirmed on a nonsectarian basis. The task of liberal theory today is to see how the principle of state neutrality can be justified without having to take sides in the dispute about individualism and tradition. In this perspective, individualism will continue to function as a political doctrine. In other words, it will continue to be an essential liberal commitment that persons as citizens are to be treated equally, in abstraction from the substantial ideals they may share with others. But there will be no appeal to individualism as a general value extending to all areas of social life.[15]

We may think of political liberalism as the effort to occupy a point between two extremes. One extreme lies in basing political neutrality, as Kant and Mill did, on individualist ideals claiming to shape our overall conception of the good life, and not just our role as citizens. The other extreme consists in basing political neutrality on solely strategic considerations. In this view, individuals who have different

---

13 Larmore, *Patterns of Moral Complexity*, p. 129

14 John Rawls, "Justice as Fairness: Political Not Metaphysical," *Philosophy and Public Affairs* 14, no. 3 (Summer 1985), p. 245. The term "political liberalism" was coined by Rawls in "The Idea of an Overlapping Consensus," *Oxford Journal of Legal Studies* 7, no. 1 (1987), p. 24. I discuss Rawls's own "political liberalism" in Section 5 of this chapter.

15 For more on this, see my *Patterns of Moral Complexity*, p. 106.

ideals of the good life, but are roughly equal in power, may strike a
bargain, according to which the political principles to be established
will not favor any of these rival ideals. This approach is basically a
Hobbesian one, since it aims to ground a moral principle (neutrality)
on nonmoral, purely prudential motives.[16] It has two important defects. It seems inherently unstable, since it is hostage to the shifting
distribution of power: individuals will lose their reason to uphold the
agreement if their relative power or bargaining strength increases
significantly. Also, the attempt to explain the special authority of moral
principles in terms of prudence (maximization of individual preference satisfaction) has never yet succeeded, so there seems little reason
to suppose it ever will.

Only by finding a mean between these two extremes can liberalism
work as a minimal moral conception. We must look to a core morality
that is, as much as possible, common ground. It may be too hopeful to
expect that this moral basis will escape every element of controversy.
But it must certainly be neutral enough to accommodate people who
value belonging and custom, for Romantic ideals have become an
enduring part of our culture. At the same time, of course, it must be
powerful enough to justify the principle of political neutrality. Although the moral basis of liberalism must be minimal, it cannot be
trivial. Nor is the form of political association it secures of small importance. No doubt we have seen enough in this century to abhor the
darker political visions that the rejection of liberal ideals has so often
spawned. But this conviction, by itself, will not answer the question
concerning the foundations of liberalism. It will not show that liberal
thought can keep its promise of offering a political conception acceptable to people having very different views about the human good, and
in particular about the merits of individualism and community. With-

16 This approach is what Rawls calls a "modus vivendi" ("The Idea of an Overlapping
Consensus," section 3). I should observe that it is not what I called a modus vivendi
in *Patterns of Moral Complexity*, which instead resembles the position Rawls himself
favors; this is a merely terminological difference. A recent example of the Hobbesian
approach is David Gauthier, *Morals by Agreement* (Oxford University Press, 1986).
The crux of his argument, to which many critics have pointed, is whether he
has indeed shown that prudence alone can move agents to become "constrained
maximizers" (pp. 157–89), complying with rules of cooperation instead of taking advantage of those who comply with them. See Chapter 2, footnote 9, this
volume.

out an answer to this question, liberalism lacks the strength that would come from really being what it purports to be.[17]

3. Rational Dialogue and Equal Respect

The justification of liberal neutrality that best meets these conditions is one that relies on the two norms of rational dialogue and equal respect. In calling the justification the best, I do not mean to deny that there are other rationales that, within particular moral perspectives, are equally sound. To those who prize the values of autonomy and individuality, for example, Kant and Mill may well have given cogent reasons for adopting the liberal principle. The special virtue of the justification I propose is that it is a minimal one. It appeals to elements of a core morality. It can be accepted even by those who are convinced that autonomy and individuality have serious drawbacks and that much of what makes life worth living is less a matter of choice than of tradition. This does not mean, I should add, that the norms of rational dialogue and equal respect are implicitly contained in the bare notion of reasonableness to which I alluded earlier. The point is not to show that reasonable people, no matter what else they believe, must affirm them. Liberalism is a historically contingent form of political life resting on moral assumptions that we cannot suppose will recommend themselves to all humanity by the idea of reason alone. What remains true, however, is that these two norms have been central elements in Western thought and generally shared by Romantic critics of autonomy and individuality.

The broader appeal of this justification of political neutrality makes it a more fitting response to the basic political problems which liberalism has sought to solve. We may think of it as providing the terms in which a liberal state ought to *announce publicly* the basis of its legitimacy. In an earlier book, *Patterns of Moral Complexity*, I showed how this justification works. Here I go through it again, amplifying the discussion of specific points and bringing out important assumptions I did not see clearly before.

First, the *norm of rational dialogue*. In discussing how to solve some

---

17 I should note that in this chapter I discuss the nature of liberalism without making much mention of democracy. Liberalism and democracy are separate values whose relation consists largely in democratic self-rule being the best means for protecting the principles of a liberal political order. For more on this, see Chapters 8 and 10.

problem (for example, what principles of political association they should adopt), people should respond to points of disagreement by retreating to neutral ground, to the beliefs they still share, in order either to (a) resolve the disagreement and vindicate one of the disputed positions by means of arguments that proceed from this common ground, or (b) bypass the disagreement and seek a solution of the problem on the basis simply of this common ground. I think the validity of this norm should be obvious, but let me say here a bit in its defense. The first part of the norm turns on the distinction between proof and justification. Whereas a proof consists simply in the logical relations among a set of propositions, a justification is a proof directed at those who disagree with us to show them that they should join us in believing what we do. It can fulfill this pragmatic role only by appealing to what they already believe, thus to what is common ground between us.[18] The second part of this norm becomes relevant once there seems little chance that the points of disagreement will prove resolvable by argument. If the people still wish to solve the given problem, and if they are committed to solving it through rational discussion, then they have no choice but to find the solution on the basis of the beliefs they share.

This norm governs one crucial function of the *public realm* in a liberal political culture. That role is to be the forum in which we try to convince others of the worth of our views so that they can become part of the shared allegiances the state should promote. Sometimes common ground can thus expand, perhaps contrary to first expectations. It is because its guiding aim is to reach a decision about political principles that this sort of public discussion, following the norm of rational dialogue, must proceed from common ground and heed the constraint that, where reasonable disagreement persists, the decision must remain neutral. But decision need not be the only goal of public discussion about political principles. The public realm also serves the function of disclosure, of letting people see where they all stand. People must then be free to explain to one another in full their comprehensive visions of the good life, and not just those parts that can be laid out on the basis of common ground. In this capacity, public discussion will properly turn out to be more unbridled and rife with controversy. Today, liberalism is sometimes criticized for being blind

18 Cf. John Rawls, *A Theory of Justice* (Cambridge, Mass.: Harvard University Press, 1971), pp. 580–1.

or hostile to this more expansive conception of the public sphere.[19] But in reality liberal neutrality, and the argument for it which I propose, need not deny a place to this function of public discussion. A liberal polity benefits greatly from people coming to know the full extent of their reasonable disagreements. The recognition of our differences is necessary for exercising the equal respect we owe one another as beings capable of affirming a vision of the good life. But we must also be careful not to confuse these two separate functions of the public realm. Citizens of a liberal polity must be able to distinguish between the unconstrained activity of mutual disclosure and the self-limitation, arising from the norm of rational dialogue, that is required for making decisions about the principles that will govern political life.

The norm of rational dialogue does not suffice by itself, however, to yield the liberal principle of neutrality.[20] It tells us what to do, *if* we want to talk together with an eye to deciding what political principles to establish. It does not tell us that we ought to continue this discussion once we discover points of disagreement about what principles to set up. In other words, it does not rule out resorting to force, instead of discussion, to achieve a political settlement.

What demands that we go on talking, what in other words requires political principles to be the object of reasonable agreement, is the additional norm of *equal respect* for persons. The norm I have in mind comes close to the Kantian rule that we should never treat other persons solely as means, as mere instruments of our will; on the contrary, people should always be treated also as ends, as persons in their own right.

But this is rather nebulously expressed. To make it more specific, I shall first observe that moral principles fall naturally into two groups. There are those with which we believe people can be legitimately forced to comply, and there are others that we do not think are legitimate items of enforcement, whatever disapproval or even outrage we may feel at people who break them. The first group alone has the

---

19 This criticism is often made by thinkers influenced by the work of Jürgen Habermas. See, e.g., Seyla Benhabib, "Models of Public Space: Hannah Arendt, the Liberal Tradition, and Jürgen Habermas," pp. 73–98 in C. Calhoun (ed.), *Habermas and the Public Sphere* (Cambridge, Mass.: MIT Press, 1992); Kenneth Baynes, *The Normative Grounds of Social Criticism* (Albany, N.Y.: SUNY Press, 1992), pp. 74–6; Rainer Forst, *Kontexte der Gerechtigkeit* (Frankfurt: Suhrkamp, 1994), pp. 158, 200.

20 See my "Liberal Neutrality: A Reply to Fishkin," *Political Theory* (November 1989), pp. 580–1.

status of *political* principles. For an association is political precisely insofar as it relies upon the legitimate use of force to secure compliance with its rules. This is why the basic question of political philosophy is to determine what moral principles ought to be backed up by coercion.

Now forcing people to comply with principles of conduct is to treat them as means: their compliance is seen as conducive to public order, or perhaps to their own reformation. In itself the use or threat of force cannot be wrong, for otherwise political association would be impossible. What is prohibited by the norm of equal respect is resting compliance only on force.[21] For the distinctive feature of persons is that they are beings capable of thinking and acting on the basis of reasons. If we try to bring about conformity to a political principle simply by threat, we will be treating people solely as means, as objects of coercion. We will not also be treating them as ends, engaging directly their distinctive capacity as persons. True, they will not be able to be moved by threats except by exercising this capacity, by finding good reasons to fear them. But their distinctive capacity as persons will be something that we simply intend to make use of to achieve the goals of compliance. It will not be something we engage in the same way that we engage our own distinctive capacity as persons. We will not be making the acceptability of the principle depend on their reason just as we believe it draws on our own. To respect another person as an end is to insist that coercive or political principles be as justifiable to that person as they are to us. Equal respect involves treating in this way all persons to which such principles are to apply.

It is the fundamental role played by this ideal of equal respect that makes liberal principles characteristically embody only some of all the moral commitments we have, and abstract from others we value profoundly. In other words, equal respect does not simply figure in the moral conception that is liberalism; it also explains why this moral conception cannot but be a minimal one. For in modern times we have come to appreciate how naturally conceptions of the human good become controversial among reasonable people. As I pointed out in earlier chapters, this modern experience has been the impetus for

---

21 Note that Kant did not declare that treating others as means is morally wrong. What he condemned was treating them solely as means and not also as ends. See *Grundlegung zur Metaphysik der Sitten*, Akademie-Ausgabe (Berlin: Preussische Akademie der Wissenschaften, 1900–), vol. 4, p. 429.

finding a core morality on which we can agree despite the views of the good life that divide us. The norm of equal respect makes this project imperative, when we ask what should be the principles of our political life, to be enforced by coercion where the need arises. Not all the elements of a core morality are essential to political association, of course, or can be made the object of enforcement. But it is a commitment to equal respect that requires our political principles to belong among them.

I have also observed, however, that one of the central items of reasonable disagreement has become the respective value of individuality and belonging. Kant produced the great moral philosophy of individual autonomy, of course. But he also articulated the idea of equal respect in so authoritative a form (the treatment of others never merely as means, but always also as ends) that I, no less than many others, have been unable not to follow his lead. The question arises whether the norm of equal respect I have invoked is really so independent of Kant's individualist philosophy as I have said it must be for liberalism to keep its promise today.

It is worth noting first of all that I have not taken over Kant's attempt to understand the whole of morality in terms of treating others always as ends in themselves. I have connected the norm of equal respect solely to the acceptability of coercive principles, not to the acceptability of moral principles in general. This is because coercion, or the use of force, seems to me the only clear-cut case of treating a person as a means. If we censure someone for breaking a moral rule but do not seek his or her compliance by force, we are not, in any obvious sense, treating that person as a means. Thus, I do not think that moral rules of this sort can be valid only if justifiable to all people to whom they apply.[22] (Certain kinds of deception may also count as treating persons as means; but refusing to base compliance solely on deception as well as on force leaves room for there being some moral norms we apply even to those to whom they are not justifiable.)

But where the norm of equal respect does play a role in my account of liberalism, can it really be detached from Kant's ideal of autonomy,

---

22 This account of coercive principles is quite similar to what T. M. Scanlon calls "contractualism" in "Contractualism and Utilitarianism," pp. 103–28 in Amartya Sen and Bernard Williams (eds.), *Utilitarianism and Beyond* (Cambridge University Press, 1982), except that, apparently unlike Scanlon, I do not think it should be extended to the whole of morality. See also Thomas Nagel, *Equality and Partiality* (Oxford University Press, 1991), p. 159.

which it is our aim to leave aside? I believe it can. Observe that the idea of a person, to which my formulation of the norm of equal respect appeals, involves simply the capacity of thinking and acting on the basis of reasons. Nothing is said about the source of a person's reasons. It is left open whether persons themselves decide what shall count as valid reasons or whether they see their reasons as stemming from a tradition to which they belong. The norm of equal respect seems neutral with regard to the dispute between individualism and tradition. Some further remarks should make this clear.

Consider the case in which political decisions required by equal respect conflict with the furtherance of our ideal of the good life. For political liberalism, the norm of equal respect must then take precedence. But this does not mean that our allegiance to the ideal ceases to exist, or ceases to be constitutive, or that we cannot continue to pursue it within the bounds set by the norm of equal respect. The point should become clear if we consider the nature of value conflict. Values may conflict in two quite different ways. One is that the values themselves may contradict one another, such as the way the gluttonous life conflicts with health. When we find our values in this sort of conflict, we ought to reject one of them, for our commitments are logically inconsistent. The norm of equal respect does conflict in this way with certain conceptions of life (virulent forms of racism, for instance). But our concern here lies with the different kind of conflict that arises when two values, though mutually consistent themselves, recommend in given circumstances courses of action that cannot both be carried out. The proper way to resolve this sort of conflict is not to withdraw our commitment to one of the values, but instead to seek some means of weighing them against one another, to find which of the rival courses of action is to be preferred.

To return to the case at hand, recall that constitutive ideals of the good life belong to our very sense of what is valuable, to the basis of our choices. Where the pursuit of such ideals conflicts with the norm of equal respect it must give way. But this does not change the integral attachment we have to these ideals if the norm of equal respect, too, forms a constitutive commitment. I believe, indeed, that this is the shape our commitment to equal respect assumes, and I have more to say about this at the end of the chapter.

The norms of rational dialogue and equal respect do, of course, make a certain individualism overriding within the political realm. That is, the rights and duties of citizens must be specifiable in abstrac-

tion from any controversial ideals they may share with others. But the
two norms do not imply that a broader individualism concerning the
very sources of value must pervade the whole of social life. Private
associations cannot violate the rights of citizens. Yet they can continue
to conduct their internal, extrapolitical affairs according to "illiberal"
principles – principles that deny their members equal rights and require them to defer to traditionally constituted authority. The Catholic
church, for example, is a legal institution in our society even though it
does not handle its ecclesiastical affairs on the basis of toleration. It
may not burn heretics, for that is contrary to their rights as citizens,
but it may still excommunicate them. So, too, the principle of equal
respect requires that people as citizens not be kept a part of any private
association against their will. That is, they may leave such organizations
without any compromise of their legal and political standing. But this
right to exit does not imply endorsement of the general idea that
people should regard even their most basic commitments as open to
revision. There are certain vows, perhaps, of marriage or of priesthood,
from which individuals cannot release themselves before God. In a
liberal state, however, this eventuality would not deny them the right,
in their capacity as citizens, to call off these commitments and their
membership in the institutions that define them (be it at the peril of
their souls).[23] Such is political liberalism's distinction between *homme*
and *citoyen,* which has already become, indeed, a part of our way of life.

It is also true that by requiring citizens to rank the norms of rational
dialogue and equal respect above their other commitments, political
liberalism must encourage them to reflect critically upon these commitments from the impartial standpoint involved in these two norms.
But this does not mean that constitutive commitments to some substantial ideal of the good life, whose value cannot be manifest to an
impartial, distanced point of view, must be undermined. Standing back
critically from our ideal of the good life to see whether it conflicts with
our overriding commitment to the norm of equal respect is quite a
different matter from standing back critically from it to see whether it
is valuable at all (which is what Kant and Mill demanded). In the first
case, we are determining whether one value we hold runs contrary (in
the circumstances) to another value we rank higher. In the second, we

---

23 This is my reply to Kymlicka's criticism (*Liberalism, Community, and Culture,* p. 60)
    that the liberal right to exit assumes the general moral principle that all commit-
    ments must be considered revisable.

are determining whether we ought to affirm the first value at all. There seems no reason to think, therefore, that liberal neutrality, if understood in the way I have proposed, must harbor any special affinity for individualist views of the good life.

None of the preceding is meant to imply that the liberal ideal makes no demands of our overall moral outlook. On the contrary, it requires, as I have said, that we rank the norms of rational dialogue and equal respect above our other values. It also relies on our being able to abandon "the cult of wholeness" and to embrace a certain differentiation between our role as citizens, free of status and ascription, and our other roles where we may be engaged with others in the pursuit of substantial ideals of the good life. Since these commitments have scarcely been affirmed in all societies but instead are largely confined to modern Western ones, there is some point to talking of a "liberal conception of the person." What is crucial to observe is that this conception carries no commitment to a general individualism. Just such a commitment, however, is what "the liberal conception of the person" has usually been thought to involve, both by its partisans and by its adversaries. This is why liberalism has come to seem a necessary enemy of tradition and constitutive ideals. It is to oppose such views that I have claimed that liberalism need not be a "philosophy of man."

4. Liberal Community

At the heart of the minimal moral conception that is political liberalism lie, therefore, the two norms of rational dialogue and equal respect. I trust it is clear how, abstractly speaking, these two norms work together to yield the liberal ideal of political neutrality. If the principles of political association are to be rooted in a commitment to equal respect, they must be justifiable to everyone whom they are to bind. Where in trying to make the fundamentals of our political life transparent to all we meet with reasonable disagreement, we thus should fall back on common ground and determine what principles can be set up on that basis. This is why acceptable political principles must conform to the cardinal principle of neutrality toward controversial views about the good life.

Clearly, a great deal more needs to be said to get a fuller picture of what this view of liberalism amounts to and what it requires of our political life. I will focus here only on two key assumptions that underlie this argument and need to be made explicit. The first is that, strictly speaking, the argument applies only to the ideal case in which everyone in the society already accepts the norms of rational dialogue and equal respect, and accords them supreme importance. Nothing has been said so far about how we ought to converse with those who, in determining the principles of political association, refuse rational dialogue or about how we ought to respect those who refuse to show us respect. This point is significant. With those who reject the norm of equal respect or rank their view of the good life above it, we will usually be unable to converge on any political (coercive) principles that are as justifiable to them as to ourselves. Though we must believe such people could come to value that ideal through appropriate training, we cannot expect that reason alone can justify so basic an element of our core morality (see Chapters 1 and 2). In this regard, therefore, there is a limit to the "rational transparency" liberalism can hope for in its political principles. The public justification a liberal polity offers for its principles must presume that citizens share a form of life that embodies a commitment to equal respect. How then should we understand the way these principles are addressed to those who do not share that commitment? The proper answer would seem to be that they should be justifiable to these people as well, though with the justification premised on the (counterfactual) supposition that they do prize most highly the norms of rational dialogue and equal respect.

The argument for liberal neutrality turns on another crucial assumption as well. It applies only to people who are indeed interested in devising principles of political association. It assumes that they share enough to think of themselves as engaged in this common enterprise. In particular, it supposes that they regard these bonds as setting them off from other people, since their aim is presumably to live with one another, but not with everyone else, in political association. Or at least this last supposition is necessary if liberalism is not to become a cosmopolitan doctrine of world government, but can instead be at home in a world where political life takes the form of a system of nation-states. For my part, I do not regard this accommodation as a mere surrender to historical reality. On the contrary, it expresses a recognition of the conceivable roots of political allegiance today.

In short, therefore, the people to whom this argument for liberal neutrality applies must already think of themselves as "a people" or "a nation." They must have a common life *before* they can think of organizing their political life according to liberal principles. This is not only true of the version of liberalism I am proposing. It must hold for all liberal theories that undertake, as indeed they must, to find principles that individuals otherwise divided by disagreement can agree to accept; without a common life, the disagreements would give ample grounds for the individuals to disband or to switch their allegiance elsewhere.

With the notable exception of Ernest Renan, whose "Qu'est-ce qu'une nation?" (1882) remains in many respects the best treatment of the question, liberal thinkers have generally not said enough about this assumption. Locke did recognize that an "*original Compact,* whereby [a man] with others incorporates into *one society,*" must precede the contract by which political rights and obligations, and the structures of government, are determined (*Second Treatise of Government,* VIII.97 and XIX.211). But he left this point undeveloped. I do not think, however, that it undermines the coherence of the liberal outlook. Present-day communitarians, of course, have called attention to the distinctive common life necessary for political association and have argued that it must embody substantive visions of the good and feelings of belonging that go beyond the formal principle of equal respect. There is a grain of truth behind their view, but they have missed it. The common life necessary for the liberal project to make sense need not involve the sort of controversial ideals toward which a modern liberal state must aim to be neutral.

The important mistake of these communitarians is to suppose that the common life constituting a people, and their commitment to a separate political existence, must rest on shared values besides a common devotion to liberal principles. There exist other mechanisms of social unity – none is probably sufficient by itself, or even necessary, but when several of them work together they can be of considerable moment. Geography and a common language, for example, can serve to hold a people together and set them off from others. But most important of all is a common historical experience, including the memory of past conflicts, even civil war, that were sparked by opposing ideals of the good life but are seen now as having given way to a shared practice of equal respect.

This is what Ernest Renan had in mind when he noted (famously though paradoxically) that "every French citizen must have forgotten the St. Bartholomew's Day massacre."[24] He did not really mean that French citizens must have forgotten the Catholic massacre of Protes-

24 Ernest Renan, *Qu'est-ce qu'une nation? et autres essais politiques,* J. Roman (ed.) (Paris: Presses Pocket, 1992), p. 42.

tants in 1572 (many had not, and anyway Renan was addressing this statement to his French readers). His aim was to underscore a common memory rather than a shared amnesia. French citizens, Renan believed, are joined together by remembering the theological-political passion, the urge to anoint political life with religious confession, that they have now outgrown. Not in this case alone has a common sense of citizenship been forged by the memory of what has been left behind. In contemporary Western societies there exist powerful forces that imperil the vitality of historical memory. One thinks of the pervasive news and entertainment media with their fixation on ephemeral amusement. Against this threat, liberal polities must keep alive a sense of the past experience from which they derive.

Although the necessary assumption of an existing common life does not render liberalism incoherent, it does show that the liberal conception of politics is by nature a *latecomer*. It is addressed to a people whose common life has not proven immune to disagreement about matters of deep significance. As a rule, it makes its appearance only in a society that has left behind a homogeneous culture (or more accurately, perhaps, the pretense that it possesses one) and suffered through the violence of political attempts to reimpose it. The common life on which a liberal order depends must involve, therefore, an allegiance to the past that is more reflective than just a sense of continuity. It must be the life of a people united by what they have learned together from the things that once came to divide them.

5. The Goals of Political Liberalism

Liberalism understood in this way seems to satisfy the need for a minimal moral conception. It depends on moral commitments, but on ones that are neutral with respect to the general ideals of individualism and tradition. In this form, liberalism does not take sides in one of the most important moral and cultural controversies of the past two centuries. It becomes again what it was in early modern times with regard to religious controversy: an appropriate response to the problem of reasonable disagreement about the good life. Because this version of liberalism does not assume the validity of individualist views of the good life, I have called it "political liberalism." The idea is that, in this view, the individualist treatment of persons as separate from the substantial ideals they may share with others is a strictly political norm, applicable to persons in their role as citizens. It does not express a broader individualism about the sources of value, contrary to what both defenders and opponents of liberalism have often believed.

The term "political liberalism" is likely, nonetheless, to give rise to two misunderstandings I want to caution against. First, no contrast is intended between "political" and "moral." Political liberalism is a moral conception based on the norm of equal respect, even if its ambition is to be a minimal one. Second, in political liberalism, at least as I conceive of it, the norms of rational dialogue and equal respect, as well as the principle of neutrality they justify, are understood to be correct and valid norms and not merely norms that people in a liberal order believe to be correct and valid. No contrast is intended between "political" and "philosophical." It is true that political liberalism aims to occupy a common ground between the champions of individualism and the defenders of tradition. But what makes this common ground an appropriate basis for principles of political association is not the mere fact that it is common ground, an object of agreement. It is, rather, that this common ground includes the norms of rational dialogue and equal respect. Political liberalism is the view that these are norms we ought to affirm, and that if we do we ought to embrace the principle of political neutrality as well.

In other words, the guiding aim of political liberalism is not to devise political principles by appeal simply to whatever might turn out to be common ground among divergent views. It is instead to base such principles precisely on the moral norms that impel us to seek common ground as far as possible. These norms may themselves fail to belong to the common denominator of existing opinion. It would therefore be wrong to object to political liberalism that there are many in our society who show no commitment to these norms. That would be unfortunate if true. But it is not a reason to reject political liberalism.

Of course, the essential claim of political liberalism is that it provides a basis for justifying political neutrality that both parties to the dispute between individualism and tradition can affirm. So it will fail as a solution to this crucial problem of reasonable disagreement if the norms of rational dialogue and equal respect are alien to our moral thinking. But this is palpably false. These norms have been a part of Western moral thought for centuries, even if they have not enjoyed universal acceptance in the West. Moreover, they have figured among the moral commitments of many of the thinkers who have challenged the cogency of individualist conceptions of the good life. This is why political liberalism is so important: it shows the critics of modern individualism that they still have good reasons – and moral reasons, not just prudential ones – to affirm the value of a liberal political order. It shows that Romantics can also be liberals.

I wish to insist on the fact that political liberalism is to be understood as a correct moral conception and not just as an object of consensus, because many people have taken the contrary view of the "political liberalism" that John Rawls has defended in recent writings. Consider the following rather typical statement of Rawls's present position:

> The aim of justice as fairness as a political conception is practical, and not metaphysical or epistemological. That is, it presents itself not as a conception of justice that is true, but one that can serve as a basis of informed and willing political agreement between citizens viewed as free and equal persons.[25]

To many, this disclaimer of truth has seemed a surrender of Rawls's earlier claim (in *A Theory of Justice*) that his theory of justice as fairness (the liberty and difference principles, etc.) is the correct theory of justice. It has seemed a retreat to the weaker but also inadequate and even false view that his theory is simply one on which people in modern Western societies will agree.[26]

If this is an accurate interpretation of Rawls's present views, then I would wish to dissociate my version of political liberalism from his. But as a matter of fact, I do not believe that this construal grasps the point he is intending to make. I am convinced that the norm of equal respect lies at the basis of Rawls's own theory of justice, though I will not go through my reasons here.[27] I also find myself in agreement with a great

---

25 Rawls, "Justice as Fairness: Political Not Metaphysical," p. 230; also idem, *Political Liberalism*, p. 94.

26 William A. Galston, "Pluralism and Social Unity," *Ethics* 99, no. 4 (July 1989), pp. 723–5, and Jean Hampton, "Should Political Philosophy Be Done Without Metaphysics?" ibid., pp. 807–13; also John Gray, "Contractarian Method, Private Property, and the Market Economy," pp. 37–8 in John M. Chapman and J. Roland Pennock (eds.), *Nomos 31: Markets and Justice* (New York University Press, 1989); Joseph Raz, "Facing Diversity: The Case of Epistemic Abstinence," *Philosophy and Public Affairs*, 19, no. 1 (Winter 1990), pp. 3–31.

27 See Ronald Dworkin, *Taking Rights Seriously* (Cambridge, Mass.: Harvard University Press, 1978), pp. 150–83, and also Rawls's reply in "Justice as Fairness: Political Not Metaphysical," pp. 236–7 (note 19).

deal of what he has written about political liberalism. It may thus be useful to an understanding of my own view (and of his) if I point out where I think this interpretation of Rawls goes wrong.

When Rawls declines to call his theory of justice "true," his intention is not to withdraw the claim that it is correct, that it is one we ought rationally to accept whether or not we do in fact believe it. On the contrary, his point is that its rational acceptability is independent of the claim that it is true of "*an independent metaphysical and moral order,*" as he writes in the very paragraph containing the sentences quoted here. His aim is to have political liberalism suspend judgment in a continuing controversy about what the correctness of a moral conception consists in. One side in this controversy, which Rawls calls "rational intuitionism" and attributes to philosophers such as Samuel Clarke, G. E. Moore, and W. D. Ross, is that moral beliefs are "true or false in virtue of a moral order of values that is prior to and independent of our conceptions of person and society, and of the public social role of moral doctrines."[28] The other side he calls "constructivism" and associates with Kant: it holds that the correctness of a moral belief consists in its being derived by a procedure of construction (e.g., Kant's universalizability test) from a conception of moral personality; there is no domain of moral facts independent of this conception of moral personality of which moral beliefs can be true or false. Rawls himself seems to have considerable sympathy for Kant's moral constructivism. But it is a commitment, like the contrary commitment to rational intuitionism, from which he wants his political theory to abstain.

The notion of truth that he withholds from his theory of justice is thus a specific one, implying the existence of an independent order of moral facts. It is an explanation (as is moral constructivism) of what we mean by calling a moral belief correct or rationally acceptable. Rawls's claim is that we do not have to accept either of these explanations to recognize that some moral beliefs are supported by good reasons and others are not. (Of course, we may deploy a weaker notion of truth, one that is equivalent to rational acceptability, and then assert that political liberalism is true.)

One possible source of confusion is that Rawls also uses the term

28 John Rawls, "Themes in Kant's Moral Philosophy," p. 95 in Eckart Förster (ed.), *Kant's Transcendental Deductions* (Stanford, Calif.: Stanford University Press, 1989); also idem, *Political Liberalism*, pp. 91–2.

"constructivism" for the way in which political liberalism employs this neutral notion of rational acceptability. Political liberalism is "constructivist" in that valid political principles are defined as those on which we would agree if we reasoned according to certain constraints (expressed in the terms of Rawls's "original position"). In his recent book *Political Liberalism* (1993) he calls this "political constructivism," distinguishing it from the general account of moral objectivity that is "moral constructivism."[29] It is clear why he wants to separate these two views. Kant, he argues, adopted this conception of moral validity only because of the ideal of autonomy: to think that moral beliefs are true or false, depending on an independent moral order, would be to put our moral worth out of our control.[30] And the aim of political liberalism, Rawls maintains, is to avoid assuming the validity of the ideal of autonomy.[31] For my part, I do not think that moral constructivism, in contrast to intuitionism, is a viable view (see Chapter 5, this volume). But I do think that when we consider Rawls's reluctance about "truth" in its proper context as a sign of his wish to keep liberalism free of a deep and long-standing controversy about the nature of moral validity, we will see that it involves no surrender of the claim that liberalism is a correct moral conception. The idea that objectivity in ethics need involve only rational agreement, and not also truth concerning an independent moral order, goes back in fact to Rawls's earliest writings.[32]

It is in these terms that we should understand his notion of an "overlapping consensus" as the basis on which liberal constitutional

---

29 Rawls, *Political Liberalism,* pp. 125–9.
30 Rawls, "Themes in Kant's Moral Philosophy," pp. 93, 97. Rawls also points out (p. 93) that Kant connected his constructivism with his assertion of the priority of the right over the good – i.e., with the claim that moral principles are categorically binding on the agent whatever his or her conception of the good. However, the categorical character of moral duties can favor constructivism only if it is first thought to imply the ideal of autonomy. And this implication seems to me unfounded (for details, see Chapter 1). The priority of the right over the good is neutral between constructivism and intuitionism.
31 Rawls, *Political Liberalism,* p. 98.
32 John Rawls, "Outline of a Decision Procedure for Ethics," *Philosophical Review* 60 (April 1951), pp. 177–97. Consider also his claim in the *Dewey Lectures* (*Journal of Philosophy* 77, no. 9 [September 1980], pp. 554, 569) that moral (i.e., political) principles, as "constructions," are to count as reasonable, not true. This view of ethical objectivity is developed further in his "Political Constructivism and Public Justification."

principles should be justified. Rawls does intend this overlapping consensus to encompass as broad a domain of agreement as possible. That is why it is to exclude Kantian and Millian ideals of autonomy and individuality, which remain controversial. But breadth of agreement is not the only desideratum. The agreement must also be, as Rawls writes, "free and willing"; it must be an agreement between "citizens viewed as free and equal persons."[33] Such phrases indicate that something like what I have described as the norm of equal respect serves to define the sort of consensus that, for him, counts as a legitimate basis of political principles. This norm is therefore assumed to be correct and not merely agreed on. It belongs to the constraints according to which acceptable political principles are "constructed" in "public justification," to use Rawls's language. I do think it fair to say that Rawls should be more explicit about the role that the norm of equal respect plays in his political theory.[34] But he seems clearly not to believe, contrary to some of his recent critics, that the commitments on which his political liberalism rests are simply those that people in modern Western societies share as a matter of fact. What he holds is that these commitments would be the object of consensus to the extent that people view themselves, as they should, as free and equal citizens.

Rawls often writes that the basis of his political liberalism is drawn from notions implicit in our political culture.[35] That does not mean that it is important only that these notions are widely affirmed, and not that they express valid principles. The point is rather that valid principles, which are also alien to a culture, can be of no help in solving its problem of finding terms of political association amid reasonable

---

33 Rawls, "The Idea of an Overlapping Consensus," pp. 5, 7; also *Political Liberalism*, pp. 39–40, and "Justice as Fairness: Political Not Metaphysical," p. 230; and see especially the sentence on pp. 229–30: "Justification is addressed to others who disagree with us, and therefore it must always proceed from some consensus, that is, from premises that we and others publicly recognize as true; or better, publicly recognize as acceptable to us for the purpose of establishing a working agreement on the fundamental questions of political justice. It goes without saying that this agreement must be informed and uncoerced, and reached by citizens in ways consistent with their being viewed as free and equal citizens." Since this point about justification already occurs in *A Theory of Justice*, pp. 580–1, it seems wrong to see it (as Galston does in "Pluralism and Social Unity," p. 723) as signaling a change in Rawls's conception of the status of his theory.

34 Although see Rawls, *A Theory of Justice*, pp. 337–8, 511, 585–6, and his *Dewey Lectures*, p. 521.

35 For example, Rawls, "Justice as Fairness: Political Not Metaphysical," p. 225.

disagreement about the good life.[36] If we understand the basis of political liberalism as consisting in the norms of equal respect and rational dialogue, as I have proposed, then this condition of relevance will have been met. These norms have been a central element in Western thought. There can be no doubt that many of us (if not all) consider them to be valid principles for living together.

Some may ask, particularly about the norm of equal respect, what our reasons can be for holding it to be correct. How can we justify it to people (in our own culture or elsewhere) who do not already accept it? This is a hard question, and I have no ready answer to it. But I do want to point out that this difficulty is of no immediate consequence to the viability of political liberalism, at least as I understand it. For first of all, we are not required, I believe (see Chapter 2), to justify to ourselves an existing belief except where we have discovered a reason for thinking that by our own lights it may be false. And as for justifying to others the cardinal commitments of liberalism, I have observed that reason alone cannot carry this burden; without some shared moral outlook involving norms of precisely the fundamental character that equal respect possesses, political argument proves impossible. Moreover, I am inclined to regard the difficulty of finding any deeper principles to justify the ideal of equal respect as less a philosophical defect than a sign that this ideal has come to belong to our very sense of what we are as moral beings. It makes up, as I also suggested in Chapter 2, the form of life from which we draw our moral bearings. If we cannot see how to justify it, that is because it defines the framework of what we understand moral argument to be.

But in addition to these general points (which some may no doubt dispute), it is important to remember that political liberalism is intended chiefly as a response to a problem within our own culture, the Romantic critique of modern individualism. Like every doctrine, it draws its point from its context. Its goal is to refute the claim (which is one of the mainstays of antiliberal polemic) that liberalism makes sense only as the affirmation of individualist views about the good life. It tries to show that liberalism carries no such broad commitment,

---

36 I believe that Rawls has in mind another point as well: in moral argument, as in other domains, we do not reason from scratch, but rather build on beliefs that we already have and that we have (so far) no positive reason to doubt. I share this view of moral epistemology (see Chapter 2, this volume). But since many still hold older, more foundationalist views, it is probably best to minimize its role within political liberalism.

that the moral principles on which it relies are compatible with the affirmation of the value of tradition and belonging. Since these principles have been a major part of Western culture, since indeed most of the Romantic critics of modern individualism have also shared these principles, political liberalism needs to show no more than that.

I hardly wish to deny that modern society harbors many forces that work against the Romantic values of belonging and tradition. I would agree, moreover, that one of these forces has been a conception of liberalism as a general way of life, an overall exaltation of the values of autonomy and individuality. But this "liberal view of man" is not the only form that liberalism can take. Political liberalism seeks to detach the principle of political neutrality from the fate of that view. In fact, it offers those opposed to full-scale individualism the best means for blocking a chief way that ideology has come to play such a large role in our culture, namely, by riding piggyback on the liberal principle of political neutrality.

The danger in making liberalism yet another controversial and partisan vision of the good life is that it will cease to be a plausible solution to one of the most pressing moral and political problems in modern times. It will become just another part of the problem. A distinctive feature of modern thought is the insight that the nature of the good life is not likely to be the object of reasonable agreement. On matters concerning the meaning of life, discussion among reasonable people tends naturally not toward consensus, as Aristotle thought, but rather toward controversy. The more we talk about such things, the more we disagree – even with ourselves, as Montaigne observed.[37] Liberalism has been the hope that, despite this tendency toward disagreement about matters of ultimate significance, we can find some way of living together that avoids the rule of force. It has been the conviction that we can agree on a core morality while continuing to disagree about what makes life worth living. In the end, this conviction may turn out to be baseless. Liberalism may necessarily be just one more partisan ideal. But if that is so, then unless the modern experience is to dissolve in the light of the one irresistible, all-encompassing Good, our political future will indeed be one "where ignorant armies clash by night."

37 Michel de Montaigne, "De l'art de conférer," *Essais* III.8, *Oeuvres complètes* (Paris: Gallimard, 1962), pp. 901–2, as well as idem, "De l'expérience," *Essais* III.13, ibid., pp. 1043–4.

7

PLURALISM AND REASONABLE DISAGREEMENT

1. Political Liberalism

Liberalism is a distinctively modern political conception. Only in modern times do we find, as the object of both systematic reflection and widespread allegiance and institutionalization, the idea that the fundamental principles of political association, being coercive, should be justifiable to all whom they are to bind. And so only here do we find the idea that these principles should rest, so far as possible, on a core, minimal morality that reasonable people can share, given their expectably divergent religious convictions and conceptions of the meaning of life. No longer does it seem evident – as it did, let us say, before the seventeenth century – that the aim of political association must be to bring man into harmony with God's purposes or to serve some comprehensive vision of the good life.[1] The causes of this transformation are various, and not all of them lie at the level of moral principle. But a change in moral consciousness has certainly been one of the factors involved. As Hegel observed,[2] modern culture is inherently a *reflective* one: notions of principle are essential to our self-understanding and thus to the stability of the social forms in which we

---

1 For this characterization of liberalism, see Chapter 6, this volume.
2 G. W. F. Hegel, *Vorlesungen über die Asthetik,* "Einleitung," p. 24–5 in *Werke,* vol. 13 (Frankfurt: Suhrkamp, 1970).

participate. Modern culture has no room for a dichotomy between "in principle" and "in practice." It is worth determining, then, what new moral conceptions have been responsible for the emergence of modern liberalism. Not only will we thereby better understand how we have become who we are, we will also have a surer grasp of the principles that sustain our political life.

A prevalent view about the moral sources of liberalism is that it arose out of the acceptance of value pluralism. Liberalism and pluralism are indeed often thought to be intimately connected ideas. Pluralism is often considered an essential part of the basis of liberal principles of political association. And a liberal political order is in turn often perceived as one that guarantees and fosters a pluralistic society.

I believe that this view is significantly mistaken. Liberalism does not draw its rationale from an acceptance of pluralism, nor must it seek to promote its virtues. But this is not because pluralism is a form of error from which liberalism would do best to free itself. On the contrary, I think that pluralism – once its content is carefully defined – is a truth we should accept. My point in this essay is instead that it is a truth without the special relevance to liberalism that many have believed it to have, and indeed a doctrine on whose truth or falsity liberalism need not pronounce. The mistaken association of liberalism and pluralism has arisen, I shall argue, because pluralism has not been properly distinguished from a very different idea, one that does lie at the heart of what should be the self-understanding of liberal thought. This idea is the recognition that reasonable people tend naturally to disagree about the comprehensive nature of the good life.

A recognition of the inevitability of reasonable disagreement about the good is indeed often described as the acceptance of pluralism. (That, I believe, is why pluralism is so closely tied to liberalism.) John Rawls, for example, identifies what he calls "reasonable pluralism" with the fact that "a modern democratic society is characterized by a pluralism of incompatible yet reasonable comprehensive [religious, philosophical, and moral] doctrines. No one of the doctrines is affirmed by citizens generally."[3] In such a society "a diversity of conflicting and irreconcilable – and what's more, reasonable – comprehensive doctrines will come about and persist if such diversity does not already obtain."[4] But if pluralism is meant also to be the outlook with which

3 Rawls, *Political Liberalism*, p. xvii.
4 Ibid., p. 36. See also Rawls's *Dewey Lectures*, p. 542.

we are so familiar from the writings of Isaiah Berlin, if it is the conception that life affords "a plurality of values, equally genuine, equally ultimate, above all equally objective," that "there are many objective ends, ultimate values, some incompatible with others,"[5] then we are faced with a confusion. There have indeed been some who have equated explicitly Rawls's concern with Berlin's.[6] Yet the two cannot possibly be the same. What Rawls (like others) *calls* pluralism is the expectable inability of reasonable people to agree upon a comprehensive conception of the good. What Berlin has so memorably described as pluralism, however, is precisely a deep and certainly controversial account of the nature of the good, one according to which objective value is ultimately not of a single kind but of many kinds. Doctrine and reasonable disagreement about doctrine can hardly be the same thing.

Which of these two really deserves to be termed "pluralism" is in many regards unimportant. There is nonetheless one good reason to reserve the term "pluralism" for the view that Berlin has advocated. Pluralism is naturally contrasted with monism, and then at least it is understood as one of two contrary doctrines about the nature of value: are the ultimate sources of value one or many? Henceforth I shall mean by "pluralism" just such a doctrine.

What is really of significance, of course, is that we recognize the difference between pluralism and reasonable disagreement, whatever we may call them. The point is not simply one of conceptual clarity. In addition, reasonable disagreement bears an essential relation to the basis of political liberalism, which, as I have mentioned, pluralism does not really possess. Whether true or false, pluralism is an eminently controversial doctrine. It has been, as Berlin has emphasized, a peripheral view in the history of Western thought. It is incompatible with the religious orthodoxies that have sought in God the single, ultimately harmonious origin of good. If political liberalism rested essentially on the acceptance of pluralism, it would itself amount to a very controversial doctrine. Yet liberalism's primary ambition, I believe, has been to find principles of political association expressing certain fundamental moral values that, to as great an extent as possible, reasonable people may accept despite the different views about the good and about religious truth that divide them. Though we should not expect the

5 Isaiah Berlin, *The Crooked Timber of Humanity* (New York: Knopf, 1991), pp. 79–80.
6 Despite his misleading use of the term "pluralism," Rawls himself does not do so. At one point, indeed, he seems close to acknowledging the difference between the two notions. See his "Domain of the Political and Overlapping Consensus," *New York University Law Review* 64, no. 2 (May 1989), p. 237, footnote 7.

principles of liberalism to stand above every element of controversy – for they are principles, however minimal, that we should regard as correct, and not just as widely shared – pluralism still seems to me too controversial a doctrine, far too exclusive of many views well represented in our culture, to have a rightful place among such principles. Indeed, these reflections show that what liberalism is essentially committed to accepting is the very different phenomenon of reasonable disagreement. Pluralism is itself the object of reasonable disagreement in our culture. So liberalism must aim to make its guiding principles independent of it.

2. The Nature of Pluralism

To understand this important point fully, we must look more closely at the distinctive features of pluralism and reasonable disagreement. Let us begin with pluralism. As I have said, a far from insignificant fact is that it is a doctrine, opposed to monism, about the ultimate nature of value. (From the standpoint of political liberalism this is the most significant fact about it.) Yet what more precisely does pluralism assert?

A first observation is that pluralism may be an affirmation about the nature of morality or about the nature of human self-realization. Often it presents itself as both. Yet the two positions are logically independent. Morality is not the same thing as self-fulfillment or the good life. There are other things of value besides doing what we ought morally to do. It may not, of course, be possible to find, or wise to seek, a precise and permanent distinction between the two. Nonetheless, if we mean to spurn moralism, morality can figure as but one ingredient in the good life. More exactly, though some will dispute this, it should be understood as embodying, in its most fundamental requirements, the constraints we should observe in pursuing the other elements of the good life. One might, then, conceivably be a pluralist about morality without being one about the other aspects of the good life, or vice versa. Kant, for example, seems to have been a pluralist about happiness, though obviously not about morality.

What, however, does pluralism assert about morality or about the good life? In its broad form it asserts that the kinds of moral claims upon us and the forms of self-realization we can admire are in the end not one, but many. It is, in other words, a doctrine about the *sources*[7]

---

7 I should note that by "source of value" I mean here an ultimate value and not, as in Chapter 2, the source of authority for a moral conception.

of value. Moral pluralism, in one plausible version, is the view that our moral convictions cannot all be conceived in terms of the consequentialist principle of bringing about the most good overall. Some duties do fit this principle. But others are better understood as strict (deontological) demands that we respect people's inviolable rights, whatever other people may do as result of what we do, and thus whether or not our action maximizes the total good of all affected. Still other duties (such as duties of friendship or loyalties to particular cultural traditions) present themselves as ours only because we stand in particular bonds of affection to the people to whom we owe them.[8] Similarly, pluralism about the good life is the view that the value we find in different ways of life cannot be explained in terms of their all expressing or promoting a single kind of good such as pleasure or freedom. These different forms of the good life call on the diverse concerns and interests that make up our malleable and complex nature, that constitute what Berlin, turning Kant's phrase to his own purpose, calls "the crooked timber of humanity."

It is in terms like these that Berlin characterizes his own position. Pluralism, he writes, may be best understood as the rejection of a Platonic ideal that has been at the heart of Western thought, the ideal that every genuine question must have but one true answer, that there is a dependable path toward its discovery, and that these true answers are compatible with one another.[9] The correct view, he claims, is that the genuine question of how we should live has more than one true answer. There is a plurality of objective, ultimate ends that reasonable people may pursue, and that indeed are in many cases not mutually realizable, but conflicting.[10] To the old Platonic problem of the one and the many, pluralism urges the opposite answer to the one Plato and so many after him have given.

Pluralism is often linked, by Berlin and others, to an appreciation of the conflicts among our values and to the regretful recognition that not all good things can exist together in an individual life and in society as a whole. This is not wrong, but it can be a misleading view of pluralism. Monism, too, leaves room for value conflict and regret, as sophisticated utilitarians like R. M. Hare are eager to point out.[11] Once we consider pluralism as fundamentally a doctrine about the multiple sources of value, we can see that value conflict can have a special

8 For more details, see my *Patterns of Moral Complexity*, pp. 131–53.
9 Berlin, *Crooked Timber of Humanity*, pp. 5, 24, 209.   10 Ibid., pp. 11, 79.
11 R. M. Hare, *Moral Thinking* (Oxford University Press, 1981), pp. 25–49.

significance for the pluralist, not because of its prevalence, but because of its frequent difficulty, and this because of its ultimate explanation. Monism offers in principle an easy way with conflicts: the purportedly single source of value should be able to provide a common basis for determining, in given situations, the respective weights of the conflicting commitments. Pluralism harbors no such guarantee of solvability. In its lights, conflicting values can stem from different ultimate sources, and when this is so, there can be no assurance of a resolution. By that I do not mean that a reasonable settlement is impossible. On the contrary, sometimes we can find a solution to such a conflict not by appealing to a common denominator of value but simply by recognizing that one consideration carries more weight than the other. Value commitments may be, in other words, *comparable* without being *commensurable*, the directives they offer in a given situation being rankable without appeal to a common standard providing the reasons for the ranking. About this last distinction, which is evidently controversial, I shall have more to say shortly. For now we may agree that, if the distinction proves acceptable, pluralists will still have to admit that such resolutions of value conflict are likely to spark disagreement. They will also have to recognize that many conflicts among values of different sources cannot be reasonably settled by any means. In these two ways, value conflicts can display for the pluralist a difficulty they will not have for the monist.

Before I return to the proposed distinction between commensurability and comparability, it will be helpful to survey the different *kinds* of value consideration that may conflict.[12]

(1) *Duties* may conflict, as when we find ourselves in a situation where refusing to lie would lead us to seriously harm another.

(2) *Ideals* may conflict, as when it is said that one of the enduring problems of modern liberal democracies is how the ideals of liberty and equality often run contrary to one another.

(3) Comprehensive *conceptions of the good*, views about the meaning of life, may conflict.

(4) So, too, may different *forms of moral reasoning*, such as the consequentialist principle that right action consists in bringing about the most good overall, and the deontological conviction that, on the contrary, some things should never be done to others, even at the cost of not effecting the most good overall.

12 Cf. Steven Lukes, *Moral Conflict and Politics* (Oxford University Press, 1991), pp. 5–7.

Because the distinctive feature of pluralism is what it asserts about the sources of value, conflicts of the third and fourth types are the ones on which the monist and the pluralist stand fundamentally opposed. For the monist, conflicting comprehensive conceptions of the good can at best prove to be opposing means to, or opposing specifications of, what is the one source of value in life; there cannot be ultimately divergent forms of the good life. So, too, for the monist about morality there cannot prove ultimately to be conflicting forms of moral reasoning that are equally authoritative for our practical evaluations. For the monist, conflicts between ultimately divergent conceptions of the good, as well as between fundamentally different forms of moral reasoning, can only be apparent: further reflection must lead to a revision of the alternatives or a dissipation of the conflict. But for the pluralist, such conflicts can be real. They can then lead in turn to conflicts of duties and of ideals of a sort that the monist, unlike the pluralist, must refuse to acknowledge.

3. Pluralism and Value Conflict

It is also appropriate to look at the different *ways* values may conflict:

(1) Some commitments may be logically incompatible, impossible ever to carry out together; in this case we should perhaps always revise them for the sake of coherence.

(2) Some commitments may be logically compatible, yet offer incompatible directives in given (not in all) situations.

(3) To some conflicts of this sort a solution may not be available, *either* because we do not yet have the information needed to resolve them (and so we should suspend judgment about what to believe is the best course of action, though we may still have to act),[13] *or* because we have good reason to think no new information will ever be uncovered about how to decide the issue. This second case is the truly irresolvable value conflict. To the extent that we continue to believe we should act on the commitments in conflict (which is likely to be so when they are of fundamental moral importance), we must see the world itself as deficient, as too narrow in its possibilities for us to do what we know we ought to

13 Isaac Levi, *Hard Choices* (Cambridge University Press, 1986), chapter 2.

do. However fascinating philosophically, this case is not one I shall pursue further here.[14]

(4) To other conflicts between logically compatible commitments a solution may instead be available. That is, we can reasonably rank what the one value-commitment directs us to do, in the given set of circumstances, above what the others enjoin us to do there. It should be noted that often a solution will consist in thus ranking certain courses of action recommended by the values, and not in ranking the values themselves. The latter is also possible, but only when we can uniformly rank the options recommended by the commitments in all foreseeable situations of conflict. (Sometimes, of course, a solution may consist in finding the directives to be of equal weight.)

On what basis can such a solution by ranking arise? One way is very familiar: it occurs when we regard the conflicting values as being valuable because they promote or express some underlying value, and we can describe this common value in terms that permit us to rank in importance what the conflicting values direct us to do in the given situation. In this case, the values are certainly thought to be *comparable*. But in addition they are understood as *commensurable*, their directives rankable with respect to a common denominator of value. This sort of ranking can be of different types. It may be a *cardinal* ranking, as when classical utilitarians asserted that different options are to be weighed in terms of precisely how much pleasure they produce. (In this case, pleasure is understood as the ultimate source of value.) It may instead be an *ordinal* ranking, as when one ranks different actions as more or less pleasurable, or ways of life as more or less saintly, without specifying by how much. Or, third, the ranking may be, as I shall say, *imprecisely cardinal*, as when one deems one action "a lot more" pleasurable than another, without believing that there is any more precise amount by which the two differ in pleasure. In general, values are commensurable if they can be compared in terms of the extent to which they promote or express some common value. Value commensurability takes different forms, depending on whether this extent is a matter simply of more or less or of how much more or less.

That all values are thus commensurable (in one of these three forms, though not necessarily with respect to pleasure) is, of course,

14 See my *Patterns of Moral Complexity*, pp. 149–50.

the conviction that distinguishes the monist from the pluralist. If commensuration were the only way values could be compared and their implications for action ranked, pluralism would not be wrong. But the pluralist would then have to admit that all conflicts between values deriving from different ultimate sources are rationally irresolvable. Should the pluralist accept this consequence of his views? Many believe he must. As we shall see, Isaiah Berlin himself seems to be one. But I do not share this conclusion, for I believe that values may be comparable without being commensurable.

Consider, for example, a situation in which, having made a rather unmomentous promise to one person, we discover that a friend of ours badly needs our advice on an important decision he must make, and that we can meet with him in time only if we do not keep the promise to the other individual. I will assume we agree that we should put helping our friend first and indeed that morally we ought to do so. The duties of friendship, when urgent and within certain moral bounds, take precedence over the (deontological) duty of promise keeping when the latter is not of great moment. The two values are thus comparable. But is there a common denominator of value with respect to which they are commensurable? What could it be? It is not from a deontological perspective, focusing on the inviolable rights of others, that we judge that our friend's need comes first. For the duties of friendship are not deontological in character: they do not purport to be binding on us whatever our own interests, as deontological duties do, since we should do for our friends what friendship requires only if we want to be friends with them. Nor do we weigh the two values as we do by aiming to bring about the most good overall. For however the good is concretely specified, the consequentialist framework requires that we regard each individual involved as of equal weight ("each counting for one and only one"); yet what our friend expects of us, and what we express in putting our friendship for him first, is that we attach greater importance to him than to others.

This seems, then, a clear case in which values can prove comparable without being commensurable. Of course, in believing that morally we ought to put friendship first, we are supposing that there is a *common perspective* – the point of view of morality, in which the two values are being weighed against one another. Two things cannot be compared except from some point of view. But for all that, the framework of comparison does not itself have to embody a common denominator of value. It need not be such as to show how the values being compared are more or less valuable, depending on whether they promote or express that common denominator to a greater or lesser extent. It need not be a source of value, explaining the value of what is being compared. It is in this sense that I mean that the two values, though comparable, need not be commensurable. The point may be easier to accept if we observe that part of it must be granted by any pluralist, even by one holding that heterogeneous values cannot be compared. If it is to be claimed that the sources of moral value are not one but many, these many sources must share enough to be grouped (though perhaps not compared) within the common perspective of morality, though they will not share so much as to be derivative in their value from some superior value.

Many pluralists have denied that heterogeneous values can be compared. (So, too, have many monists, to make their own opposing view appear all the more attractive.) The guiding assumption of these pluralists is that values can be compared, weighed against one another, only by determining how they may promote or express some superior value that is their source. As I have mentioned, Isaiah Berlin is one such pluralist. Pluralism, he has written, asks us

> to look upon life as affording a plurality of values, equally genuine,
> equally ultimate, above all equally objective; incapable, therefore, of
> being ordered in a timeless hierarchy, or judged in terms of some one
> absolute standard. . . . The fact that the values of one culture may be
> incompatible with those of another, or that they are in conflict within
> one culture or group or in a single human being at different times . . .
> does not entail relativism of values, only the notion of a plurality of
> values not structured hierarchically; which, of course, entails the perma-
> nent possibility of inescapable conflict between values.[15]

Berlin seems to believe that, being equally ultimate, not derivable from a single form of good, plural values cannot be weighed together and their directives ranked and ordered hierarchically. This being so, we apparently cannot believe, in Berlin's view, that where our values differ in this way from those of others, our own are legitimately superior. The only universally valid principles of cultural evaluation would have to be the very meager set expressing values that everywhere are held to be of paramount importance.[16]

I am not alone, however, in believing that pluralism need not take

---

15 Berlin, *Crooked Timber of Humanity,* pp. 79–80.
16 For evidence that Berlin does think there exist some universally shared values, see
    Claude Galipeau, *Isaiah Berlin's Liberalism* (Oxford University Press, 1994), pp. 65–
    8, 82.

this form, that instead it can permit us to rank the recommendations of heterogeneous values and thus arrive at some universal standards of cultural evaluation. Oddly enough, J. G. Herder, who has been one of Berlin's inspirations, held just this sort of view. "Ist nicht das Gute auf der Erde ausgestreut?" ("Is not the good dispersed about the earth?") is the exclamation with which he announced his conviction that the good is ultimately various.[17] But he did not draw from it the conclusion that the forms of good are thus incomparable. On the contrary, in his *Briefe zur Beförderung der Humanität* (1793–7),[18] for example, Herder professed agreement with Kant that there exists an ethic of unconditional duties binding on all. He was, to be sure, no Kantian in the sense that makes Kant's a monistic outlook: he did not believe that all moral value derives from the rational self-legislation of autonomous agents. So he was keen to point out the moral costs of this ethic, the other forms of good incompatible with it, such as the intense family loyalties of the heroic ethic. But he did not believe that the heterogeneity of these goods precluded their comparability. On this point I think we should follow Herder. Can we not in good conscience consider our own moral universalism as superior to earlier and very different tribal moralities, while acknowledging that thereby we have also lost the possibilities of good they embodied? The weighing of heterogeneous goods is not likely to yield a cardinal ranking. But surely we can have reason to believe that some such goods are more important than others, in the given circumstances or overall, and even a lot more important.

I suspect that many will regard these remarks about how incommensurable values may still be comparable as just so much assertion. If not by appeal to a common denominator of value, then how, they will ask, are the values weighed against one another? I admit that I have no fully satisfactory answer to this question.[19] Nonetheless, an inability to solve this problem is not, I believe, as damaging as it might seem. Sometimes we can legitimately claim to know something without knowing how we know it. This can be so, for example, when we make the claim directly, without having to go through any explicit reasoning. In

17 J. G. Herder, *Auch eine Philosophie der Geschichte* (Frankfurt: Suhrkamp, 1967), p. 46.
18 Herder, *Briefe zur Beförderung der Humanität*, Sechste Sammlung, § 79.
19 Recent "particularist" accounts of moral judgment may be helpful here (e.g., David McNaughton, *Moral Vision* [Oxford: Blackwell, 1988]), though I think the idea of "moral perception," with which they are often combined, is misleading. See Chapter 5, this volume.

this case, any account of the basis of the claim may be somewhat speculative and less certain than the claim itself.[20] It seems to me that the example of ranking a friend's needs above an unmomentous promise is just like this: we know directly that the one should count for more than the other without having any systematic account of why this is so – though we can exclude its resting on any common denominator of value.

4. The Modern Character of Pluralism

So far our discussion has focused on the structure of pluralism. But another significant aspect is its historical character. Is pluralism about the right and the good a distinctively modern doctrine? Or, however much a minority view, has it also had distinguished exponents in premodern times? This question is clearly important for anyone who considers pluralism a central source of the distinctively modern outlook that is political liberalism. This customary association of pluralism with liberalism has been challenged, in effect, by some recent neo-Aristotelian thinkers. In general, the neo-Aristotelian revival has been devoted to showing that Aristotle's ethics, far from being so alien as is sometimes supposed, serves to confirm and also to deepen many of our cherished ethical convictions. In particular, there have been a number of attempts to demonstrate that Aristotle himself was a pluralist at heart, though obviously he was no liberal.[21] Recall that Berlin presented his pluralism as the rejection of the Platonic view that all goods are ultimately one. The neo-Aristotelian argument may be seen as claiming that a similar rejection already lies at the core of Aristotle's own critique of Platonic ethics (as expounded, for example, in *Nicomachean Ethics* I.6).

I, too, believe that the association of pluralism with liberalism is misconceived, but not for this reason. On the contrary, not only does

---

20 Cf. G. E. Moore, "Four Forms of Scepticism," p. 222 in his *Philosophical Papers* (New York: Macmillan, 1959).

21 See J. L. Ackrill, "Aristotle on Eudaimonia," pp. 15–33 in A. Rorty (ed.), *Essays on Aristotle's Ethics* (Berkeley and Los Angeles: University of California Press, 1980); Martha Nussbaum, *The Fragility of Goodness* (Cambridge University Press, 1986), pp. 373–7; and idem, *Love's Knowledge* (Oxford University Press, 1990), pp. 56–66; J. O. Urmson, *Aristotle's Ethics* (Oxford: Blackwell, 1988), pp. 13–15, 119–21; Ronald Beiner, "The Moral Vocabulary of Liberalism," pp. 145–84 in *Nomos XXXIV: Virtue* (New York University Press, 1992). Some of my remarks here are drawn from my "Limits of Aristotelian Ethics," pp. 185–96 in ibid.

the pluralist interpretation fail to fit Aristotle's thought, but pluralism is indeed a distinctively modern doctrine. It belongs to a disenchanted vision of the world, which sees itself as having abandoned the comfort of finding in the harmony of the cosmos or in God's providential ordering of the world the one ultimate source of value. There is good reason, then, to show that pluralism has no place in Aristotle's ethics, if only to understand better how it can be a modern phenomenon without being, as I also shall argue, a central source of political liberalism.

What makes the pluralist interpretation of Aristotle's ethics attractive is the apparently broad, "inclusivist" (as it is called) claim of Book One of the *Nicomachean Ethics* that our end is to unify our various strivings in a coherent conception of the good life (1097b14–20). This seems to acknowledge the heterogeneous character of the different activities reasonable people hold to be good. Yet the obvious obstacle to the interpretation is the clear assertion of X.7–8 that the contemplative life of *theoria* is superior to the practical life of moral excellence. Perfect happiness, Aristotle wrote there, consists in contemplation (1177a17–19), and the life of moral excellence achieves happiness only in a secondary sense (1178a9). This perfect happiness is reserved for the gods (1177b26–7; 1178b21–2). But from this admission Aristotle did not draw the conclusion that the neo-Aristotelian pluralist would want him to draw, namely that the best human life consists in a reasonable mix of contemplation and action, a mix determined by *phronesis* (judgment).[22] Instead, Aristotle urged that our aim should be as far as possible to become like gods, leaving behind the human sphere and putting on immortality (*athanatizein:* 1177b33, also 1178b23). Such views seem difficult to house within a pluralist conception of the good.

The pluralist interpretation of Aristotle's ethics has typically chosen to ignore these passages of Book Ten or else to banish them from the true core of Aristotle's thought. Martha Nussbaum, for example, has suggested that they may be either an interpolation or a residue of a Platonic ethics that elsewhere Aristotle had outgrown.[23] J. O. Urmson remarks that Aristotle's "enthusiasm" for his own scholarly life has momentarily gotten the better of him.[24] The fact, however, is that the aspiration to divinity is not confined to Book Ten. It also stands in the

22 Nussbaum, *Fragility of Goodness,* p. 374; Beiner, "Moral Vocabulary," pp. 161–2.
23 Nussbaum, *Fragility of Goodness,* pp. 373–7.
24 Urmson, *Aristotle's Ethics,* p. 125.

background of Book One, where Aristotle states that "the good for man is an activity of soul in accordance with virtue, or if there are more kinds of virtue than one, in accordance with the best and most complete kind" (1098a16–18). Nussbaum tries to yoke this passage to her pluralist interpretation of Aristotelian *eudaimonia* by arguing that "completeness" requires "the inclusion of everything with intrinsic value."[25] But since excellences or virtues are all of intrinsic value, this passage unmistakably rules out such an interpretation: it holds that the good will consist in one excellence or virtue among others, if one is the best.

The superiority of intellectual to moral virtue is, in fact, a theme that runs throughout Aristotle's ethical writings. It follows from his overarching metaphysics, in which it is obvious that there are many things of greater value than the human affairs with which morality is concerned. The idea that Aristotle assigned to *phronesis* the task of discerning the best life by devising a mix of contemplation and action is refuted by the clear *reductio ad absurdum* of VI.7 (1141a20–2): "It is extraordinary that anyone should regard political science or *phronesis* as most important unless man is the highest being in the world." Nor will it do to suggest, as Nussbaum does, that while proclaiming the superiority of contemplation to action, Aristotle still thought our true happiness should contain both.[26] It is true that, though X is better than Y, a life given fully to X may be less good than one devoted to some mix of X and Y (there can be too much of a good thing); but her main evidence that this is what Aristotle meant here is inadequate: at 1144a2–4, Aristotle does say that *sophia* (wisdom) is, like *phronesis,* part of virtue, but this does not imply that each is part of complete happiness. "What is so hard for a modern reader to take seriously," observes Jonathan Lear – and this seems especially true of certain neo-Aristotelians, "is Aristotle's claim that man has a divine element in him. . . . Man is a composite, and yet he is *most truly* the highest element in his form. It is man's natural desire to understand . . . that propels him to transcend his nature."[27]

---

25 Nussbaum, *Fragility of Goodness,* p. 376. Cf. also Ackrill, "Aristotle on Eudaimonia," p. 28.
26 Nussbaum, *Fragility of Goodness,* pp. 374–7.
27 Jonathan Lear, *Aristotle: The Desire to Understand* (Cambridge University Press, 1988), p. 320. I also find very convincing the critique of the "inclusivist" interpretation of Aristotelian *eudaimonia* in Richard Kraut, *Aristotle on the Human Good* (Princeton, N.J.: Princeton University Press, 1989).

An important consequence of my earlier discussion of pluralism is that heterogeneous values may nonetheless be weighed against one another. So the fact that Aristotle ranked contemplation above action and understood the best life as one devoted solely to contemplation does not suffice to show that he did not have a pluralist conception of these values. We need to consider the basis on which he made this ranking. Aristotle's fundamental thesis is that happiness consists in rational activity, and that things are good to the extent that they contribute to or have a role in such activity (I.7). The arguments of X.7 in favor of the superiority of contemplation proceed by showing how contemplation is a more continuous, self-sufficient, self-directing form of rational activity. Contemplation thus expresses more purely the ideal of happiness, which is the exercise of our rational nature. Aristotle was, therefore, no pluralist. For him there was a single kind of value that the different forms of the good life exemplify to different degrees.

It is in these terms that we should understand the apparently pluralist-minded critique of Plato in I.6. Plato was wrong, Aristotle there argued, to assert that all good things, or even just all intrinsic goods, share a single form of the good. On the contrary, the different kinds of life devoted to honor, intelligence, and pleasure "have different and dissimilar accounts, precisely in so far as they are goods" (1096b23–5). This may sound like pluralism, but it is not. Aristotle assumed that a number of things can share a single form (separable or not) only if they exemplify it equally – as a man and a monkey are equally animals. There can be, he believed, no form for things related as "prior and posterior," which instead must be comprehended in terms of "focal meaning" (*aph'enos, pros hen*) or analogy.[28] Now as we have seen, Aristotle's argument for the superiority of contemplation consists in showing that it exemplifies rational activity more perfectly than does action. That is why he refused to consider the two forms of life as sharing a common form of the good. But his argument is no less monistic for that, appealing as it does to a single supreme value, more or less fully realizable.

"Aristotle the pluralist" is too much like us to be much like Aristotle himself. Pluralism is a characteristically modern outlook. It is likely to

---

28 See the commentary in W. F. R. Hardie, *Aristotle's Ethical Theory* (Oxford University Press, 1968), pp. 55–6, 63–5.

appear attractive only against the background of metaphysical and religious disappointment. It recommends itself to those who continue to believe that value can be objective, something more than just the expression of our preferences, but who refuse to believe that it has its home in a harmonious cosmos (as Aristotle thought) or in God's plan. For example, the moral pluralism that accepts the mutual independence of deontological and consequentialist forms of deliberation arises from the demise of theodicy – that is, from the realization that strict deontological rules, which are undeniable, cannot be shown to be God's wise way of bringing about the most good overall.[29] Liberalism has distinguished itself from earlier political philosophies by its refusal, ever more pronounced, to base the principles of political association upon a vision of God's plan or of an ordered cosmos. So it is perhaps natural that liberalism and pluralism should be regarded as closely allied. Indeed, they are both distinctively modern in that they have something to do with the metaphysical-religious disenchantment of the world. But their relations to this phenomenon are actually very different, and we are now in a good position to see why.

5. The Nature of Reasonable Disagreement

Recall that pluralism is a doctrine about the nature of value. It asserts that the forms of moral concern, as well as the forms of self-realization, are in the end not one but many. It stands opposed, therefore, to religious and metaphysical conceptions of a single source of value. Liberalism, by contrast, does not share in this opposition. Its defining aim is different. It seeks to found the principles of political association upon a core morality that reasonable people can accept despite their natural tendency to disagree about comprehensive visions of the nature of value and so in particular about the merits of pluralism and monism. This expectation of reasonable disagreement, to which liberalism does appeal, lies at a different, one might almost say more "impartial," level than pluralism. It responds to the idea of a religiously and metaphysically disenchanted world not by affirming it, as pluralism seems to do, but rather by recognizing that like other deep conceptions of value this disenchantment is an idea about which reasonable

---

29 See my *Patterns of Moral Complexity*, pp. 134–8, and also "Théodicée et rationalité morale chez Malebranche, Leibniz et Bayle," pp. 121–38 in my *Modernité et morale*.

people are likely to disagree, as indeed they do. Ours is a culture, after all, of which religious faith remains very much a part. That is why the expectation of reasonable disagreement, unlike pluralism, belongs at the heart of political liberalism.

Recognizing the different import of pluralism and reasonable disagreement tells us something significant, not only about the aims of liberalism, but also about what we should want from a notion of modernity. It is a mistake to suppose that, in determining what is essential to modern thought and experience, we should fix upon any single phenomenon. Modernity is a multidimensional idea. It must be defined by a number of distinctive features, some of which may prove more relevant than others from a given point of view. When we aim to bring out the aspects of modern culture that ought to shape the basis of our political life, we must take pluralism into account, not as the conception of value we may happen to believe correct, but rather as a conception about which reasonable people disagree. If instead we broaden the scope of our reflection and try to determine what comprehensive conception of value most faithfully captures the many facets of our modern experience, we will no longer be able to avoid addressing directly the issue between pluralism and monism. The modernity we seek to affirm depends in part on the specific purpose we have in mind.

Since the expectation of reasonable disagreement is the modern phenomenon that animates political liberalism, we must examine it more closely. "Reasonable" people are those who think and converse in good faith and apply, as best they can, the general capacities of reason that belong to every domain of inquiry. The insight that has proven so significant for liberal thought is that reasonableness has ceased to seem a guarantee of ultimate agreement about deep questions concerning how we should live. In the early modern period the expectation of reasonable disagreement arose primarily in the realm of religion; one learned to expect that reasonable people would differ about the correct path to salvation. But over the past four centuries the scope of this insight has broadened. It has become a salient feature of modern experience that on matters concerning the meaning of life, and also concerning certain deep aspects of morality, discussion among reasonable people tends naturally not toward consensus, but toward controversy. The more we talk about such things (sometimes even with ourselves!), the more we disagree. Where there is the appearance of agreement it is likely to be the result of mutual misunderstanding,[30] or simply of people not having talked together long and hard enough. Shared forms of life based on common conceptions of the good still thrive, of course, but that is because critical inquiry is not always considered, and perhaps rightly so, the paramount value (see Chapter 6).

In its full generality, the idea that reasonable discussion leads naturally to controversy was embraced already by Montaigne, who was not so much the skeptic practicing suspension of judgment as the eager participant in the turmoil of thought. Thus he wrote:

> En subdivisant ces subtilités, on apprend aux hommes d'accroître les doutes: on nous met en train d'étendre et diversifier les difficultés, on les allonge, on les disperse. En semant les questions et les retaillant, on fait fructifier et foisonner le monde en incertitude et en querelles, comme la terre se rend fertile plus elle est émiée et profondément remuée. *Difficultatem facit doctrina.* . . . Jamais deux hommes ne jugèrent pareillement de même chose, et est impossible de voir deux opinions semblables exactement, non seulement en divers hommes, mais en même homme à diverses heures.[31]

Or as Thomas Paine put the idea: "I do not believe that any two men, on what are called doctrinal points, think alike who think at all. It is only those who have not thought that appear to agree."[32] This expectation of reasonable disagreement about ultimate questions of value has not been an idea of solely political relevance. Having become a general feature of modern life, it has shaped many of the distinctive products of modern culture. The modern novel and its concern for the individuality of human lives is, for example, inconceivable without it. "The art of the novel," writes Milan Kundera, "came into the world as the echo

30 Cf. Baudelaire, *Mon coeur mis à nu*, XLII, *Oeuvres complètes* (Paris: Gallimard, 1961), p. 1297: "Le monde ne marche que par le malentendu. – C'est par le malentendu universel que tout le monde s'accorde. – Car si, par malheur on se comprenait, on ne pourrait jamais s'accorder."

31 Montaigne, *Essais*, III.13, pp. 1043–4 in *Oeuvres complètes* (Paris: Gallimard, 1962): "By subdividing these subtleties they teach men to increase their doubts; they start us extending and diversifying the difficulties, they lengthen them, they scatter them. By sowing questions and cutting them up, they make the world fructify and teem with uncertainty and quarrels, as the earth is made more fertile the more it is crumbled and deeply plowed. *Learning makes difficulties.* . . . Never did two men judge alike about the same thing, and it is impossible to find two opinions exactly alike, not only in different men, but in the same man at different times." (Translation Donald Frame, *The Complete Essays of Montaigne* (Stanford, Calif.: Stanford University Press, 1957), pp. 816–17).

32 Thomas Paine, *The Rights of Man*, II.5 (Harmondsworth: Penguin, 1984), p. 271.

of God's laughter. But why did God laugh at the sight of man thinking? ... Because the more men think, the more one man's thought diverges from another's."[33]

An important and difficult question is *why* reasonable people should tend naturally to disagree about the meaning of life and about certain deep features of morality. After all, reasonable discussion about complicated issues does seem to lead to consensus in other areas, most notably in the sciences. The explanation cannot rest with prejudice and bias, since it is reasonable people who fail to secure agreement upon these matters. Nor should we be content to say, as Locke apparently was (*Essay Concerning Human Understanding*, IV.xvi.4), that reasonable disagreement is only to be expected about opinions that can be but probable, never certain. For that would make incomprehensible the likelihood of agreement in the sciences. A more promising explanation has recently been proposed by John Rawls. He traces "the fact of pluralism," as he misleadingly calls the phenomenon of reasonable disagreement, back to "the burdens of reason":

(1) The empirical evidence may be conflicting and complex.
(2) Agreement about the kinds of considerations involved does not guarantee agreement about their weight.
(3) Key concepts may be vague and subject to hard cases.
(4) Our total experience, which shapes how we assess the evidence and weigh values, is likely in complex modern societies to be rather disparate from person to person.
(5) Different kinds of normative considerations may be involved on both sides of a question.
(6) Being forced to select among cherished values, we face great difficulties in setting priorities.[34]

Certainly, these factors play a role. Yet as Rawls himself observes, most of them are not peculiar to reasoning about values, and so fall short of the sort of explanation we seek. For my part, I believe that (4), the great variety of life experiences created by modern society, with all its complex divisions of labor and its rich heritage of many different cultural traditions, provides the key to explaining the phenomenon.

But I also believe we will miss an important truth if we suppose, as

---

33 Milan Kundera, *The Art of the Novel* (New York: Harper & Row, 1988), p. 158.
34 Rawls, "The Domain of the Political and Overlapping Consensus," pp. 236–7; and idem, *Political Liberalism,* pp. 56–7.

we have done so far, that the peculiar fact requiring explanation is the likelihood of reasonable disagreement about complex questions of how we should live. It is perhaps a more peculiar fact, and the real departure from the ordinary course of things, that reasonable agreement should be so expectable in the sciences. This is not at all the way it has always been. Before the sixteenth and seventeenth centuries, reasonable disagreement was the norm in the study of the natural world. No two premodern physicists thought the same who thought at all. One of the distinctive features of modern science, which sets it off from the rest of the history of scientific thought, has been its remarkable ability to generate consensus. Reasonable disagreement in the handling of complex questions is perhaps just what we should expect (though our philosophical tradition has always preached that reason is what brings us together), and the extraordinary fact is that this phenomenon has largely ceased to occur in the natural sciences. How should we explain this? The conventional answer, perhaps correct, is that in this domain of inquiry we have managed to get on the track of the truth. But we should also wonder whether such an explanation does not reverse cause and effect, and whether "scientific truth" (as we now understand it) is not simply what a community of investigators will accept when they agree to subject their observation of nature to forms of reasoning designed to secure agreement.[35]

6. Reasonable Disagreement and Skepticism

As I noted, explaining why reasonable people should naturally tend to disagree about fundamental questions of value is a difficult matter. I do not propose to solve the problem here; we do not need an explanation to recognize the phenomenon. However, we do need to see how the expectation of reasonable disagreement differs from skepticism.

In a calm and careful discussion about the nature of the good life or about the precise role consequentialist and deontological considerations should play in moral reasoning, we would be foolish not to expect that our own views will meet with disagreement. From this expectation, though, we need not draw any skeptical conclusions. We need not suspend judgment about the correctness of our own views. We may

---

35 See on these lines the fascinating study by Steven Shapin and Simon Shaffer, *Leviathan and the Airpump* (Princeton, N.J.: Princeton University Press, 1985). This point of view recurs in much of the recent "constructivist" sociology of science.

still rightfully believe that, despite being controversial, they are better supported by experience and reflection than those of our opponents. This is because we can determine that a view is reasonable, though false. It may have been arrived at sincerely and in accord with generally accepted forms of reasoning, yet against the background of existing beliefs that our own viewpoint judges as false. When our own background beliefs thus clash with those of someone else, this is not (as I observed in Chapter 2) a sufficient reason for us to suspend allegiance to these beliefs and reexamine them. To call them into doubt we need some positive reason to think they may be false, one that we must be able to recognize as such by our own lights; for that, after all, is the standpoint from which we judge. Perhaps we may find this reason for doubt in the opposing position, but it must amount to more than just that we reasonably disagree.

Some recent discussions of this issue fail to distinguish adequately the expectation of reasonable disagreement from skepticism. In the preceding chapter I mentioned an essay by Thomas Nagel as one example. Nagel has claimed that reasonable disagreement of the sort I have been considering, toward which the liberal state aims to be neutral, occurs between views that fail to meet what he calls "a higher standard of objectivity." Such disagreement comes down finally to "a bare confrontation between incompatible personal points of view."[36] If this were the situation, then a skeptical suspension of judgment about such views would seem indeed the proper response, though Nagel himself denies it. But in fact, reasonable disagreement can persist even when the conflicting views satisfy the two conditions Nagel assigns to the "higher standard of objectivity." That is, we may be able to present our opponents with the reasons for our view and explain in a detailed way what errors prevent their agreeing with us (and they may be able to do the same with regard to us). The point is that when we do so, we are appealing to what we believe, to what we have so far no reason to call into doubt, and these beliefs amount to more than what reasonableness alone can underwrite. Different conceptions of the good life, and different ideas of the weight deontological and consequentialist considerations should have, generally involve rather complex and divergent structures of purposes, significances, and activities. It is on the

36 Thomas Nagel, "Moral Conflict and Political Legitimacy," *Philosophy and Public Affairs* 16, no. 3 (Summer 1987), p. 232.

basis of such structures that we can explain how opposed views go wrong. But they are also what fundamentally divide us.

From this it follows – to take another example – that Joshua Cohen goes wrong in saying that when, despite reasonable disagreement with others, we still affirm our own controversial view, we are taking the "sectarian route" of believing it "as a matter of faith," there being no further reason to regard our own view as not only reasonable but also true.[37] On the contrary, we may very well have reasons to hold our view to be true. Our allegiance to it may be much more than a matter of faith. It is simply that these reasons lie outside what is the object of reasonable agreement.

After all, good faith and common reason, the elements of reasonableness, are capacities we exercise against the background of existing belief. We should therefore not suppose either that simply by being reasonable we can adjudicate between conflicting backgrounds of belief or that, where we cannot, we must consider allegiance to such backgrounds as but an article of faith. As I have repeatedly argued, we examine the worth of an existing belief always in the light of other things we already believe, if only because we could not otherwise establish the positive grounds for doubt that alone make it necessary to seek the justification of that belief. As a result, where we have no positive grounds for doubt, we should regard our view as true, however much it may be the object of reasonable disagreement. Generally, we have good reason to believe more than what reasonable agreement with others can secure.

Thus, the idea that about matters of ultimate significance reasonable people tend naturally to disagree is distinct from both pluralism and skepticism. It lies, moreover, unlike them, at the heart of a liberal political philosophy, which seeks to base the principles of political association upon a core morality that reasonable people can accept despite the divergent conceptions of the good (and also of the right) that draw them apart. If pluralism were an essential component of liberalism's self-understanding, then liberalism would fall significantly short of its ambition to build, as much as possible, upon common moral ground. For pluralism is itself an eminently controversial doc-

37 Joshua Cohen, "Moral Pluralism and Political Consensus," pp. 281–4 in David Copp, Jean Hampton, and John Roemer (eds.), *The Idea of Democracy* (Cambridge University Press, 1993).

trine that many reasonable people, whether on religious or metaphysical grounds, do not accept; and even among themselves pluralists can achieve little agreement about what ultimate goods there are or what weight they should carry. A liberalism founded on pluralism would be too doctrinaire.

And if skepticism were an essential component of liberalism, it would be incomprehensible why the liberal project should be to look beyond the deep disagreements that divide reasonable people to the minimal principles on which they ought to unite. For if people were reasonable and skeptical about what they cannot agree upon, there would be nothing left to divide them – except at most, personal acts of faith, but certainly not systematic visions of the good. A liberalism based on skepticism would be too irenic.

The natural tendency toward reasonable disagreement, duly distinguished from other notions with which it has been confused, belongs therefore at the center of liberal thought. Yet its significance, as I have observed, extends well beyond the political domain. Our intellectual tradition has been to a large and important extent animated by the conviction that reason leads naturally to agreement, that reason is what brings us together. The aspect of modern thought I have been examining challenges this preconception. We have yet, I believe, to take the measure of all that this challenge of modernity implies.

8

CARL SCHMITT'S CRITIQUE OF LIBERAL DEMOCRACY

Carl Schmitt was one of the most famous German political theorists of this century, but it is not possible to separate his renown from the controversy that swirls around his life and work. He is notorious for his dubious loyalty to the Weimar Republic and for his active involvement with the Hitler regime. He owes his intellectual fame to a series of writings spanning more than four decades and united in their merciless repudiation of modern liberal democracy.

In this essay I pursue the limited aim of examining the cogency of this critique of liberal democracy, particularly as it is laid out in his short book of 1923, *Die geistesgeschichtliche Lage des heutigen Parlamentarismus.* I will refer only in passing to his other works, many of which might seem to be more substantial scholarly treatises, since I do not believe they add anything essential to the principal features of this critique. Also, I will focus on the quality of the arguments in the 1923 book, largely leaving aside its historical context, the rhetorical strategies Schmitt deploys, and the political agenda that lies concealed in a discourse that presents itself as detached and philosophical. But I do not mean to suggest that these are unimportant factors in understanding the nature of Schmitt's thought – far from it. My purpose in concentrating on the soundness of his arguments is to confront directly the reason most often given for why we should pay special attention to his critique of liberal democracy. Indisputably a fascist sympathizer in Hitler's Germany (between 1933 and 1936 he was a member of the Nazi party, a Prussian state counselor, and the author of a number of clearly anti-Semitic articles), Schmitt is repeatedly said to have differed from the intellectual thugs and opportunists typical of that period. He had a keen political intellect, it is urged, and developed powerful arguments that committed liberals and democrats ignore at their own peril.

That Schmitt's critique of liberal democracy represents a serious intellectual challenge was an opinion expressed in the 1930s in Germany by such notable thinkers as Herbert Marcuse and Leo Strauss. In recent years, the same claim for Schmitt's importance has reappeared, for example, in Thomas McCarthy's introduction to the new English translation of *Die geistesgeschichtliche Lage*.[1] I find it difficult to share this view of Schmitt's intellectual prowess. As I try to show here, the arguments that compose his critique of liberal democracy turn out to possess very little force. One conclusion that thus recommends itself is that Schmitt's imposing reputation as a critic of liberalism must arise from bad judgment, or else it draws on other aspects of his writings besides their intellectual caliber.

The case of Carl Schmitt deserves, however, more than just this summary verdict. Implausible though they be, Schmitt's arguments stem from fundamental mistakes about the basic features of liberal democracy, mistakes that are themselves widespread and that the crisp, steely energy of Schmitt's prose brings into uncommon focus. That is why his critique of liberal democracy does deserve our attention – not because it poses an intellectual challenge we must have the courage to face, but because it exemplifies so clearly a recurring pattern of antiliberal and antidemocratic thought.

Nor is a justifiable interest in Schmitt's thought exhausted by the exemplary mistakes he made. Underlying his argumentation is an insightful conception of the conditions of political stability in what he called "the democratic age." Schmitt believed that it must force us to move beyond the incoherencies of liberal democracy (and in a direction we would scarcely term "democratic"). But in fact this conception

---

1 See Herbert Marcuse, "The Struggle against Liberalism in the Totalitarian View of the State" (1934), pp. 3–42 in his *Negations* (Boston: Beacon, 1968); Leo Strauss, "Comments on Carl Schmitt's *Der Begriff des Politischen*" (1932), pp. 331–51 in his *Spinoza's Critique of Religion* (New York: Schocken, 1965); Thomas McCarthy, Series Editor's Foreword, pp. vii–viii in Carl Schmitt, *The Crisis of Parliamentary Democracy*, trans. E. Kennedy (Cambridge, Mass.: MIT Press, 1985). See also the special issue of the leftish journal *Telos* (Summer 1987) devoted to Schmitt.

points to a powerful argument in favor of liberal-democratic principles. Perhaps this shows how difficult it is to recognize the fundamental features of modernity and, short of self-contradiction, to resist the appeal of liberal democracy.

1. Modernity and Political Legitimacy

We must begin by looking at the central critical argument Schmitt presents in his 1923 book. The more we succeed in reducing this argument to its essentials, the more clearly will emerge, I believe, its decisive and telling weaknesses.[2]

The first, indispensable premise of this argument is that the ultimate stability of a political system depends on whether its principle of legitimacy is generally believed to be justified. In Schmitt's account, a principle of legitimacy is a normative commitment that is actually held. Such a principle lays out the basis on which the exercise of political power is to count as legitimate, but at the same time it is a principle actually proclaimed by the state, affirmed in the constitution, and invoked in the political culture. It is the fundamental norm that a political system sets itself. According to Schmitt, the stability of a political system can be assured only if its principle of legitimacy is generally thought to be justified (3, 8).

This premise explains why his critique of parliamentary democracy consists simply in arguing that its principle of legitimacy (or rather, according to Schmitt, its pair of contrary principles) cannot plausibly be affirmed. It explains why he sets aside the question whether in practice, whatever the intellectual quality of its principles, parliamentary democracy is preferable to the available alternatives. I shall later point out that this premise leads to one of the deepest flaws in Schmitt's argument. The mistake does not lie in the premise itself, that is, in his insistence on the importance of principle. It is, rather, that Schmitt fails to realize how the need for political principles to be seen as justified, which he puts at the heart of his polemic, itself becomes, under modern conditions, the basis of an important argument for liberal democracy.

Schmitt observes that a distinctive feature of politics in the modern period is the change from dynastic to democratic principles of legitimacy. There was a time when the monarch's exercise of political power

---

2 Page references in the text are to Schmitt, *Crisis of Parliamentary Democracy.*

was held to be justified by his place in a dynastic line, which was itself usually thought to be a vehicle of God's will. But since 1815 at least, not just monarchies (such as Louis-Philippe's), but nearly every form of government has laid claim to rule not by divine right but by the will of the people (29–30). This is as true of parliamentary democracy as of Bolshevik dictatorship, although the two may differ on whether they aim to represent the actually expressed or "true" interests of the governed. In general, Schmitt believes (26), the idea of democratic legitimacy rests on a supposed "identification" of those who govern with the governed ("the people"). It is in the specific form of identification that modern dictatorship differs from other kinds of democratic government.

Schmitt's assertion that "dictatorship is not antithetical to democracy" (28; see also 16, 32) is bound to appear paradoxical, and we should not discount the unsavory agenda that probably lurks behind it. But taken at face value, and given the very broad notion of democracy being invoked, it seems to me not only true, but importantly so. Modern dictatorships have indeed generally claimed to represent the will of the people, and not by accident. In modern times, the traditional view of human society as part of a larger cosmic or religious order has ceased to command widespread allegiance. As a result, the legitimacy of political power, if it is to enjoy general acceptance, can no longer be convincingly traced back to some source outside the human realm. This is an idea to which I shall return. But for now we can observe that one natural conclusion to draw from it is that legitimacy must derive from the people as such. In claiming (however disingenuously) to express the will of the people, and not to reflect some sacred or cosmic order, modern dictatorship has at least paid lip service to the spirit of modern times.

The point at which we must begin to resist the course of Schmitt's argument is his understanding of this notion of (democratic) "identification." Schmitt talks of "identification" (*Identifizierung*) because he wishes to contrast it with "identity" (*Identität*). There cannot and should not be, according to him, a perfect coincidence between the will of those who govern and that of the governed (26–8). Identity is first of all impossible, since the will of the people, to become politically effective, must find expression in some political form, and no political form (universal suffrage, referenda, reduced terms of elective office) can be guaranteed to channel faithfully the popular will. Second, identity need not be desirable, to whatever degree it might be achieved. It is

lunacy, Schmitt points out, to approve of the will of the people apart
from any consideration of the worth of what the people will. "As soon
as democracy takes on the content of a self-sufficient value," he writes
(28), "then one can no longer remain (in a formal sense) a democrat
at any price."

For both these reasons, then, Schmitt concludes (28) that "democracy seems fated . . . to destroy itself in the problem of the formation
of a will." Of course, Schmitt believes that this problem is indeed
soluble, and in terms of his broad notion of democratic (i.e., nondynas-
tic) legitimacy. But his solution calls for a frank recognition that identification, not identity, must characterize the relation between those who
govern and those who are governed. What is required is that someone
claim, and be able to enforce acceptance of his claim, that some set of
political forms, some institutional arrangement, expresses the will of
the people. That "someone" is the authority Schmitt calls the *sovereign*.
And the claim the sovereign makes is not meant to be an independently testable truth, since the faithful expression of the popular will is
neither possible nor in itself desirable. It is rather his authoritative
decision that certain institutions and procedures will count as expressing the popular will.[3] Not a true identity between government and
people, but a manufactured identification of the popular will with the
sovereign's will is Schmitt's solution to the problem of democratic will
formation. "Auctoritas, non veritas facit legem" – so Schmitt quotes
Hobbes for his own ends.[4]

Insofar as Schmitt's famous decisionism is the conclusion of an
argument (as opposed to a preexisting *parti pris*), it depends on two
assumptions: (1) that he has correctly analyzed the problems of democratic will formation and (2) that decisionism is the only viable solution
to these problems. Let us begin, then, by asking whether he is right
that there cannot and should not be a perfect match (i.e., one that
actually exists, as opposed to one manufactured by the sovereign's
dictate) between the will of those who govern and the will of the
governed. It is undeniable that any set of institutions and procedures
can fall short of faithfully expressing the will of the people. But this
scarcely entails that some political forms will not generally fulfill this
function better than others. (Compare suffrage based on property

3 Carl Schmitt, *Political Theology*, trans. G. Schwab (Cambridge, Mass.: MIT Press, 1985),
  pp. 6–10.
4 Ibid., p. 33.

qualifications with universal male suffrage and that with universal suffrage.)[5] Nor does it render pointless the use of a mix of political forms (as in a bicameral legislature) to correct for the possible failures of any single form. On the issue of feasibility, Schmitt's argument is feeble. That no setup for allowing expression to the popular will is foolproof is neither here nor there. What Schmitt would have had to show to make his case, but did not, is that no setup does better in this task than any other, or that those that do better still do not succeed to any reasonable degree or with any significant frequency. Schmitt does not even formulate the problem in these terms, and that is why here his argument lacks all force.

(I should note that Schmitt is hardly alone in resorting to the tactic of criticizing some practice simply on the grounds that it cannot guarantee success in achieving the goals it sets itself. The ploy is used by many who, instead of engaging in a reasonable discussion about the pros and cons of the available alternatives, wish only to open a breach for their own opinions.)

On the question of desirability, however, Schmitt's argument has real merit, although as he himself acknowledges it is not very novel. No one in his right mind would wish to approve of whatever the will of the people (or even a majority of them) might affirm. The "people," and majorities, are as capable of tyranny as any despot. Of course, it is not easy to see just what the "will of the people" could mean, apart from how it might be expressed through some political institution or in the form of a mass movement. Yet the point remains: given whatever expression of the popular will one favors, it cannot be acceptable to claim that it is to be upheld whatever it may affirm.

Schmitt's remarks here rehearse, however, one of the main themes of the liberal tradition. The tyrannical potential contained in the idea of popular sovereignty was already emphasized by nineteenth-century liberals such as Benjamin Constant and François Guizot,[6] and this concern has found its canonical expression in Tocqueville's notion of the "tyranny of the majority." Accordingly, liberal thinkers have insisted

---

5 Moreover, there were, historically, other rationales for universal suffrage besides its capacity to express the will of the governed. Not the least of them was its utility in discouraging *coups d'état* and revolutions, which become difficult to justify once "the people have spoken." See Albert O. Hirschman, *Shifting Involvements* (Princeton, N.J.: Princeton University Press, 1982), pp. 112–17.

6 On the liberal effort to accommodate the democratic principle during this period of French thought, see Pierre Rosanvallon, *Le Moment Guizot* (Paris: Gallimard, 1985).

on subordinating the democratic ideal of popular self-government to certain principles guaranteeing individual freedoms. This liberal-democratic position is what Schmitt himself refers to by the term "parliamentary democracy" (or *heutiger Parlamentarismus* in the original German). We must now examine why in his eyes it is, at the level of principle, an impossible position to maintain. Only if he is right about the futility of the *liberal* solution to the second problem of democratic will formation (i.e., the undeniable possibility that the popular will may prove morally unacceptable) can his own *decisionistic* solution to this problem begin to look plausible.

2. The Coherence of Liberal Democracy

Schmitt's basic point is that the very idea of liberal democracy is incoherent since it rests on two distinct principles of legitimacy (15, 34).[7] The democratic principle, as already noted, maintains that legitimate political power has its source in the collective will of the people. By contrast, the liberal principle claims, according to Schmitt, that there are true or objectively valid principles of government, that public discussion is our means of access to them, and that parliament forms the best organ for bringing this public discussion to bear on the exercise of political power. It is from this fundamental principle connecting truth, public discussion, and parliament, he claims, that the familiar liberal norms – the protection of free speech and of free association and the division of powers – are derived (36).

During the nineteenth century, writes Schmitt (2, 15), contingent historical factors led to a convergence of liberal and democratic thought: they often had the same advocates and the same opponents. But by their nature, the two principles pull in contrary directions, as we can see now, Schmitt insists, in contemporary parliaments: the liberal principle has largely given way to a degenerate version of the democratic principle, since government by discussion is increasingly replaced by negotiation among representatives of special-interest groups, and debate on the floor of parliament superseded by committee work (5, 49–50). To grasp the antagonism between the two principles, Schmitt remarks (3), we need only reflect upon the quandary a

---

7 Schmitt's claim that there is a *fundamentaler Gegensatz* between liberalism and democracy cannot be explained away as simply a ploy in what is a partisan pamphlet. It recurs in his later systematic treatise, *Verfassungslehre* (Munich: Duncker & Humblot, 1928), pp. 201, 233, 309.

member of parliament in a liberal democracy must face; is it his duty to seek the truth or to faithfully represent the interests of his constituency?

How good is this argument that liberal democracy is by its nature an oxymoron, a square circle? There is no doubt that the liberal and democratic principles can pull in opposite directions; that is hardly a novel insight. Not only was it a constant theme of a turn-of-the-century elite theorist such as Gaetano Mosca, but it was also, as I noted earlier, a central concern of liberal thinkers throughout the nineteenth century. But contrary to what Schmitt supposes, the possible opposition between the two principles does not imply that liberal democracy is an intellectual hodgepodge, sustained by the blind hope that the two principles will not conflict too often. Instead, liberal democracy consists in a *ranking* of the two principles, a subordination of one to the other. The liberal freedoms set limits to democratic government, and in particular to the form it usually takes, majority rule. Nor is this ranking a mere makeshift. On the contrary, democracy is made subordinate to liberal principles precisely because the value of democratic institutions is held to lie chiefly, if not exclusively, in their being the best *means for guaranteeing* liberal freedoms.

One of the astonishing things about Schmitt, in this and in other writings, is that he does not even mention this principled way of combining and ordering the two principles. Perhaps the oversight is not so inexplicable, or indeed unrepresentative. In this century there has been a tendency to suppose that the ideal of democratic self-rule must aim to stand on its own, that popular sovereignty must present itself as the ultimate source of political principles. Democracy has been trumpeted as the supreme value, the single fundamental ideal of political association. As I argue more thoroughly in the last chapter of this book, this view of democracy does not in the end make sense. Democratic self-rule, in any form likely to command our assent, must itself rest on an antecedent, "liberal" respect for individual freedom. Strangely enough, Mosca himself, whose disabused opinions of parliamentary practice preceded and surely influenced Schmitt's own, came around to just this conclusion in his later defense of "mixed government," particularly in the new edition of his *Elementi di scienza politica* of 1923, the year in which Schmitt's book appeared.[8]

8 See Gaetano Mosca, *The Ruling Class*, translation of *Elementi di scienza politica* by Hannah D. Kahn (New York: McGraw-Hill, 1939), pp. 147, 244, 428, on mixed government combining liberal and democratic principles. For his distinction between

Liberal democracy, so understood, continues to present, of course, problems of interpretation and justification. My point is that, failing to grasp the basic character of liberal democracy, Schmitt can be expected to have little to contribute to the solution of these problems, despite the now-increasing interest in his writings. This must suffice for Schmitt's principal argument against the coherence of liberal democracy. He also makes two subsidiary criticisms, each of which deserves some remarks.

First, there is his observation (20, 49) that modern parliaments rely more and more on committees instead of open discussion, as well as on the negotiation of compromises between special-interest groups. The fact was undeniable in Schmitt's day as in our own. But what is its significance? Why should it signal a fatal flaw in liberal democracy? Some issues might indeed be handled more fairly if they were brought before the parliament as a whole and if they were addressed head-on instead of being merely deferred by ad hoc compromises. Schmitt offers no reasons, however, for thinking that liberal democracies lack the means for making these corrections.

But also, why should reliance on committees and the search for compromises be in themselves unacceptable or incompatible with the ideals of liberal democracy? Committee decisions, unlike the majority-rule decisions of assemblies, can often be positive rather than zero sum. Whereas voting generally makes some winners and others losers, logrolling – the favorite mechanism of committees – allows some to win on one issue in return for letting others win on another.[9] Consequently, some problems will be better handled in committee, that is, with greater justice: individual rights will be better respected and greater attention given to the strength of different convictions in society. Compromise has frequently a similar advantage, when each of the opposing sides is allowed to win something, but not everything. Bargain and compromise need not imply betrayal of principle, though a certain strand of German political thought has often suggested that they do.

Second, there is Schmitt's claim that the liberal principle of govern-

---

the two principles, see pp. 254, 395, 409. In my final chapter, I criticize Jürgen Habermas for believing that democratic self-rule can serve as the ultimate value of political association. It is ironic that in one point, then, Habermas makes the same mistake as Schmitt, whom he has otherwise regarded for so long as a philosophical bête noire.

9 There are some insightful remarks on this subject in Giovanni Sartori, *The Theory of Democracy Revisted* (Chatham: Chatham House, 1987), vol. 1, pp. 227–32.

ment by discussion involves a "comprehensive metaphysical system" (35). The author of *Political Theology* (1922) was not the sort, of course, to use the term "metaphysical" as necessarily a reproach. His complaint was rather that (1) liberalism has refused to acknowledge its metaphysical core, and that (2) liberal metaphysics, though consistent enough, is either implausible or politically inept. According to Schmitt, liberalism assumes that open discussion converges naturally on the truth. This is either because some sort of preestablished harmony is supposed to connect the two ("that the truth can be found through an unrestrained clash of opinion and that competition will produce harmony," 35) or because truth is thought to be nothing more than ongoing discussion itself ("truth . . . becomes a mere function of the eternal competition of opinions," 35).[10] The first version rests but on a pious hope, while the second, Schmitt notes triumphantly, shows more clearly still how little understanding liberal thought has of the reality of political life. "The political," in Schmitt's view, has to do essentially not with discussion, as liberalism supposes, but instead with containing the ever-present threat of disorder through authority and decision.

It is true that nothing recommends either of the two positions Schmitt assigns to what he chooses to call "liberal metaphysics." But what have they to do with liberalism?

Schmitt selects François Guizot (1787–1874) as his chief example of the liberal metaphysician. So it will be instructive to look indeed at Guizot's way of justifying the principle of government by discussion. In reality, nothing could have been further from Guizot's mind than to declare that open discussion leads inherently to the truth. His point of view was, rather, a thoroughgoing *fallibilism* (no doubt connected with his Calvinist upbringing): no individual or group has been given an inside track, a prior guarantee of discerning the moral and political truth. His doctrine of the *souveraineté de la raison* was meant to exclude any political form, even the people, from counting as the unquestionable source of truth, as the sovereign source of authority. It is precisely this fallibilism that, according to Guizot, makes representative government and, more broadly, public opinion, necessary features of a just regime. Their function is to pool as many different opinions as possible since the validity of none of them can be assured a priori, and to keep open the possibility of changing decisions already made should better arguments come to light.

10 Schmitt's *Political Theology*, too, refers to a "liberal metaphysics," which "wants to dissolve metaphysical truth in a discussion" (pp. 62–3).

Consider the following passage from Guizot's *Histoire des origines du gouvernement représentatif* (1821):

> Sovereignty belongs as a right to no individual whatever, since the perfect and continued apprehension, the fixed and inviolable application of justice and of reason, do not belong to our imperfect nature. Representative government rests upon this truth. . . . The representative form of government, never forgetting that reason and justice, and consequently a right to sovereignty, do not reside fully and constantly in any part of the earth, presumes that they are to be found in the majority, but does not attribute them to it as their certain and abiding qualities. At the very moment when it presumes that the majority is right, it does not forget that it may be wrong and its concern is to give full opportunity to the minority of proving that it is in fact right, and of becoming in its turn the majority.[11]

As this passage shows, Guizot did not believe, contrary to Schmitt's allegation, that parliamentary government leads inherently to the truth. Instead, his view was that no form of government does so – not monarchy, not democracy, not majority rule, not even parliament, and that it is just this fact that offers the basic rationale for parliamentary government. Since a sounder view is always possible, open discussion is necessary to ensure the revisability of decisions. Though not foolproof, parliament is thus a mechanism more likely to disclose the truth.[12] Guizot himself appealed to the "sovereignty of reason" to limit the franchise, believing that those without sufficient property could not be trusted to look beyond their own needs toward the common good. But precisely a fallibilist outlook shows, of course, how unfounded this sort of discrimination is.

---

11 François Guizot, *Histoire des origines du gouvernement représentatif* (Paris: Didier, 1855), pp. 93, 111–12; translation from idem, *Historical Essays and Lectures* (University of Chicago Press, 1972), pp. 45, 57.

12 Cf. François Guizot, "Philosophie politique: de la souveraineté" (1821–3), § 21: "Le droit de la liberté ne se fonde que sur la chance de l'illégitimité du pouvoir. . . . il exige que, sur cette question, le débat demeure toujours ouvert, qu'aucune force, majorité ou autre, ne se prévale de l'obéissance qui lui est due pour se soustraire à l'examen. L'homme doit obéissance au pouvoir dont la légitimité est probable, mais c'est seulement à des probabilités qu'il obéit. Le meilleur gouvernement est celui qui les donne plus grandes; aucun système de gouvernement ne peut donner rien de plus: et celui-là seul est fondé sur la vérité, celui-là seul respecte et garantit le droit, qui prend cette condition de l'homme pour principe fondamental et ne la perd jamais de vue soit dans ses doctrines, soit dans ses institutions"; reprinted in P. Rosanvallon's edition of Guizot's *Histoire de la civilisation en Europe* (Paris: Hachette, 1985), pp. 377–8.

Whether Guizot's fallibilism is "metaphysical" or not seems a matter of terminology. It is, in any case, something that liberals need not (and have not been inclined to) fear acknowledging.

Our conclusion, then, is that Schmitt's critique of liberal democracy is astonishingly weak. He is right that having the exercise of political power depend on the actual will of the people is unacceptable. But he offers no sound arguments against the ability of the liberal principle to correct for the defects in democratic will formation. He fails even to perceive this two-tiered character of liberal democracy. As a result, Schmitt provides no good reason to accept his decisionism – that is, his thesis that only decisions by fiat, emanating from the true sovereign and manufacturing what shall count as the popular will, can put the democratic principle in an intellectually respectable form.

3. Discussion and Stability

These remarks suffice, I believe, to show that Schmitt's thought does not really pose the serious challenge to liberal democracy that many have supposed. Yet I have one more objection, an important one and of a different kind, since it points out how a fundamental assumption of Schmitt's thought works against his own antiliberal, antidemocratic commitments.

As I observed at the outset, a key premise of Schmitt's argument is that the stability of a political system depends on whether its principle of legitimacy is perceived as justified. This is why his criticisms of parliamentary democracy focus throughout on the tenability of its principles. Now it is time to show why this strategy of argument subverts Schmitt's own agenda. Intending thus to expose liberal democracy at its weakest point, Schmitt has unwittingly provided the materials for recognizing one of its strongest supports.

In Schmitt's conception, a principle of legitimacy is the fundamental norm that a political system sets itself. Naturally, this conception leaves open the possibility of concluding that a given principle is in fact unjustified, even morally unacceptable. But more significant for Schmitt's purposes (and for our own) is that this conception does not imply that the political system actually lives up to its announced principle of legitimacy. There is an important difference between a principle of legitimacy and actual practice. As a result, we may find ourselves regretting that a political system's practice does not match its principles. Conversely, we might actually welcome a disparity between practice and principle if we believe that although the principle is intellectually insupportable, actual practice is largely beneficial.

Precisely this second sort of mismatch between principle and practice is what Schmitt claims to find in contemporary parliamentary democracy. At the level of principles of legitimacy, he believes (for the reasons I have discussed) that it is incoherent. But he is willing to admit that in practice it is preferable to the available alternatives (3) and that the liberal freedoms it actually secures are not to be abandoned (50). How sincerely he means this we may leave aside. Still, the crucial first premise of Schmitt's argument is that parliamentary democracy cannot continue on the basis that in practice, if not in principle, it is superior to the alternatives (3, 8). To welcome this sort of mismatch between principle and practice is, according to Schmitt, shortsighted. In the long run, people cannot maintain their allegiance to a political system simply by repeating to themselves "What else?" (3). They need to be able to give themselves positive reasons for thinking their form of political association justified. It is in these terms, stressing the need for political allegiance to be animated by principled justification, that in the preface to the second edition of his book, Schmitt dismisses Richard Thoma's objection that practically (despite the conceptual untenability of its principles) parliamentary democracy remains viable.

This basic premise of Schmitt's argument seems indeed correct. Political stability does not always require that actual practice live up to announced principles; generally, it demands only that there be the feasibility of reforms that will overcome this sort of disparity. But political stability does rest on a widespread confidence that the principles are themselves in good order and not subject to reasonable doubt. For political principles (in contrast to other sorts of norms) are ones that people will not only be judged by, but also be compelled to comply with, by force if need be. The use of force will not long meet with acceptance if it is seen to be unjustified. The point has not been lost on the many different political regimes that make up human history: not one has failed to offer some account of its legitimacy.

Yet this premise, though correct, dooms the conclusions that Schmitt ultimately intends to draw. Far from revealing the intellectual and thus practical fragility of liberal democracy, it points to one important reason that the liberal principle of government by discussion is indispensable. For can we believe that some political principle is not open to doubt if we are kept from discussing it freely and openly? To the extent that we have been shaped by certain modern developments, and precisely by those Schmitt himself assigns to the modern "democratic" age, we cannot. If we no longer believe – and Schmitt is no exception – that the ultimate court of appeal for normative questions is divine revelation or the natural order of the cosmos, we cannot hope to achieve general acceptance of political principles except insofar as they can become the object of free and open discussion. Under modern conditions, political legitimacy cannot succeed by deferring to revelation or to the evidence of nature. It must draw upon a public realm of argument and discussion.

I should observe that this rationale for government by discussion, based as it is on the need for political stability, is not the only argument (nor indeed the principal one) that can be offered for liberal democracy. Stability is not the ultimate value by which a political system is to be judged. Justice is a more important political value, though stability is itself often a sign of justice. Moreover, it is best, as I explained in the previous chapter and will explore further in the last, not to identify the political significance of modernity with the demise of religious and teleological worldviews. No doubt their waning has been a feature of the modern age. But from the standpoint of liberal democracy, the significant aspect of modernity must be the realization that reasonable people tend naturally to disagree about the merits of such worldviews and of so-called postmetaphysical attempts to replace them.[13] Liberal democracy must aim to appeal even to the many who continue to affirm older conceptions of sacred or natural order. For these reasons, basing the system of government by discussion on the principle of equal respect for all who are to be subject to political principles seems to me more central to the self-understanding of our political life.[14]

It remains true, nonetheless, that in insisting on the link between political stability and the perceived legitimacy of declared principles, and not merely on the preferability of actual practice, Schmitt has not, contrary to his intention, uncovered the Achilles' heel of liberal democracy. He has instead uncovered one of its strengths.

---

13 See Chapters 7 and 10, this volume. In the French version of this essay (*Modernité et morale*, pp. 207–20), I wrote that to the extent that Schmitt refused to align himself with the idea that in questions of normative justification we can no longer defer to revelation or cosmic order, but only to public argument, his political thought is irrelevant to modern problems of political order. This verdict now seems to me unfair. It rests on too narrow a conception of modernity, as I indicate here.

14 See Chapter 6, this volume.

9

MODERNITY AND THE DISUNITY
OF REASON

One of the enduring concerns of modern thought has been the nature of modernity itself. Since the sixteenth century fundamental shifts in orientation have transformed religion, science, ethics, and art. These changes have seemed connected with the emerging features of modern society – technological progress, capitalism, liberal democracy. But in addition, modern thought has been from the beginning characteristically self-reflective. The cultural and social transformations of the modern age have often been driven and absorbed by the image modern thought has projected of itself as having broken decisively with the outlook of former times. Today this self-image surely seems too stark, and yet a new sense of continuity with the past is itself part of modernity's ongoing reflection upon itself.

During the nineteenth century modernity was often regarded as an age of transition. In thinkers otherwise as diverse as Chateaubriand, Comte, Mill, and Arnold there recurs the view that modern times are a troubled interregnum between one epoch of order (the Middle Ages) and another yet to come. The delayed arrival of the new order was seen as a burden to be met with intellectual courage, as when Arnold described himself as "wandering between two worlds, one dead, the other powerless to be born."[1] This view, too, seems not very attractive.

---

1 Matthew Arnold, "Stanzas from the Grande Chartreuse," 85–6.

Not only has the new age of faith still not come, but the pace of transformation, the creation of conditions setting us off from the past, has accelerated. To a large extent, change itself has become the status quo.

It is therefore more promising to look at modernity in its own terms, not as a way station to something else. Max Weber's theory of rationalization is surely the most influential example of this approach. Modern thought, according to Weber, is characterized by an increasingly "disenchanted" view of the world. In earlier times the ultimate purposes of life were seen as part of the fabric of the world, as part of the Greek "cosmos" or of Christian "creation"; the description of fact and the affirmation of norms were not sharply distinguished. The modern era, by contrast, has recast rationality as simply the calculation of efficient means to given ends. This narrower, instrumental conception of reason was what, in Weber's eyes, brought about the unprecedented increase in knowledge and power, prediction and control, characteristic of modern science. But it has also meant that ultimate purposes, and the good and the beautiful generally, have come to seem a matter of merely subjective conviction. For Weber, this development was as unstoppable as it was terrifying. Not surprisingly, other thinkers have wondered whether the rationalization of our knowledge of the world must entail the irrationality of morality and art.

One of the most impressive efforts to work out a broader view of reason and a more hospitable view of modernity has been the recent writings of Jürgen Habermas. Against Weber, he has insisted that we must understand modernity in terms that allow scientific knowledge, morality, and art all to embody forms of rational thought. In his view, the course of modern thought does not lie in the "Dialectic of Enlightenment" the earlier Frankfurt School of Horkheimer and Adorno evoked, in which the expansion of our scientific control of the world goes hand in hand with the erosion of recognized moral limits to its use, and where the promised means of human emancipation become new "mind-forg'd manacles" of enslavement.

At the heart of Habermas's thinking is the idea that fundamentally reason is not instrumental, but *communicative*. By this he means that the exercise of reason consists in thinking or acting on the basis of reasons that we suppose others, too, under suitably ideal conditions of discussion, would acknowledge. It is through language and its three distinct functions – to describe facts, to invoke rules, and to express states of mind – that we exercise this capacity. So being rational involves supposing that one has reasons for the truth of the factual claims one makes, reasons for the correctness of the rules or norms one invokes, reasons for the truthfulness or sincerity of one's efforts at self-expression.

Though I share Habermas's search for an ecumenical conception of reason, I have doubts about his "communicative" theory of ideal discussion, which I explain in the following chapter.[2] What I want to examine here is a further and distinctive element of his theory of modernity. Habermas argues that science, morality, and art are all forms of rational activity because each focuses centrally (if not exclusively) on one of the three forms of rational thought just distinguished – describing the way the world is, devising rules of conduct, and expressing states of mind.[3] He thereby assumes that Weber was right on a very important point. This is the idea that modern thought has brought about a *differentiation* between scientific knowledge, morality, and art. He holds on to this Weberian thesis even as he insists that such a differentiation rests on an underlying *unity of reason*. As a result, Habermas is able to believe that modernity is fundamentally at one with itself. The legitimacy of modern science does not impugn the legitimacy of morality, nor does either deny the legitimacy of art, so long as all are properly understood as specializations of a single idea of reason. By thus giving each of these three activities a specialized task within the unity of reason, Habermas's theory of modernity aims indeed to renew the perspective of Kant's three critiques.

The crucial question, however, is whether this conception of modernity is too harmonious to be true. I am convinced that it is, and that this is a central example of the modern theme to which I have referred repeatedly in this book – the recognition that on issues of ultimate value reasonable people tend naturally to disagree. There is not the unity of reason Habermas supposes, because modern science, morality, and art have in fact been deeply at odds with one another. Have not, for example, some of the greatest works of modern art undertaken to challenge the scientific conception of the world – countering "Newton-

---

2 See also my *Patterns of Moral Complexity*, pp. 55–9.
3 For Habermas's account of communicative reason, see particularly "Was heisst Universalpragmatik?" especially pp. 427–40 in *Vorstudien und Ergänzungen zur Theorie des kommunikativen Handelns* (Frankfurt: Suhrkamp, 1984); and idem, "Wahrheitstheorien," ibid., pp. 127–83. For his differentiation theory of modernity, see "Aspekte der Handlungsrationalität," ibid., pp. 441–72; and *Der philosophische Diskurs der Moderne* (Frankfurt: Suhrkamp, 1985), pp. 30, 137, 360–8, 393.

ian" reason with the imagination, seeking to overcome the attitude of detached manipulation in which the scientific mind confronts the world?

To see the force of this question, consider the precise role that Habermas's theory of modernity assigns to art. The function of art can no longer be to tell us something important about life or to urge us to change the way we live, for these matters belong to the special provinces of knowledge and morality. Art can undertake only to express, however powerfully, the particular perspective or cast of mind of the artist. We are to value the artist's vision independently, it seems, of what he has seen or whether it should matter. Otherwise we will be crossing the legitimate bounds of art, asking questions of it that can be answered only in other domains. It must be said that this is a rather trivializing view of art (though there are many who share it). It makes the work of art little more than the artist's personalized calling card. Habermas himself seems unsatisfied with it, since he also assigns to art another more substantial function, which is to disclose worlds of meaning (*Welterschliessung*).[4] The trouble with this claim is not that it is wrong, but that it confuses the neat division of labor that Habermas's theory of modernity sets up among science, morality, and art. Are not scientific breakthroughs and moral insights also ways of disclosing new meanings? And is not problem solving, which Habermas in this context contrasts with disclosure, just as important in the work of art as in scientific and moral thinking? The result seems to be that science, morality, and art cannot be so finely compartmentalized as Habermas supposes. And this means that the different domains of modern thought may be genuinely at odds with one another in a way that Habermas disallows.

Few people have explored this possibility so insightfully as Karl Heinz Bohrer, in the series of books he has devoted to the place of aesthetic sensibility within modern thought. (Their focus has been almost exclusively on literature.) Professor of literature at the Universität Bielefeld and editor of the prestigious review *Merkur,* Bohrer has become one of the philosophically most talented and provocative literary theorists in Germany today.[5] Against theories of modernity like that

---

4 Habermas, *Der philosophische Diskurs der Moderne,* pp. 241–3.
5 In this essay I am concerned chiefly with the following books by Bohrer: *Die Ästhetik des Schreckens* (hereafter, AS) (Frankfurt: Ullstein, 1983; originally 1978); *Plötzlichkeit. Zum Augenblick des ästhetischen Scheins* (P) (Frankfurt: Suhrkamp, 1981); *Der romantische Brief. Die Entstehung ästhetischer Subjektivität* (RB) (Frankfurt: Suhrkamp, 1989;

of Habermas, he has argued that the venerable model of "identity in difference" does not fit the import of artistic development since the early Romantic age. There is, according to Bohrer, no underlying notion of reason in modern thought that unites art with science and morality. On the contrary, modernity is fundamentally a disunity: the modern aesthetic sensibility, Bohrer claims, stands opposed to the rationalization characteristic of modern science and ethics. I shall look in some detail at Bohrer's arguments in order to follow one fault line in the disunity of modern reason. Since Bohrer believes this opposition of modern aesthetics to the reigning ideas of science and ethics has its roots in Romantic thought, the discussion will bring out a dimension of Romanticism's contribution to our modern condition besides the one I examined in Chapter 6.

Bohrer holds that a common ground between the different domains of modern thought does exist in what he calls an outlook of "artificiality." This notion seems identical with what Weber called "disenchantment" – the disappearance of the conviction that nature itself speaks directly of our ultimate purposes.[6] Modern thought, he writes, generally proceeds after the demise of nature, "nach der Natur," in the words of the title of one of his recent books. If this thesis is meant to imply that the world itself has no room for value, then I do not myself think it is correct (see Chapter 5). But there is no denying the prevalence of this point of view in modern thought, and here the important thing is to see what effect Bohrer finds it has had on the modern aesthetic sensibility. Without seeking to re-enchant the world and to return to the more innocent view that nature and culture are congruent, the modern aesthetic is sharply at odds, he claims, with the rationalizing spirit in which modern science and morality have coped with disenchantment. The hallmarks of this rationalizing spirit have been a conception of nature as the object of prediction and control and a conviction in the inherent (if not inevitable) tendency toward moral progress. Against this outlook the modern aesthetic, according to Bohrer, has set the power of the aesthetic imagination. Not only has it abandoned the "classicist" assumption that the work of art should reflect reality, that the beautiful is a species of the true, but its pursuit

---

originally 1987); *Nach der Natur* (NN) (Munich: Hanser, 1988); *Die Kritik der Romantik. Der Verdacht der Philosophie gegen die literarische Moderne* (KR) (Frankfurt: Suhrkamp, 1989).

6 NN, p. 210. Cf. also RB, pp. 13–14.

of irony and fantasy poses a challenge to the hegemony of the reality principle according to which the world is to be known in order to be controlled. Similarly, not only has it left behind the view that art must be morally instructive, but it has shown a fascination for the phenomena of evil, violence, and horror for their own sake that seems hardly compatible with the goal of moral progress. In general, the modern aesthetic expresses a disenchantment with modern reason itself. Bohrer's thesis is that we must learn to acknowledge modernity's "Janus-faced origin – namely Enlightenment and Romanticism, teleology and destruction."[7]

According to Bohrer the roots of this aesthetic lie in Romanticism. One of his constant aims, therefore, has been to counter the "legend" that Romanticism, particularly in Germany, was a reactionary movement, a retreat from the reality of modern life.[8] Bohrer does not deny the presence of feudal nostalgia in the writings of such figures as Novalis and the later Friedrich Schlegel. But this is not, he insists, the whole story. It leaves out the aesthetic innovations of *irony* and *fantasy* that made German Romantic thought anything but a return to the past. If the cliché of Romantic reaction has endured, reaffirmed again and again in German philosophy from Hegel's time to today, it is because, Bohrer claims, these aesthetic revolutions have been ignored or misconceived. They have not been seen for what they are, precisely because of the widespread modern confidence in scientific and moral rationality that they disavow. They have brought about an *autonomy* of the aesthetic realm that differentiation theories of modern rationality, from Kant to Weber to Habermas, cannot comprehend.[9]

Bohrer cites some exceptions to this general insensitivity to German Romantic aesthetics. Walter Benjamin is one. Another is Heine, whose *Die romantische Schule* (1835) was drawn between Enlightenment-inspired censure and enthusiastic appreciation of Romantic fantasy. The formidable obstacle Bohrer sees standing in the way of a proper appreciation, however, is the "classicist" view that the work of art is to be judged in terms of its capacity for truth. It is because classicism was

---

7 NN, p. 209. For his view of the *"Zwiespalt der Moderne,"* see AS, pp. 19–20; RB, pp. 8, 14, 50, 266; NN, pp. 110, 224–6; KR, pp. 18, 203, 308.
8 NN, pp. 143, 153; KR, pp. 7, 9, 12, 17, 203.
9 For Bohrer's conception of the autonomy of the aesthetic, see AS, pp. 59, 64, 489; P, p. 125; RB, pp. 14, 50, 61, 161; NN, pp. 95, 110, 220; KR, pp. 14, 27, 82, 145, 168, 191, 273. For his explicit criticisms of Habermas, see P, p. 214; RB, pp. 11, 25, 217; NN, pp. 110–12, 159, 209, 222.

so powerfully enshrined in Hegel's aesthetics, and because it has been so widely shared generally, that the verdict of principleless frivolity that Hegel lodged against the Romantics has been so influential.

Consider for a moment the basic elements of Hegel's classicism. Art is a vehicle of truth, Hegel argued, in that it presents imaginary forms of life and nature as expressions of a deeper reality. Being dependent on the sensuous image ("appearance"), art is not as high a mode of thought as philosophy or religion, which can proceed in pure thought; but it remains a kind of knowledge, not mere play. Since according to Hegel the mind's understanding of the relation between appearance and reality and of its own relation to truth has developed historically toward ever more adequate conceptions, his lectures on aesthetics were devoted to charting the history of art in these terms. It was thus that Hegel made his famous declaration that for us moderns, art must be "a thing of the past." The claim was not that there would be no art, but that art would no longer have the significance it once possessed. This is because, Hegel observed, ours is a "reflective culture," committed to explaining the world and our conduct within it in terms of general principles. Art is seen as an unnecessary detour: the truths it contains are ones that now, if not in earlier times, we can grasp directly in abstract thought.

In Hegel's eyes, German Romantic thought, particularly the notion of irony developed by Schlegel, was a perverse symptom of the modern transcendence of art. Irony consists generally in standing back and refusing to identify with whatever particular form of thought and action one at the same time affirms. Hegel argued that it came to play a central role in Schlegel's aesthetics, according to which the modern work of art makes a point of not affirming itself wholeheartedly, precisely because art itself can no longer command our full conviction. Schlegel extolled irony as a way of life and so did no more, Hegel charged, than preach frivolity, because he would not budge from the standpoint of art even after reason itself had left art behind.[10]

The important thing to note about Hegel's classicism and his condemnation of the German Romantics is that it does not depend on the peculiarities of his own speculative philosophy. It is instead a rather

---

10 For Hegel's critique of Romantic irony, see *Vorlesungen über die Ästhetik* (Frankfurt: Suhrkamp Theorie-Werkausgabe, 1970), vol. 1, pp. 92–9. For his view that art is now "a thing of the past," see ibid., vol. 1, pp. 23–5. And for Bohrer's view of Hegel's aesthetics, see KR, pp. 138–81.

widespread view about the nature of art and the apparent irrelevance of art in modern times. Bohrer holds that this conception of art is irresistible so long as we accept its underlying premise, namely that the function of art is to express truth, to reflect reality. Just this premise, however, is in his view what German romantic aesthetics and modern art generally have sought to overthrow. The modern aesthetic, according to Bohrer, refuses to see art as a form of reason, now outdated, precisely because it sees art as a challenge to what reason has become in modern times.[11]

The two central Romantic contributions to this modern aesthetic were according to Bohrer the notions of irony and fantasy.[12] The first derived more from the early Jena-centered group of Novalis, Schlegel, and Tieck (1790s), the second more from the later period of Kleist, von Arnim, and Brentano (first decade of the nineteenth century), though both were present throughout. They differ in the sort of opposition they express to the modern notion of reason. Irony operates with what might be called a *surplus* of consciousness. It challenges the idea that the function of thought is to represent and control reality, by making thought turn on itself and draw back from what it appears to assert. It is important to note, Bohrer insists, that irony as Schlegel championed it is not a subjective attitude of the artist toward his work, but rather an objective feature of the work itself, a dimension of its style and organization. Through various devices, the work of art calls attention to its own fictionality, warding off the inclination to measure it against reality. Precisely because irony aims to ensure the aesthetic autonomy of the work of art, and thus to resist the hegemony of modern standards of reason, it is wrong according to Bohrer to discount it as just a sign of a lack of conviction. Hegel, and those who have followed his lead, have failed to see what is at stake. Irony, as Schlegel himself maintained, is in "the most holy earnest."[13]

11 See, e.g., Bohrer, KR, p. 308: "Wenn die metaphysischen Bestände einerseits nicht mehr verfügbar scheinen, die moderne Lebenswelt andererseits nicht das von der Aufklärung verheissene 'Glück' garantieren kann, tritt die moderne Kunst an die leere Stelle, indem sie romantisiert."

12 KR, pp. 11, 40, 174, 181, 242, 272. Bohrer himself does not distinguish between irony and fantasy in terms of a surplus and deficit of consciousness, though this is in keeping with what he does say about them. I explore these Romantic notions further in *Romantic Legacy*.

13 See F. Schlegel, "Über Goethes Meister" (1798): "Man lasse sich also dadurch, dass der Dichter selbst die Personen und die Begebenheiten so leicht und so launig zu nehmen, den Helden fast nie ohne Ironie zu erwähnen und auf sein Meisterwerk

Fantasy, by contrast, opposes modern rationality by means of a *deficit* of consciousness. It consists generally in freeing the imagination from control by considerations of what is reasonable or appropriate. The cardinal example is Tieck's effort in his stories (*der blonde Eckbert, der Runenberg*) to blur the difference between the everyday and the marvelous. "There is a way," Tieck once remarked, "of regarding the most ordinary life as a fairy-tale, and similarly we can come to feel at home with the most marvelous as though it were the most everyday."[14] Another example is Kleist's brilliant essay, *Über die allmähliche Verfertigung des Gedankens beim Reden* (1805–6), in which Kleist argued that often the best way to work out an opinion on some subject is not to stand back and reflect upon the subject, but instead simply to begin talking about it to someone, so that "l'idée vient en parlant." Bohrer views Kleist's essay as one of the best accounts of what he calls "the aesthetic moment" of "suddenness" (*Plötzlichkeit*), the disruption of rational expectations in a moment of revelation, which has become a distinctive feature of the modern aesthetic (particularly in surrealism).[15] Romantic fantasy, as Bohrer is keen to point out, may also involve suspending the claims of morality, not just the standards of perception. Many of the German Romantics (Tieck, Brentano, and Hoffmann), followed by Baudelaire (*Les fleurs du mal*), Flaubert (*Salammbô*) and Lautréamont (*Les chants de Maldoror*), have undertaken a literary exploration of evil and violence for their own sake, unqualified by moral judgment. In general, the function of fantasy is for Bohrer the same as that of irony, however different may be their methods: to secure the autonomy of the aesthetic domain from the norms of science and morality. Implicit in this function, he argues, is a protest against what modern reason has become in these two areas. The fantasy of a Kleist cannot be written off, as Hegel did, as simply the expression of sickness and madness.[16]

Bohrer seems to me right in his basic conviction that the leading strands of modern thought are not so easily harmonizable as thinkers

selbst von der Höhe seines Geistes herabzulächeln scheint, nicht taüschen, als sei es ihm nicht der heiligste Ernst" (p. 266 in *Schriften zur Literatur* [Munich: Hanser, 1970]).

14 L. Tieck, *Schriften*, 28 vols. (Berlin: Reimer, 1828–54), vol. 4, pp. 128–9.

15 Bohrer, P, pp. 20, 80. For a discussion of "the aesthetic moment" generally, see besides P, also AS, pp. 29, 146, 297, 331, 337, 342, 360.

16 Hegel, *Vorlesungen über die Ästhetik*, vol. 1, pp. 314–15, also 288–89. See Bohrer's discussion of Hegel on fantasy in KR, pp. 158–81.

such as Kant and Habermas have believed. The influential aspects of Romantic aesthetics that Bohrer has emphasized cannot be understood as simply the project of giving powerful expression to interesting, because novel, states of mind. They involve instead a challenge to the hegemony of the forms of scientific and moral thought (prediction and control of nature, moral progress) that have indeed established themselves in modern times. All the same, it is hard not to conclude that Bohrer's own thinking is caught in a contradiction. On the one hand, he argues that the modern aesthetic stands opposed to modern science and morality. On the other hand, he describes the goal of this aesthetic as the autonomy of art. How, we must ask, can the modern aesthetic challenge modern science and morality unless it proposes alternative conceptions of the true and the good? And if it does this, how can its aim be coherently conceived as making art autonomous or independent of a concern with the true and the good?

It is the notion of the autonomy of art that flaws Bohrer's otherwise very penetrating diagnosis of the disunity of modern thought. During the past two centuries there have, of course, been currents of artistic thought that have aspired to the ideal of *l'art pour l'art*. But the aestheticism of a Gautier or a Pater does not incorporate the forms of the modern aesthetic that challenge the other domains of modern thought. Bohrer would seem eager to subscribe to a statement such as this: "We praise a work, not as 'true', but as 'strong'; our highest praise is that it has 'affected' us, has 'terrified' us." But the person who wrote these words, Thomas Carlyle, spoke for many of the Romantics when he went on to add in protest, "All this, it has been well observed, is the 'maxim of the Barbarous', the symptom, not of vigorous refinement, but of luxurious corruption."[17] Certainly the German Romantic thinkers in whom Bohrer seems most interested were very far from an aestheticist devotion to the autonomy of art.

To see this, we must look more carefully at their understanding of the relation between art and truth. There are, in fact, two distinct ways in which art may be seen as a vehicle of truth. According to one conception, the function of art is to present in a particularly vivid form what we can recognize to be true by other, if less memorable means. This is the mimetic conception of art, which holds that the beautiful

17 Thomas Carlyle, "Signs of the Times" (1829), p. 81 in his *Selected Writings* (Harmondsworth: Penguin, 1971).

imitates the true. But a different conception is that the work of art may be an indispensable means for grasping truths we cannot adequately express or, at least, would not have discovered by other means. In this view art is not imitation, but revelation. The German Romantics were certainly opposed to restricting the truth content of art to imitation, since this makes art basically a second-class, dispensable form of thought. But they did not therefore reject, as Bohrer supposes, all connection between art and truth. On the contrary, their conviction was that art was unique in its capacity to disclose truths of a fundamental importance. Novalis's remark was typical: "Poetry is genuinely absolute reality. This is the core of my philosophy. The more poetic, the truer."[18]

For the Romantics, the truth it is the mission of art to disclose is the Absolute or being itself, the way things are in themselves as distinct from how they look from any given perspective. Their guiding premise was that the Absolute can never be the direct or intended object of our thought. Reflection, they maintained, always shapes to some extent the conception of its object in accord with its own presuppositions and interests. (At its most basic level this distorting role of reflection consists in the very distinction between subject and object whereby the object of thought must be understood as different from the knowing subject that reflects upon it.) The idea that the Absolute eludes the grasp of reflection finds its most famous expression in Hölderlin's essay *Urteil und Sein* (1795), but it also runs throughout the writings of Novalis and Schlegel. "We *seek* everywhere the Unconditioned," Novalis observed, "and always *find* only things."[19] The importance of the idea was that in their view art can do what reflection – and that means, not only modern science and morality, but philosophy itself – cannot. It can reveal the Absolute. "Where philosophy ends," Schlegel once quipped, "there must poetry begin."[20] The means by which the Roman-

---

18 "Die Poesie ist das ächt absolut Reelle. Dies ist der Kern meiner Philosophie. Je poetischer, je wahrer" (Novalis, *Schriften,* 4 vols. [Stuttgart: Kohlhammer, 1960–75], vol. 2, p. 647). For an excellent discussion of how the German Romantics worked out this second, nonmimetic conception of "aesthetic truth," see Manfred Frank, *Einführung in die frühromantische Ästhetik* (Frankfurt: Suhrkamp, 1989), pp. 16–18, 29, 140, 149, 223–6, 360.

19 Novalis, *Vermischte Bemerkungen* [*Blüthenstaub*], §1 (in *Schriften*, vol. 2, pp. 412–13).

20 F. Schlegel, *Ideen* (1800), §48 (in *Athenaeum. Eine Zeitschrift 1798–1800* [Munich: Rowohlt, 1969], vol. 2, p. 140).

tics believed that art could accomplish this paradoxical task of representing the unrepresentable were precisely irony and fantasy. Bohrer is
right that they were the key notions in the German Romantic aesthetic;
but he is quite off the mark in holding that their aim was to immunize
art against considerations of truth.

The function of irony, according to the Romantic aesthetic, is to call
attention to the fact that the perspective created by the work of art is
indeed but a perspective, and so is not to be taken as an absolute view
of its subject. By drawing back from what it represents, the work of art
is able to *suggest*, if not portray directly, the Absolute of which it falls
short. As Schlegel liked to say, it *intends* to be taken as a *fragment*, a part
of a larger whole, to which it nonetheless alludes.[21] Of course, the
effort to fix precisely the content of this suggestion or allusion will
meet the fate of all reflective thought and fail to express the Absolute.
That is why irony, when successfully deployed, will involve a suggestion
of the Absolute whose meaning can never be made quite clear. "A
poem," Novalis wrote, "must be completely *inexhaustible*, like a human
being or a good aphorism."[22] This is also why the German Romantics
often claimed that the successful work of art expresses an aspiration
toward the infinite: it embodies a continual dissatisfaction with the
limited views it recognizes that we cannot help but hold.[23]

The Romantics' love of fantasy was similarly fueled by the conviction
that art alone can circumvent the antagonism between the Absolute
and reflective thought. But the strategy was quite different. Instead of
being a form of thought that suggests the Absolute by underscoring its
own limits, fantasy consists in simply suspending the rules and rational
expectations belonging to reflective thought and in letting the imagination move freely. Still, the goal was not to turn the work of art in

---

21 See Schlegel, *Athenaeumsfragmente*, §15: "Viele Werke der Alten sind Fragmente
geworden. Viele Werke der Neuern sind es gleich bei der Entstehung" (in *Schriften
zur Literatur*, p. 27).
22 Novalis, *Schriften*, vol. 3, p. 664.
23 The idea that the aim of art is to suggest the infinite is widespread in European
Romanticism. See, for example, Wordsworth, *The Prelude* (1805), VI. 538–42: "Our
destiny, our nature, and our home, / Is with infinitude, and only there; / With hope
it is, hope that can never die, / Effort, and expectation, and desire, / And something evermore about to be" (also II. 330–41). See also Baudelaire's famous statement in "Qu'est-ce que le romantisme?": "Qui dit romantisme dit art moderne –
c'est-à-dire intimité, spiritualité, couleur, aspiration vers l'infini" (*Oeuvres complètes*
[Paris: Gallimard, 1961], p. 879).

upon itself, as Bohrer maintains, but again to show how only art can open out onto a dimension of truth that would otherwise escape us.

Take, for example, the artistic exploration of evil and violence for their own sake, which began with Romanticism and has become an integral part of the modern aesthetic. According to Bohrer's discussion in *Nach der Natur,* this form of fantasy comes into its own only when the interest in evil is no longer blasphemous but intrinsic, and scenes of horror and carnage are presented without any ulterior meaning intended. In this way art secures its autonomy from morality. Flaubert's *Salammbô* (1862), with its repeated depiction of "sheer massacre" in the war between Carthage and its mercenary army, is his paradigm.[24] But if sheer massacre is presented for its own sake, without any ulterior significance, how can it be understood *as evil*? "Aesthetic evil" is a category that necessarily intersects with the domain of moral evaluation. Bohrer is quite right that secularized forms of theodicy, the conceptions of moral progress so popular since the eighteenth century, have been unable to comprehend, and have only condemned the aesthetic of evil (see the essay "Die permanente Theodizee" in *Nach der Natur*). But that is just the point. The aim of this aesthetic has been to point to the permanence of evil, the inevitability of violence, to which optimistic views of history refuse to face up. The meaning behind the "*style cannibale*" of *Salammbô* was surely a disgust with the modern world and its self-complacent notions of progress. Even Bohrer cannot avoid proposing, in another writing of his, an interpretation of *Salammbô*'s violence, "die Verdächtigung des Geistes im Namen der Natur" (casting suspicion on the spiritual in the name of what is natural).[25] The aesthetic of evil is not, contrary to Bohrer, an expression of the autonomy of art. The rational expectations that here fantasy suspends are those belonging to the confidence in moral progress. The aesthetic of evil aims to provide a truer vision of the moral universe.

Bohrer has in general very little to say about this problematic of reflection and the Absolute that underlay the German Romantic interest in irony and fantasy. The "reflexivity" (or irony) that the Romantics sought in art is for him not a strategy for suggesting more than can

---

24 Bohrer, NN, pp. 119, 124–5, 129, 134.
25 See Bohrer, "Friedrich Schlegels Rede über die Mythologie," p. 68 in idem (ed.), *Mythos und Moderne* (Frankfurt: Suhrkamp, 1983). For Flaubert's own motives, see his letter to Mlle. Leroyer de Chantepie of 18 March 1857.

ever be said outright, but rather a means for making art autonomous or an expression of the intensity of modern self-consciousness – or both, as when he speaks of the "aesthetic subjectivity" peculiar to Romantic and modern thought and cites the modern aesthetic as the best proof for the ineliminability of the concept of the subject ("Ich reagiere ästhetisch, also bin ich").[26] This view may fit to some extent the "late Romanticism" (*Spätromantik*) of Brentano and von Arnim, which was not very articulate philosophically. And at times Bohrer seems to express a preference for the *Spätromantik* over the *Frühromantik* (Novalis, Schlegel).[27] But certainly Kleist, another *Spätromantiker*, cannot be properly understood in terms of a view that disconnects art from considerations of truth. In his intellectual crisis of 1801, the crisis that signaled his emergence as a great writer, Kleist did give up his earlier confidence in the rational intelligibility of the world and in moral progress. But it was precisely this insight into the human condition, the unreality of Enlightenment ideals and of the Weimar classicism of Goethe and Schiller, that he sought to evoke in his work (notably in *Das Erdbeben von Chili*).

Furthermore, Bohrer's approach to German Romanticism misses the essence of Hegel's influential critique of the German Romantics. What separated Hegel from the Romantics was not his assumption that art is a vehicle of truth. Their point of difference was instead the kind of truth – mimetic or revelatory – of which they thought art capable. The core of Hegel's position, the conviction that raises his critique above the peculiarities of his own philosophy, was that there is no truth that cannot be adequately grasped by reflective thought. Thus, even the Absolute can and must be grasped reflectively, in the "system of speculative idealism." There could not, therefore, be a special function for art, as the Romantics believed, to disclose a truth we could not apprehend by any other means. And that is why he claimed that art must be a "thing of the past" for a culture so thoroughly reflective as our own. Hegel would in fact have been far less alarmed by an aesthetic that extolled the autonomy of art from considerations of truth. It

---

26 NN, p. 217. See also NN, pp. 167, 213–14; RB, pp. 24, 66, 107–8. In KR, pp. 146–50, he does mention Schlegel's connection between irony and the Absolute, and warns against viewing Romantic irony as merely an expression of subjectivity – but only in order to insist that it is instead a purely aesthetic process isolated from considerations of truth (p. 146).

27 RB, p. 72 and KR, p. 7 (though at p. 61 he disclaims any preference).

would have offered no competition to his own deepest philosophical conviction.[28]

The aesthetic of the German Romantics did not seek, therefore, to detach art from the true and the good. Irony and fantasy were intended instead to uncover truths we are otherwise in danger of missing. This is the spirit of Novalis's famous definition of Romanticism: "The world must be romanticized. That is the way to its *original meaning*. . . . In giving a noble meaning to the vulgar, a mysterious appearance to the commonplace, the dignity of the unknown to the known, the semblance of infinity to the finite, I romanticize it."[29] The same seems to be true of those elements of the modern aesthetic that grew out of Romanticism and that Bohrer seems most to prize. Precisely to the extent that the modern aesthetic has challenged the hegemony of the form of scientific rationality that consists in the prediction and control of nature, and of the form of moral rationality that produces a confidence in moral progress, it has projected an alternative vision of the true and the good.

The alternative has not always been the one the German Romantics proposed – the Absolute and the ineliminability of evil. Modern art has also strived to recapture a sense of the individuality of human lives (this is particularly true of the modern novel), as well as to evoke the poignancy of losses that can never be made good.[30] But in any case we should recognize that modern thought is, as Bohrer himself insists, riven by discord (*Zwiespalt*). This means that modern thought cannot be understood in terms of the harmonious division of labor postulated by differentiation theories such as those of Kant and Habermas. But it also means that Bohrer betrays his own insight in supposing that the idea of autonomy, or independence from the concern with truth and morality, can grasp the place of art in modern thought. The situation is rather one in which the contours of the true and the good remain controversial. The oppositional character of modern art is the refusal to accept the view that prediction and control of nature, as well as

---

28 Manfred Frank has developed a very interesting contrast between "Romanticism" and "Idealism" (Hegel) along the lines of this relation between reflection and the Absolute. See his *Einführung in die frühromantische Ästhetik*, pp. 222, 227, 229, 287, 297, 307.

29 Novalis, *Schriften*, vol. 2, p. 545 (my emphasis).

30 Cf. Milan Kundera, *L'art du roman* (Paris: Gallimard, 1986); Walter Benjamin, *Geschichtsphilosophische Thesen*, §9.

moral progress, offer the best means for understanding the world and ourselves. Naturally it would be wrong to think of modern art as simply a conduit for heterodox theorizing. There is such a thing as aesthetic pleasure that makes art more than just the propounding of an idea.[31] Still, it would also be wrong to think that the peculiar pleasure we derive from a work of art is independent of what the work lets us see about the world. Otherwise, art would be a far less important form of experience than it is.

---

31 Stendhal's warning is always appropriate: "Sans ce plaisir en quelque sorte instinctif ou du moins *non raisonné* du premier moment, il n'y a ni peinture ni musique. Cependant j'ai vu les gens de Koenigsberg arriver au plaisir, dans les arts, à force de raisonnements" (*Rome, Naples, et Florence,* 7 November 1816, in *Voyages en Italie* [Paris: Gallimard, 1973], p. 321).

10

THE FOUNDATIONS OF MODERN
DEMOCRACY: REFLECTIONS
ON JÜRGEN HABERMAS

Jürgen Habermas is one of the very few indisputably great moral and
social thinkers of our time. We must situate our own thought with
respect to his in order to know what it is we truly think, even when we
then find that we must disagree. Over a number of years, Habermas
has been working out a new conception of moral philosophy that he
calls "discourse ethics" (*Diskursethik*). To some extent, this line of
thought has developed at a very abstract level. Perhaps its most prominent feature has been the attempt to find the source of morality in a
general principle of universalization that any agent must assume just
by virtue of being a competent speaker with an understanding of the
concept of reasons for action. It cannot be said that this attempt has
met with evident success. Like all efforts to draw some fundamental set
of moral obligations from the notion of practical rationality as such,
Habermas's reflections at this level seem caught in a well-known but
inescapable dilemma: either the idea Habermas proposes of practical
rationality (or "communicative reason," as he terms it) proves too weak
to deliver any moral principles, or it is made to yield the desired
conclusions only by virtue of moral content having been built into it
from the outset (see Chapter 2).

These exercises in "first philosophy" have been, however, only one
part, and doubtlessly not the most deeply felt, of Habermas's project
of a "discourse ethics." Far more important has been the vision of a

truly democratic politics that has driven this project. That is why one of Habermas's most recent books, *Faktizität und Geltung*, represents so significant an event.[1] In it, Habermas's political philosophy and his guiding conception of radical democracy have finally achieved the detailed articulation they deserve. This book allows us to take a more just measure of the contribution that Habermas's discourse ethics can make to an understanding of the nature and promise of political association.

1. Argument and Context

In the book, Habermas sets out to reply to the frequent objection that his discourse ethics promotes a sort of excessive moralizing that betrays a lack of contact with the reality of the modern liberal-democratic state. The general form of Habermas's response is to argue that reality (*Faktizität*) and validity (*Geltung*) form a relation of tension, which his political philosophy pursues in two opposing directions. On the one hand, he aims to show that social reality, even in the most elementary aspects of language use, rests on a normative dimension. Whenever we act or think reasonably, or believe we do, we make a "validity claim" (*Geltungsanspruch*): we suppose that the reasons we have possess a certain objectivity and would command the rational assent of others in an appropriately conducted discussion (*Diskurs*). No satisfactory theory of the political life of modern societies, however complex they may be, can therefore ignore or dismiss the normative claims of the modern liberal-democratic state. This conclusion is familiar from many of his earlier works, particularly from his *Theory of Communicative Action*.

But on the other hand, Habermas also acknowledges that the cultural and social realities of modern society impose certain tasks and constraints upon our attempt to make sense of the proper nature of political association today. Modern societies are highly complex, he observes, in that they can no longer be understood as politically constituted. In functionally differentiated or "decentered" societies such as our own, where different social domains (or "subsystems") such as law, the economy, political life, and religion take on specialized tasks in accord with their own criteria, the state may no longer serve, he claims, as the expression and guarantee of the goals and ideals of society as a

---

1 J. Habermas, *Faktizität und Geltung* (Frankfurt: Suhrkamp, 1992). All page references to this book appear in parentheses in the text.

whole (65, 365–6). For my part, I think one might better say that modern societies are so complex that such holistic conceptions are likely to have considerably less appeal, and not that they have only now become untrue. For probably they were never really adequate to their object. Be that as it may, Habermas is surely right to maintain (here principally in opposition to Niklas Luhmann's systems theory) that we need not think society to be politically constituted in order to suppose that the collectively binding decisions of the legal system and the underlying principles of our political life have a normative basis and can become an appropriate object of reflection for moral philosophy (70–2). Sensitivity to the complexities of social reality cannot replace our need to reflect upon the validity of the principles by which we live together.

In the course of his book, however, Habermas presents two distinct notions of the "validity claims" that we raise whenever we make a moral or any other sort of judgment. The one conception seems to me correct, the other not. When aiming for philosophical rigor, he says that in asserting something we presuppose that the assertion can be justified, not merely on the basis of standards we already accept, but also under highly idealized conditions that transcend all locally embedded forms of understanding and stand at the end of an infinitely extended conversation (30–1, 36–7). We assume that the assertion would be justified according to the best standards there could ever be. The difficulty with this conception of justification, which Habermas has drawn from C. S. Peirce and advocated, of course, for some time, is that we can discern as little content in such extremely idealized justification conditions as in any other notion of the unconditioned.

It is therefore not surprising that at other times Habermas concedes that in reality we always determine what will count as a "sufficient" justification of an assertion by looking to the standards of our existing argumentative practices. "The concept of argument," he then admits, "has inherently a pragmatic character. As a matter of fact, we end an argument, under favorable conditions, precisely when reasons, within the horizon of hitherto unproblematic background assumptions, co-alesce in a coherent whole to such an extent that an unforced consensus about the acceptability of the disputed validity claim comes into being" (279, 278; also 31, 37).

I myself would not describe very differently a conception of justification that, despite Habermas's own reservations, seems not only attractive but also able to stand on its own. It is, as Habermas notes, a "pragmatic" conception, and one more truly pragmatic than the transcendent conception he has taken over from Peirce. It does not need to be backed up by appeals to the remoter ideal of a justification that reaches altogether beyond our present standards of warranted belief. When we make an assertion, we do presuppose that it can be justified under idealized conditions. But the crucial point is that the ideal conditions we then assume embody standards that we already accept – if not all the standards we currently employ, then at least those to which we are most strongly committed. Otherwise, we would have no idea of what we are actually presupposing.

What counts against the adequacy of this conception? Nothing, it seems to me. Naturally, our accepted standards have to be revised from time to time, as Habermas observes (55). But just as the justifiability we assume our assertions to have must be understood in relation to standards and beliefs we already accept, so, too, we understand the need to revise a hitherto accepted standard always by appeal to other standards and beliefs that remain unproblematic. In no case must we extend our claims of justification beyond our existing argumentative practices and into the realm of the unconditioned. Of course, it is also the case that in asserting something as true, we do not mean that it is true only for us or for those who share our standards. We presume that the assertion is true for everyone universally. Nonetheless, we can still claim that someone has missed a truth without our having to suppose that we must be able to justify to him the change of perspective that would make this truth accessible to him. In such situations, we then take for granted simply that we have no positive reason (and that is something we ought to judge by the light of our own perspective) to question our standards and take seriously his contrary ones. Claims to universal truth need not imply, therefore, claims to universal justifiability. The *visio sub specie aeternitatis,* even in the secularized form that is the hypothetical outcome of an infinite conversation, is not a necessary postulate of reason (see Chapter 2, this volume).

What Habermas seems particularly to fear is the "contextualism" he finds in the writings of Richard Rorty (85). To the extent, however, that Rorty would agree to the pragmatic conception of justification I have just sketched, he is not obliged to adopt as well the thesis for which Habermas reproaches him the most – namely, that democratic ideals cannot and need not be justified by appeal to principles. A contextualist notion of justification that dispenses with all appeals to eternity does not imply the disappearance of the search for principles, whatever Rorty himself may think. It does not celebrate, in Habermas's words, "the normative power of whatever exists" (16). Such an epistemology holds, and rightly so, that justification by appeal to principles is conceivable only as a historically situated activity and not as an attempt to tap into the unconditioned. At the same time, the principles we thus invoke may also serve as the basis for criticizing existing practice and for refining our democratic ideals, and they may even undergo revision in the way I described.

This issue is not merely abstract; it has a number of moral and political consequences. Habermas's indecision between two general conceptions of justification reappears in his understanding of moral argumentation. "Moral" discourse, which in Habermas's terminology focuses on social justice by contrast to "ethical" debate about questions of the good life, must heed, he claims, "communicative presuppositions that require a break with the certainties of the life-world and most of all a hypothetical attitude toward the norms of action and claims of validity that have been made the object of attention" (202).

This statement is ambiguous. Obviously, our attitude toward a problematized norm of action must be a hypothetical one, for we are then engaged in weighing reflectively its validity. But this activity does not require a break with the certainties of the "life-world." On the contrary, we must rely upon existing certainties in order to discern the reasons for problematizing the norm in question, and also to locate the reasons for solving the problem then before us. It seems, moreover, that Habermas's transcendent ideal of justification also underlies his understanding of the political ideal of popular sovereignty. For in his view, popular sovereignty, understood as practical argumentation among citizens, cannot assume the validity of any norms (in particular, of any individual rights) other than those that it can itself generate and justify (610). The ideal of context-transcendent justification seems to me, however (for reasons I will present later), just as unrealizable in this political application as it is inconceivable at the abstract level.

The contextualist view of justification I favor has also a philosophical consequence that Habermas may be particularly loath to welcome. Once we admit that the "ideal conditions" under which we suppose an assertion we make would be justified are ones embodying our own best standards of warranted belief, the idea of discussion (*Diskurs*) ceases to play a substantial role in the theory of justified belief. For instead of saying that we must suppose our assertion to be rationally or "discursively" acceptable to others under ideal conditions, we may simply say that we must assume it to be justified by our own best standards of warranted belief. In Habermas's preferred – that is, context-transcendent – conception of justification, "discussion" does play an essential role. But that is just because the notion of "ideal conditions" then lacks all discernible content and must draw instead on the idea of an infinitely extended discussion, which itself, however, eludes our grasp as well. *Diskurstheorie,* as a general account of rationality, is of a piece with Habermas's investment in transcendence.

All this being said, I do not want to suggest that Habermas's commitment to discussion is without merit. His mistake, it seems to me, has been to transfigure a practical concern into a transcendent ideal. For in two regards his insistence on the importance of discussion is to the point. Typically, we can learn of the concerns of others that morally we ought to respect, only by actually talking with them instead of trusting to our own conception of their interests. And within the political realm, public discussion is itself an intrinsic and fundamental value, though as I have indicated, I cannot agree with all that Habermas says about it. To this last point I will return, after first examining the moral and political heart of Habermas's book.

2. Politics and Modernity

In Habermas's view, the moral self-understanding of modern political association must today satisfy the requirements of "postmetaphysical thought" (24, 127, 135, 492). One might well wonder just how postmetaphysically Habermas himself is disposed to think when he resorts so freely to his ideal of the unconditioned. But let us begin by looking more closely at what he means by postmetaphysical.

According to his earlier book, *Post-Metaphysical Thought* (*Nachmetaphysisches Denken*), our epoch requires that, in place of metaphysical modes of thought, we regard reason as finite, fallible, oriented toward achieving intersubjective agreement, and tied to procedural rationality.[2] Habermas's most recent book defends basically the same conception. Concepts of justice, and the legal systems corresponding to them, are constructed in a postmetaphysical fashion, he claims, when they aim to remain neutral with respect to religious and metaphysically conceived forms of life that have themselves become problematic and disputed. The normative foundations of the modern liberal-democratic state must consist in procedural principles of justice that do not pre-

2 J. Habermas, *Nachmetaphysisches Denken* (Frankfurt: Suhrkamp, 1988), pp. 41–2.

suppose the validity of controversial ideas of the good life (375–6). Here the right, as he says, must be prior to the good. Societies such as our own, which are functionally differentiated and culturally heterogeneous, have no common good other than a legal system that treats free citizens equally and deals with their conflicts according to standards of procedural justice. If patriotism is the virtue of loyalty to the common life underlying political association, then Habermas's position, succinctly put, is that only a "constitutional patriotism" (*Verfassungspatriotismus*) is truly coherent today (642).[3]

With this in mind, Habermas turns a cold eye on some of the recent revivals of the "civic republican" tradition. To the extent that these revivals have taken a "communitarian" form (Habermas cites the work of Frank Michelman and Charles Taylor), and long for citizenship to express the substantial ethic (or *Sittlichkeit*) of a common vision of the meaning of life, they do not fit with the exigencies of modern political life (338–9, 642). I agree. But I should point out that in reality the republican tradition is not essentially communitarian. The strand of republican thought represented paradigmatically by Machiavelli's *Discorsi* and recovered today in particular by Quentin Skinner appeals not to the fusion of politics around a common ideal of the good life, and in particular not to the idea that political participation is itself the highest form of activity, but rather to the importance, limited but real, of the virtues of active citizenship and to the need to nurture the rule of law necessary for individual liberty.[4] As such, republicanism ought to be a central ingredient in the self-understanding of the modern liberal-democratic state and of Habermas's own political philosophy.

A principle of neutrality similar to Habermas's, expressed as the demand that liberalism take the form of a "political," not a "comprehensive" doctrine, lies at the heart of the theory of justice John Rawls has made so famous. It is also a principle that I have defended, as in Chapter 6, this volume. Despite this common ground, which Habermas is kind enough to point out (376–8), there are several respects in which I find myself in disagreement.

The first objection concerns an important matter, though it does not affect, I believe, the basic contours of Habermas's position. It

3 This formulation appears in a celebrated essay, "Staatsbürgerschaft und nationale Identität" (1990), reprinted at the end of *Faktizität und Geltung*, pp. 632–60.

4 See Quentin Skinner, "Two Views on the Maintenance of Liberty," pp. 35–58 in Pettit (ed.), *Contemporary Political Theory;* and Chapter 6, Section 1, this volume.

seems to me that, though he rightly rejects the communitarian longing to have politics express a common vision of the good life, Habermas underestimates the depth of the common life necessary, even today, for the fundamental principles of political association to command allegiance. Our common life as citizens must run deeper than just constitutional patriotism. If the political identity of a people did not extend beyond that level, if it consisted therefore only in the affirmation of procedural principles of equal freedom and respect, which clearly purport to govern political life everywhere, then such a people would have to espouse as its ultimate goal the construction of a world political order. Its fundamental political aspiration would have to be cosmopolitan. Whether or not this goal is really desirable, it seems to me wrong to regard it as inscribed in the very logic of the modern liberal-democratic state. Political allegiance today, even when its object is liberal democracy, remains essentially shaped by the conviction that a people can rightly enjoy a form of political association that sets it off from other peoples, even from those sharing the same fundamental political values.

How then should we understand this further dimension of common life, which gives people a political identity as a people, particularly when our societies today are marked by such extensive controversy about the nature of the good life? The mistake of communitarians, but apparently of Habermas as well, is to suppose that it can consist only in a shared allegiance to additional values. That is not so. It can instead be a matter of being shaped by common circumstances. For example, a people can think of itself as a distinct people in terms of a shared language and geographical situation. Though neither necessary nor sufficient for the sense of belonging to a people, such things can certainly play a significant role.

The most important factor, however, is that a people can be bound together by a common historical experience, including the memory of past conflicts, even bloody ones, that were ignited by political programs attempting to impose contrary ideals of the good life (different religious confessions, for instance), but that have been superseded by a practice of equal respect. The political identity of a people may be forged by a shared memory of the violent struggles they have been through and the quarrels they have left behind, in addition to the principles of a "constitutional patriotism" that they have put in place of these. As I observed in Chapter 6, this was the idea Ernest Renan sought to express when he observed paradoxically (in his *Qu'est-ce qu'une nation?* of 1882) that "every French citizen must have forgotten the St. Bartholomew's Day massacre."[5] One can think of similarly formative memories in the self-understanding of other Western liberal democracies.

Only by keeping in mind this aspect of its underlying common life can we make sense of an important fact about liberal democracy. Not just as a matter of historical record, but in its very character, it presents itself as a *latecomer* among the forms of political life. Liberal democracy builds upon the memory of past conflict and the hard-won knowledge that many of the ideals that used to shape political life now form the object of reasonable disagreement. For this reason, individuals may rightly see themselves as sharing a political destiny that goes beyond the values they can affirm together in patriotic declarations. They may feel united in what they have learned together from the things that once divided them. This shared memory is itself sustained, of course, by a common allegiance to the constitutional principles of equal freedom and respect. It is, indeed, the historical coloring these principles have for a specific people, the expression of how they came to accept them. That is why a recognition of this further dimension of common life is compatible with the principle of neutrality already mentioned. It is why it can be fitted into the basic structure of Habermas's thought as well.

There are, however, two fundamental and consequential points where it seems to me Habermas goes wrong in his reconstruction of the normative basis of modern liberal democracy. The first of them concerns the very designation of postmetaphysical. In Habermas's view, reason should proceed postmetaphysically in the political realm, not in order simply to solve the problem of the principles of political association, but rather to apply to this realm the general philosophical perspective that alone, he believes, fits our contemporary intellectual situation. Again and again he insists that certain political principles (the primacy of procedural justice or the priority of the right over the good, the idea of popular sovereignty as the source of individual rights) recommend themselves because the age of metaphysical and religious worldviews is over and practical reason must thus abandon the frame-

---

5 See Ernest Renan, *Qu'est-ce qu'une nation? et autres essais politiques,* J. Roman (ed.) (Paris: Presses Pocket, 1992), p. 42; and Chapter 6, Section 3, this volume. Habermas's own essay, "Staatsbürgerschaft und nationale Identität," contains glimpses of this more complex position at pp. 643, 657.

works of natural law and of the individual subject in favor of his own model of communicative interaction (17, 24, 51–2, 127).

This argumentative strategy seems to me a mistake. It is not that I want to assert that the ambitions of metaphysics retain their plausibility or that some particular religious worldview has not really lost its authority. My own views on these matters are, in fact, somewhat more complex than Habermas's own. But the present question properly involves not all that we might reasonably believe to be true of the world, but rather what we ought to consider relevant to the establishment of principles of political association. These two perspectives are not, I continue to believe, the same.[6] So the important point here is that in modern culture such assertions about the vitality or obsolescence of metaphysics and religion are something about which reasonable people – aiming, that is, to think and converse in good faith and apply, as best as they can, the general capacities of reason – can disagree. Even today, reasonable people can come to believe that the naturalistic worldview should be replaced by a broader, metaphysical or "platonistic" vision that recognizes the existence of ideal entities neither physical nor psychological in character. Thus, I myself think that we must believe there to exist such things as reasons, which we discover by reflection, if we are to suppose that there can be normative knowledge – that is, knowledge of how we ought to think and act (see Chapter 5, this volume). Similarly, reasonable people can also find a basis for believing that the world is guided by divine providence, just as other people, equally reasonable – including Habermas himself – can conclude, to the contrary, that mind and knowledge must be understood without platonistic assumptions and that religion can belong (at best) to the realm of subjective conviction. Indeed, people can also find themselves in reasonable disagreement, as we have seen, about what should count as metaphysical and what should not.

As a political principle, the priority of the right over the good should therefore not be thought dependent on the supposed obsolescence of metaphysical and religious worldviews. This principle is not postmetaphysical, if that means it gives expression to a new, general vision of thought and world. Instead, the priority of the right should be seen as stemming from the recognition that such worldviews, like the philosophical attempts to overcome them, are and will remain the object of controversy among reasonable people. Again, it may well be the case,

6 See my *Patterns of Moral Complexity,* chapter 4.

on general philosophical grounds, that our best understanding of reason today would be along the lines of the postmetaphysical characterization Habermas gives: finite, fallible, oriented toward achieving agreement, and tied to procedural rationality. Such a conception of reason is indeed one I am inclined to share, though I think Habermas wrongly supposes that it escapes the need to assume the existence of ideal entities. But the point here is that such a conception, however ultimately correct, remains the object of reasonable disagreement. To that extent, it shows itself to be unfit to play a foundational role in what ought to be the moral self-understanding of the modern liberal-democratic state. For the priority of the right, as a political principle, expresses the conviction that in the wake of ongoing ethical, religious, and philosophical controversy, political association today must rest on a core morality that all reasonable people can accept despite their deep differences. At the heart of this core morality lies, as I explain in the next section, a principle of equal respect. This political doctrine of liberalism is "postmetaphysical" only in a trivial sense: metaphysical and religious assumptions are too controversial to have a place at its base. But the same is equally true for general philosophical conceptions of so-called postmetaphysical thought.

Habermas's aim is to bring out the fundamental dimension of modern experience that finds expression in the liberal-democratic state. This is a very sensible project. But to me it seems that Habermas has missed the relevant feature of modern experience. It does not lie in the demise of metaphysical and religious worldviews, though the widespread abandonment of such views is certainly a significant aspect of modernity. It consists instead in the growing recognition that reasonable disagreement about the nature of the good life and even about the philosophical foundations of morality is not a passing phenomenon, but rather the situation we should expect. The more we discuss the meaning of life with one another in a thoughtful and informed way, the more likely it is that we will find that we differ and disagree. The expectation of reasonable disagreement is the phenomenon that ought to guide our political thought today.

Though I have already discussed in detail this fundamental experience of modern life (see Chapter 7, this volume), let me point out again that it is far from recommending a general moral skepticism. First, there is the fact that the expectation of irresolvable controversy has been aroused most of all by questions of a speculative sort. However much such controversies may engage our deepest aspirations, they still leave generally untouched the moral commitments of everyday life. Controversy about ultimate and fundamental matters can go hand in hand with the conviction that we can nonetheless agree upon a core morality adequate for the purposes of political association. Indeed, only such a core morality can tell us that we ought to give reasonable disagreement about the meaning of life a decisive role in the establishment of political principles.

Second, that our vision of the good life is the object of reasonable disagreement does not entail that we should withdraw our allegiance to it or regard it as henceforth a mere article of faith. On the contrary, we may still have good reasons to affirm it, based on our experience and reflection. We should remember only that such reasons are not likely to be acceptable to other people, who are equally reasonable but have a different history of experience and reflection – just as their basis for their different conceptions of life will not win our assent. The good reasons that move reasonable people, disposed as they are to think and converse in good faith and to exercise, to the best of their abilities, the general capacities of reason, need not be reasons they all must share. People's grounds for belief and action draw upon their different background convictions. As their starting points differ, so do the positions at which they may legitimately arrive. Reasonable people may thus have good reason to believe in the visions that divide them; they would simply be foolish not to expect that a careful and informed discussion would keep them in disagreement.

I could sum up this criticism of Habermas, therefore, by saying that he has presented a concept of modernity insufficiently broad. Modern experience is characterized, not just by a new postmetaphysical understanding of the true and the right, but also by the expectation that metaphysics and postmetaphysics will remain an enduring object of reasonable disagreement.

The same mistake bedevils the "differentiation theory" with which Habermas argues that a single harmonious conception of reason has in modern times taken on different specialized forms appropriate to the diverse realms of science, morality, and art. As I argued in the preceding chapter, this presumed harmony of the spheres is untrue to some of the deepest facets of modern experience. The artistic imagination, for example, has repeatedly disputed the right of modern science to monopolize our image of the natural world. Modernity might be better viewed in the light of such controversies than in the hope for a cozy synthesis of the one and the many. This is, in any case, the perspective that ought to guide our thinking about the foundations of the modern liberal-democratic state.

3. Liberalism and Democracy

My second major criticism is directed at the way in which Habermas proposes to conceive the relation between basic individual rights (the rights to freedom of conscience, of speech, of assembly, and to private property) and the democratic ideal of popular sovereignty. As I have noted, he does not share the communitarian assumption that individual rights need to be nurtured and shaped by an antecedent, substantial vision of the good life (*Sittlichkeit*). But it is equally significant that he rejects the contrary standpoint of liberalism. As Habermas rightly observes, liberalism has usually assigned individual rights – at least those of a fundamental kind – the function of delimiting the proper scope of popular sovereignty (130, 329, 610). That is, liberal thinkers have generally seen fundamental individual rights as a value distinct from democratic self-rule and as taking precedence over it. This outlook finds expression in the very term "liberal democracy," but it is nonetheless one Habermas refuses. His explicit aim is to cut a middle way between the opposing camps of liberalism and communitarianism that divide between them so much of contemporary Anglo-American political philosophy.

This via media is announced in the thesis that fundamental individual rights and democratic self-rule are "co-original" (*gleichursprünglich*) values. At one level this co-originality is for Habermas a relation of mutual presupposition. Just as self-government can serve to protect individual rights, so rights are best understood as providing the necessary conditions for the exercise of popular sovereignty (133–4, 161, 610). But at bottom Habermas unmistakably privileges the second of these values. Individual rights, in his view, draw their rationale from their supposed ability to make democratic self-rule possible. Their basic purpose cannot be, as liberals generally believe, to limit the authority of popular sovereignty.

A clear sign of the priority Habermas assigns to democracy is the basic value he sees as underlying the co-originality of rights and self-government. It is what he calls "autonomy" (51–2). In a postmetaphysical age, he argues, where the appeal of metaphysical and religious world-pictures is on the wane, we have reason to consider ourselves subject to practical norms only if we are able at the same time to see ourselves as the source of these norms. Democratic self-rule is but the application of this idea of autonomy to the political realm (52, 153–4, 160). Citizens can regard themselves as legitimately bound by the rules of political association only to the extent that these rules spring from no higher source than the citizens themselves. Again, because of widespread and deeply rooted controversies about the nature of the good life, however, citizens must locate their role as the source of law not in a given substantial form of life they might already share, but instead in their own common will, which they mobilize for this political purpose alone. This is why, he argues, communitarianism is unacceptable. Citizens can form and express this collective will only in public discussion (*Diskurs*) with one another about the principles of the common life that they are to affirm.

This line of thought contains an important element that other liberal-democratic thinkers have embraced before Habermas: legitimate principles of political association must be rationally acceptable to all citizens they are meant to bind. This is why, in the face of reasonable disagreement about the good life, political association must rely on the priority of the right. But the distinctive feature of Habermas's position is the further claim that he believes to underlie this and that breaks with the usual conception of liberal democracy. It is his claim that fundamental individual rights have their proper basis only in the ideal of popular sovereignty, so that citizens will understand their collective will as the source of all the norms that bind them. In Habermas's eyes, the essentially protective function of such rights does not lie primarily in restricting the power of the state, but instead at the deeper level of empowering individuals to participate in this democratic self-rule. The right to freedom of speech, for example, is held to recommend itself as a means to the formation of a common political will. Individual rights serve not to protect us against the collective will, but rather to provide the means necessary for creating such a will.

In essence, Habermas thus wants to see democratic self-rule as the sole normative foundation of the modern liberal-democratic state. Liberal democracy ought best to be understood, he believes, not as that term itself suggests (the subordination of democracy to liberal principles), but rather as *radical democracy*. Political association must be understood as truly and thoroughly self-governing. It cannot subordinate itself to any pre-given norms. It can acknowledge only those moral norms to which it has itself given rise (123, 154). This ideal of popular sovereignty forms the heart of Habermas's political philosophy. It is why he thinks, for example, that instead of regarding fundamental

legal (i.e., constitutional) principles as the application of moral principles already held to be valid, we should understand law and morality as
equally basic, though often overlapping, specifications of an even more
general normative principle D, which gives expression to the fundamental value of autonomy (135–8): "Only those action norms are valid
to which all those who might be affected by their establishment could
assent as the result of a rational discussion."

Habermas intends his idea of radical democracy to break with the
defining features of the liberal point of view. Liberal thinkers have
always argued that political association must rest ultimately upon moral
principles that serve to protect certain basic individual freedoms. Typically, such principles have consisted in the affirmation of fundamental
rights, with the result that democratic self-rule is subordinated to the
protection of individual freedoms. The exclusive foundational role
Habermas gives to the ideal of popular sovereignty makes him something very different from a liberal.[7]

This vision of radical democracy, however, is flawed, because it
fails to understand the nature of its devotion to popular sovereignty.
Democratic self-rule, at least as Habermas understands it, depends on
an unacknowledged premise expressing an antecedent moral commitment and affirming indeed the existence of a fundamental individual
right. Other conceptions of popular sovereignty could have, no doubt,
a different character. But Habermas's conception is so constituted as
to imply that political principles ought to be rationally acceptable to
all those whom they are to bind. In fact, that demand brings his idea
of democracy back within the liberal fold, contrary to his intention.

For let us ask why we should believe that political principles ought
to be rationally acceptable to all. It will not do to reply, as Habermas
suggests, that the authority of traditional views of the world, in which
being subject to law and being the source of the law do not coincide,
has simply vanished. For that is first of all false. As I have pointed out,

---

7 Habermas does not believe, of course, that fundamental rights are to be established
   through the normal channels of democratic politics (in parliament, for example).
   They must enjoy constitutional guarantees, and so the kind of democratic self-rule
   that is supposedly their source must find expression in some extraordinary setting,
   such as a constitutional convention. Habermas's idea of radical democracy is thus a
   version of what Bruce Ackerman has called "dualist democracy," according to which
   the fundamental liberal rights have their roots in the self-legislation of constitutional
   politics. See Ackerman, *We the People*, vol. 1, *Foundations* (Cambridge, Mass.: Harvard
   University Press, 1991), chapter 1. My criticism of Habermas applies to the view
   Ackerman presents as well (however right he may be about it forming the central
   strand of the American constitutional tradition).

the authority of such worldviews remains for many the object of a living conviction. Indeed, we cannot in particular understand how there can be such a thing as moral knowledge, I have suggested, unless we suppose "metaphysically" that there exist such things as reasons that we do not create, but rather discover by reflection. It is too narrow a conception of modernity, or at least of that aspect of it relevant to the problem of political association, that fails to recognize the existence of reasonable disagreement on this point. But second, the waning of these worldviews, where it has occurred, cannot justify the idea that the principles of political association must be rationally acceptable to all. It would, for example, be just as possible under these circumstances for political principles to be geared instead to the maximization of the general welfare.

The crucial fact about the idea that the rules of political association must be rationally acceptable to all whom they are to bind is that it gives decisive importance to the way in which political principles differ from other moral principles. In general, political principles are precisely those that we believe may be enforced – imposed by coercion – if need be. The idea that such principles must be rationally acceptable to those who are to be subject to them rests on a moral view about the conditions under which norms may be backed up by force. This underlying moral commitment is that no one should be made by force to comply with a norm of action when it is not possible for him to recognize through reason the validity of that norm. Moral principles with which we do not intend to bring about compliance by force if necessary need not meet this condition. We may judge others in their light without having to suppose they would agree to their validity. There is nothing per se wrong with doing so: we do it all the time when we judge others in terms of our religious convictions or ideals of the good life, which they may well not be able to share given their own settled convictions. (Consequently, I cannot accept Habermas's view that his principle D concerns all moral norms and not just those suitable for being politically instituted.) But the matter is different with moral principles we mean to back up with coercive force. Such principles, which are precisely political in nature, we should accept only if they could command the rational assent of those they are to bind. It is, as I have said, a fundamental moral commitment that makes this so.

This moral conviction amounts, in fact, to the Kantian formula that every person is always to be treated as an end in himself. No one should be made to do, for the sake of some ulterior end, what cannot also win his rational assent. This is, at root, a norm of equal respect, according to which individuals are to be treated as beings whose exercise of their capacity for rational agency cannot be sacrificed for the sake of achieving some social goal. It lies at the heart of the core morality that can be affirmed by people who otherwise differ about the merits of metaphysical and postmetaphysical views of the world, and that sustains the political principle of the priority of the right. Most important in the present context, this moral principle gives expression to an individual right, though certainly one more fundamental than the political rights that tend to be the object of explicit constitutional guarantees. Habermas is probably correct that the familiar individual rights serve to make democratic self-rule possible. But that cannot be their entire rationale. They also give concrete expression to the deepest individual right, that of equal respect, which itself underlies the ideal of democratic self-rule. Popular sovereignty cannot form, therefore, the ultimate layer of our political self-understanding. It draws instead on a fundamentally liberal conception of the political world.[8]

This result also means that, contrary to Habermas, the concept of discussion (*Diskurs*) – be it the actual public discussion in which democratic self-rule is exercised or even the hypothetical discussion we might imagine to be carried out under ideal conditions – cannot play the fundamental role in our moral and political self-understanding. At a deeper level must lie the moral principle of respect for persons. The "ideal conditions of justification" that political argument in a liberal democracy must aim to heed have to embody at their heart this moral principle. For equal respect is precisely what makes democratic self-rule the proper form of political association. Citizens can therefore understand themselves as the source of law only insofar as they have already accepted this principle and judge the validity of their collective decisions from this standpoint. The moral principle of equal respect belongs to the innermost core of our moral consciousness. It forms the historically situated point of departure for our moral reflection, the framework within which we can conceive of moral argument.

---

8 In his response ("Postscript to *Faktizität und Geltung*," *Philosophy & Social Criticism* 20, no. 4 [1994], pp. 143–4) to an earlier version of my criticism ("Die Wurzeln radikaler Demokratie," *Deutsche Zeitschrift für Philosophie* 41 [1993], pp. 321–7), Habermas replies that "liberal rights protecting the individual against the state apparatus" cannot be primary because they emerge from citizens "recognizing one another as equals" in an expression of popular sovereignty. But my point is that this sort of recognition precisely depends (as Habermas's words imply) on a commitment to the principle of equal respect.

INDEX

223